井上雄彦

Takehiko Inoue

THIS HAPPENED A WHILE BACK, BUT THE JAPANESE WOMEN'S NATIONAL TEAM DEFEATED CHINA. CHINA IS A WORLD-CLASS TEAM THAT WON THE SILVER AT THE BARCELONA OLYMPICS.

IT CAME AT A DREADFUL TIME WHEN KUMAGAI-GUMI, A POPULAR TEAM IN THE JAPAN BASKETBALL LEAGUE, DISBANDED, AND THE STANDS AT GAMES IN CERTAIN REGIONS WERE EMPTY. I COULDN'T HELP MYSELF FROM SCREAMING WHEN I SAW THE HEADLINE 'CHINA DEFEATED' IN THE MORNING PAPER. IT GAVE ME GOOSE BUMPS. IT KINDA MADE ME SUPER HAPPY.

Takehiko Inoue's *Slam Dunk* is one of the most popular manga of all time, having sold over 100 million copies worldwide. He followed that series up with two titles lauded by critics and fans alike—*Vagabond*, a fictional account of the life of Miyamoto Musashi, and *Real*, a manga about wheelchair basketball.

SLAM DUNK
Vol. 19: Ace

SHONEN JUMP Manga Edition

STORY AND ART BY TAKEHIKO INOUE

English Adaptation/Stan!
Translation/Joe Yamazaki
Touch-up Art & Lettering/James Gaubatz
Cover & Graphic Design/Matt Hinrichs
Editor/Mike Montesa

Printed in Canada

Published by VIZ Media, LLC
P.O. Box 77010
San Francisco, CA 94107

10 9 8 7 6 5 4 3 2 1
First printing, December 2011

SLAM DUNK

Vol. 19: Ace

STORY AND ART BY

TAKEHIKO INOUE

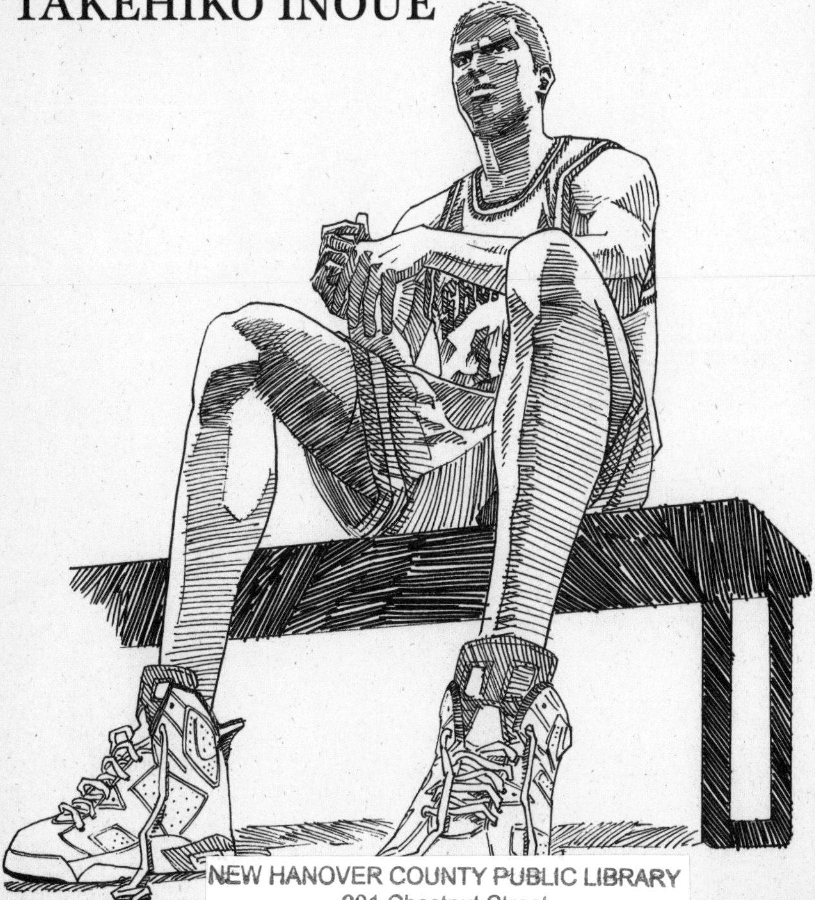

Character Introduction

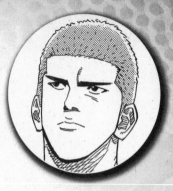

Hanamichi Sakuragi
A first-year at Shohoku High School, Sakuragi is in love with Haruko Akagi.

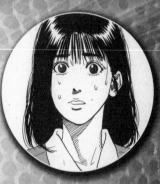

Haruko Akagi
Also a first-year at Shohoku, Takenori Akagi's little sister has a crush on Kaede Rukawa.

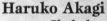

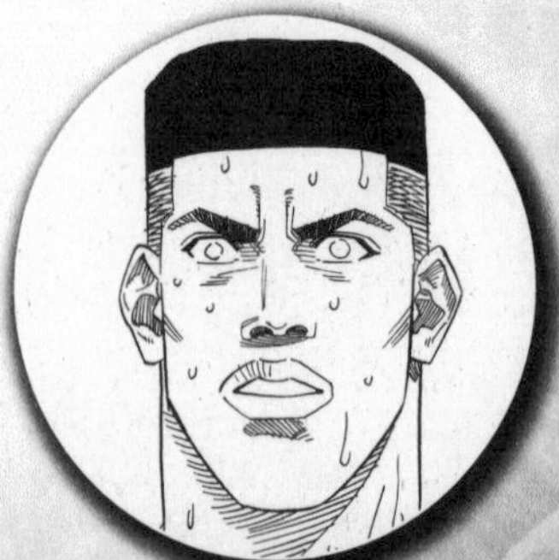

Takenori Akagi
A third-year and the basketball team's captain, Akagi has an intense passion for his sport.

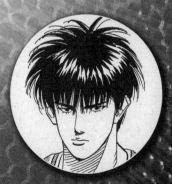

Kaede Rukawa
The object of Haruko's affection (and that of many of Shohoku's female students!), this first-year has been a star player since junior high.

Fukuda

Sendoh

Ryota Miyagi
A problem child with
a thing for Ayako.

Ayako
Basketball Team
Manager

Hisashi Mitsui
An MVP during
junior high.

Our Story Thus Far

Hanamichi Sakuragi is rejected by close to 50 girls during his three years in junior high. He joins the basketball team to be closer to Haruko Akagi, but his frustration mounts when all he does is practice day after day.

The team sets its sights on the Nationals after playing their first practice game. Then problem child Ryota Miyagi and gang member Mitsui return to the team.

Shohoku advances through the prefectural tournament to face top ranked Kainan High, but loses by two points.

Kainan then defeats Ryonan High in overtime to advance to the national tournament.

Shohoku and Ryonan begin the battle for the last remaining spot in the Nationals. With injuries slowing Akagi down and Shohoku struggling, the

Vol. 19:
Ace

Table of Contents

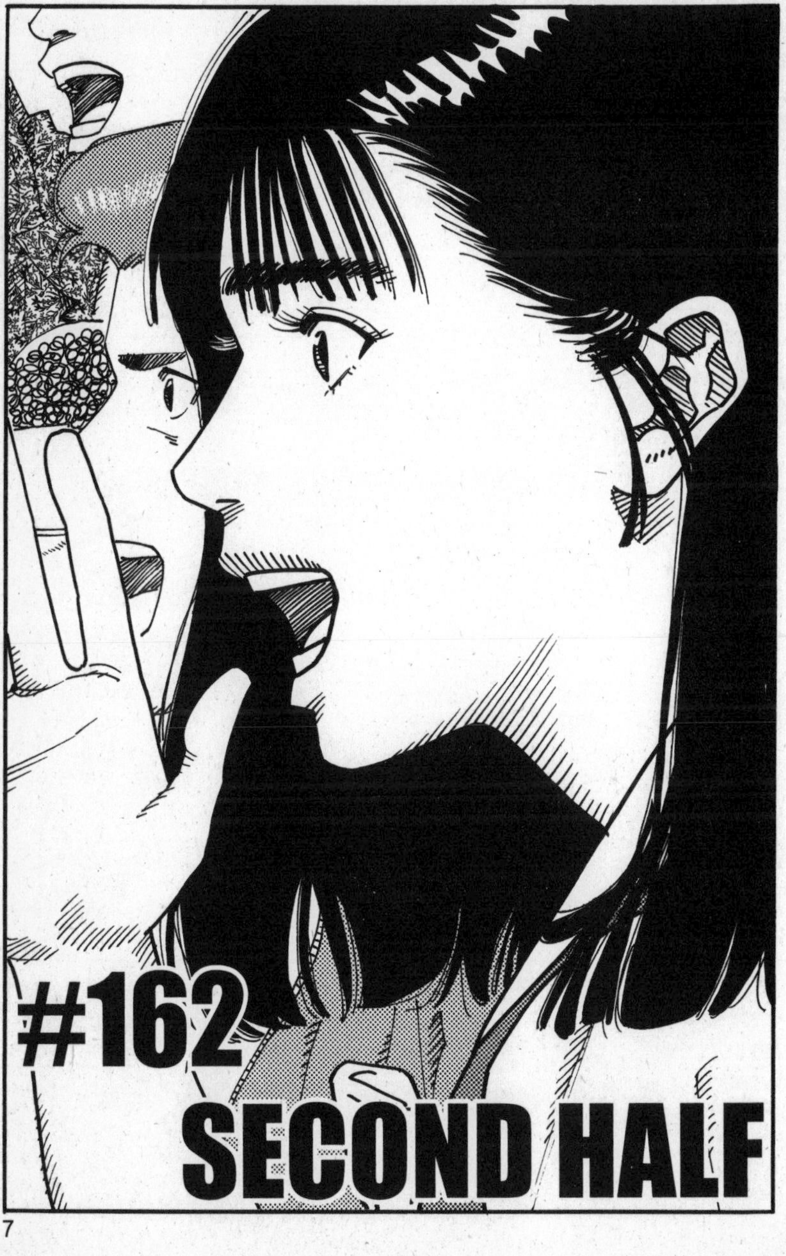
#162
SECOND HALF

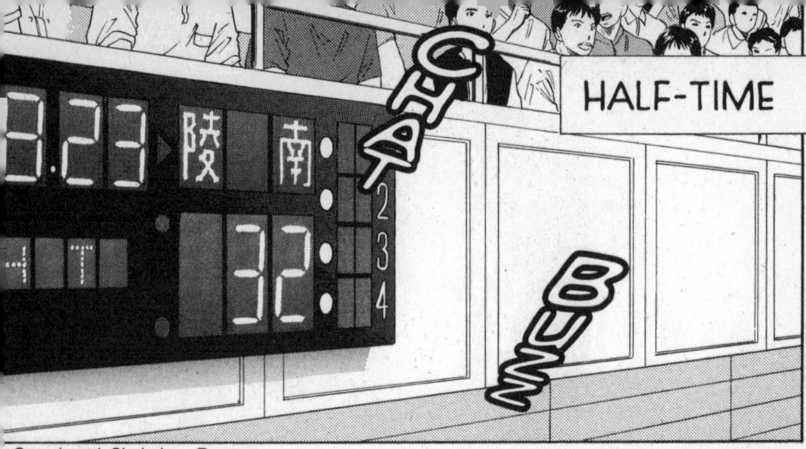
HALF-TIME
CHA
BUZZ
Scoreboard: Shohoku Ryonan

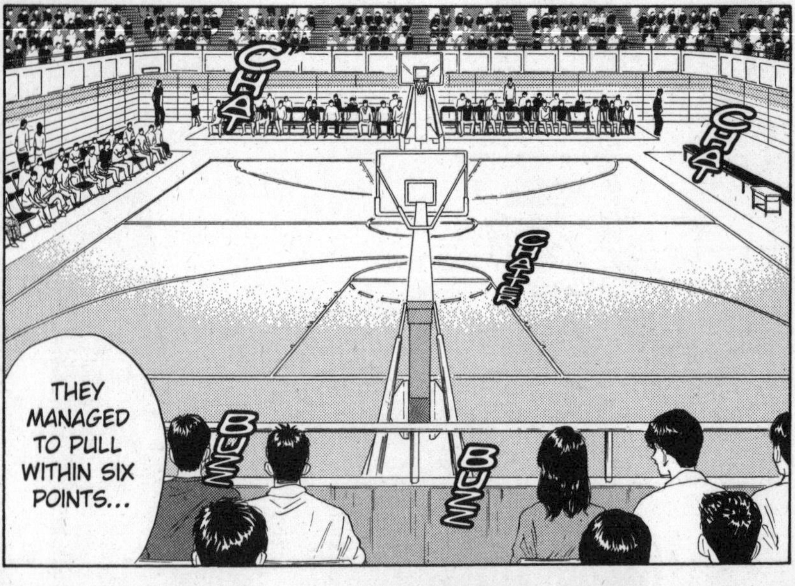
CHA
CHA
CHATTER
BUZZ
BUZZ
THEY MANAGED TO PULL WITHIN SIX POINTS...

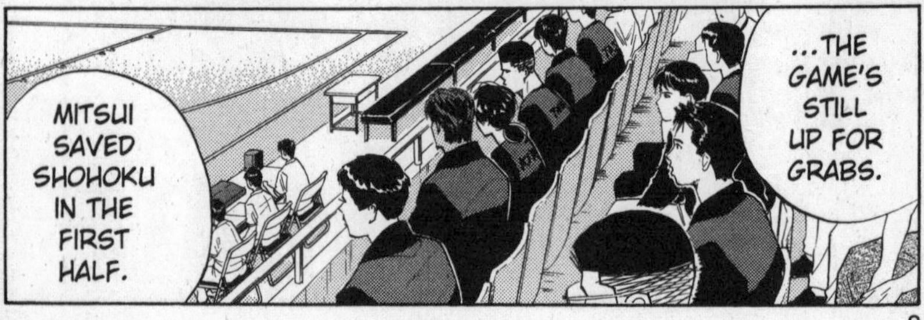
...THE GAME'S STILL UP FOR GRABS.
MITSUI SAVED SHOHOKU IN THE FIRST HALF.

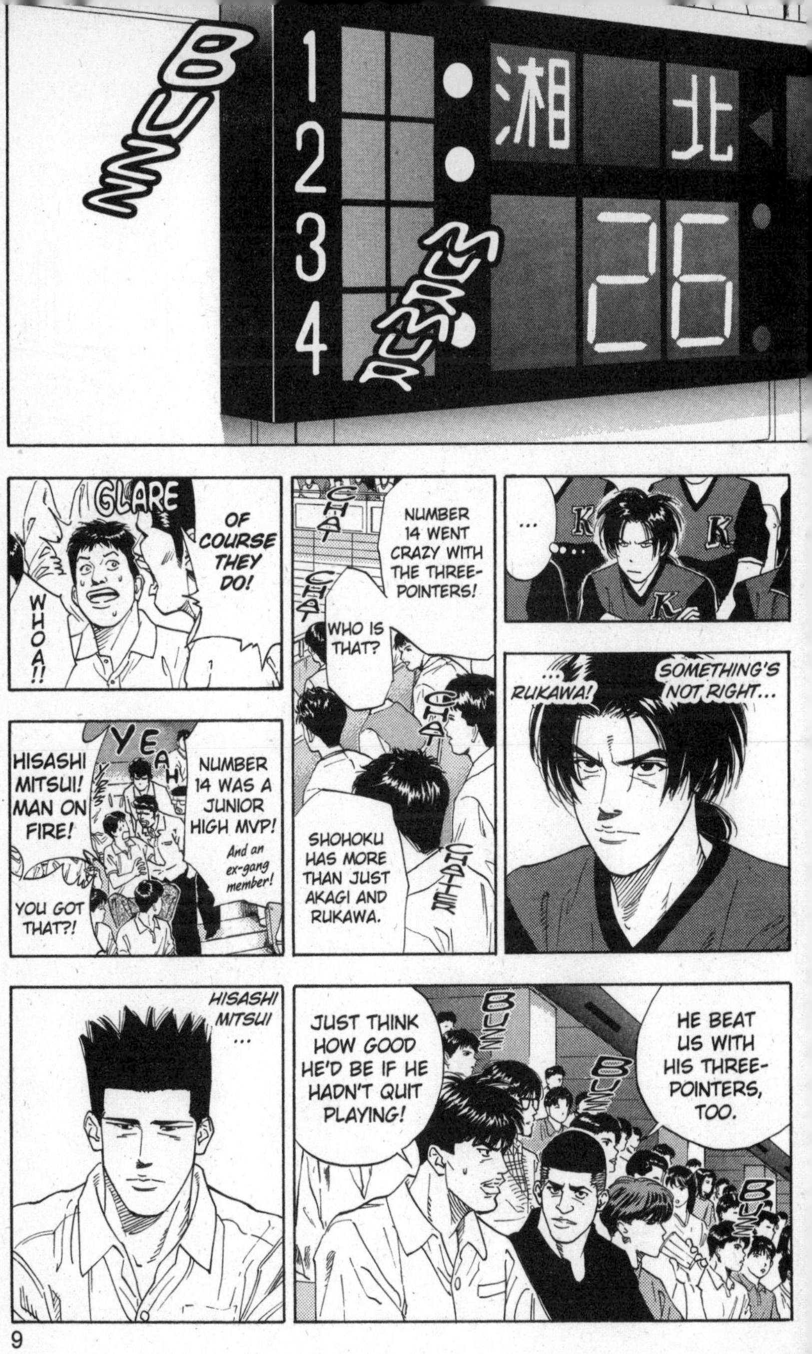
湘北
1
2
3
4
26
MURMUR
BUZZ
...
SOMETHING'S NOT RIGHT...
...RUKAWA!
NUMBER 14 WENT CRAZY WITH THE THREE-POINTERS!
CHAT
CHAT
WHO IS THAT?
CHAT
SHOHOKU HAS MORE THAN JUST AKAGI AND RUKAWA.
CHATTER
OF COURSE THEY DO!
GLARE
WHOA!!
NUMBER 14 WAS A JUNIOR HIGH MVP!
And an ex-gang member!
YEAH
HISASHI MITSUI! MAN ON FIRE!
YOU GOT THAT?!
HE BEAT US WITH HIS THREE-POINTERS, TOO.
BUZZ
BUZZ
JUST THINK HOW GOOD HE'D BE IF HE HADN'T QUIT PLAYING!
BUZZ
HISASHI MITSUI ...

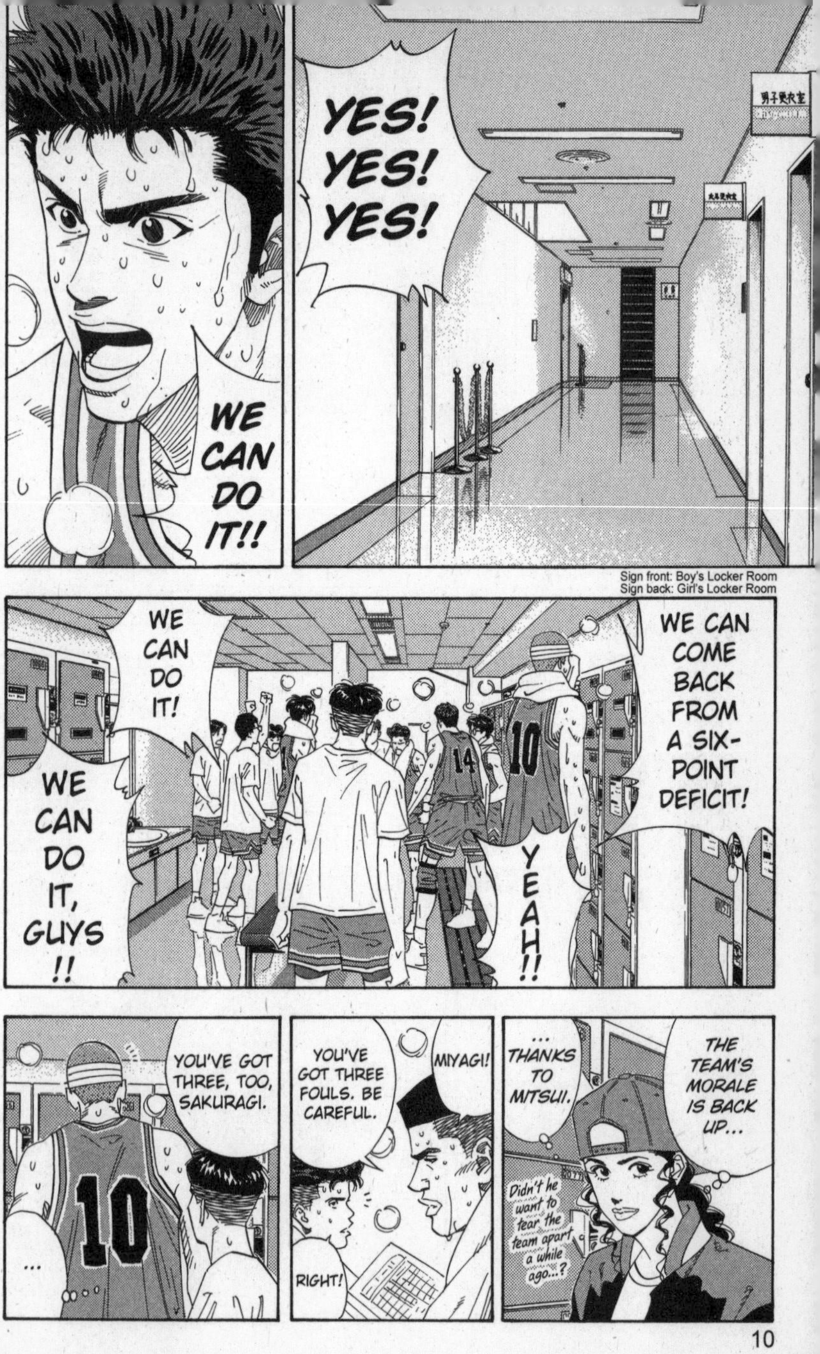
YES! YES! YES!
WE CAN DO IT!!
Sign front: Boy's Locker Room
Sign back: Girl's Locker Room
WE CAN COME BACK FROM A SIX-POINT DEFICIT!
WE CAN DO IT!
YEAH!!
WE CAN DO IT, GUYS!!
THE TEAM'S MORALE IS BACK UP...
...THANKS TO MITSUI.
Didn't he want to tear the team apart a while ago...?
MIYAGI!
YOU'VE GOT THREE FOULS. BE CAREFUL.
RIGHT!
YOU'VE GOT THREE, TOO, SAKURAGI.
...

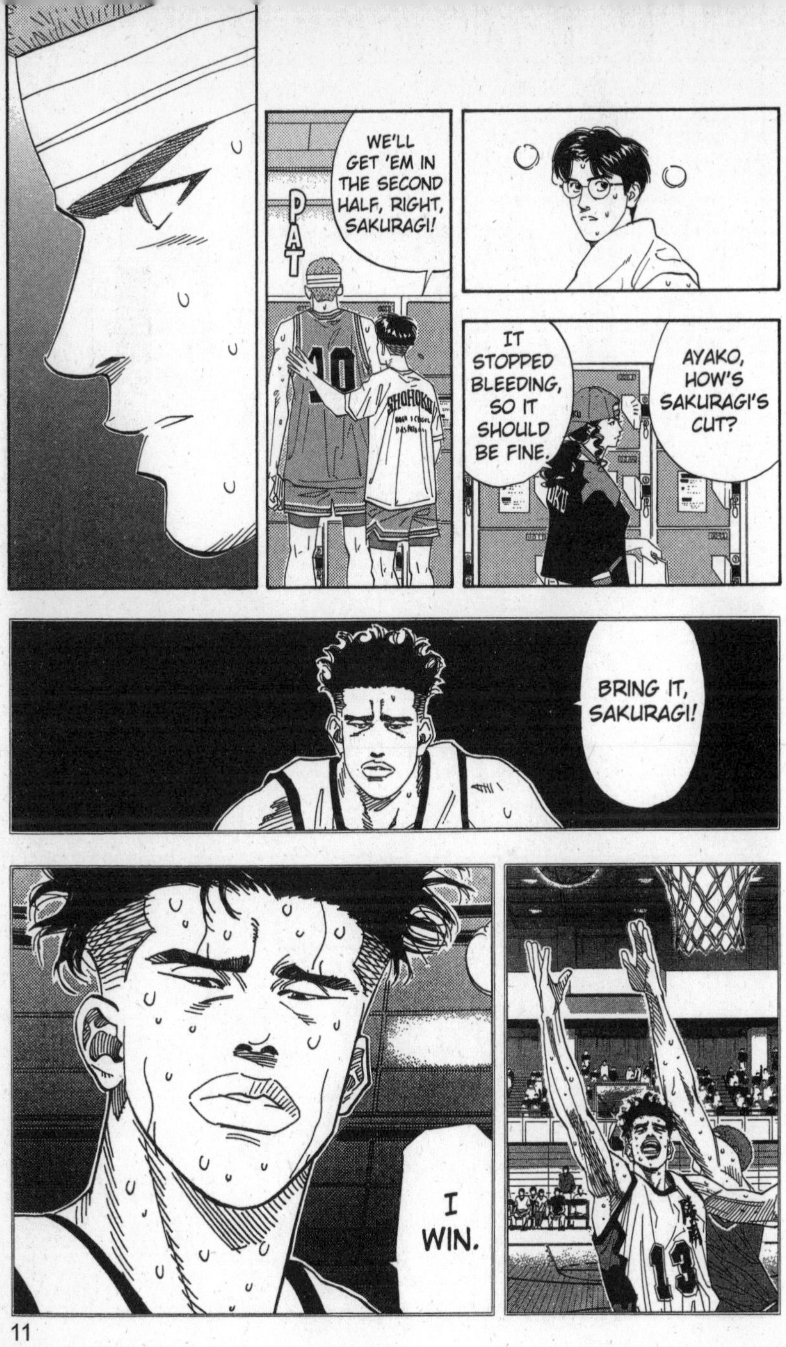
AYAKO, HOW'S SAKURAGI'S CUT?
IT STOPPED BLEEDING, SO IT SHOULD BE FINE.
WE'LL GET 'EM IN THE SECOND HALF, RIGHT, SAKURAGI!
PAT
BRING IT, SAKURAGI!
I WIN.

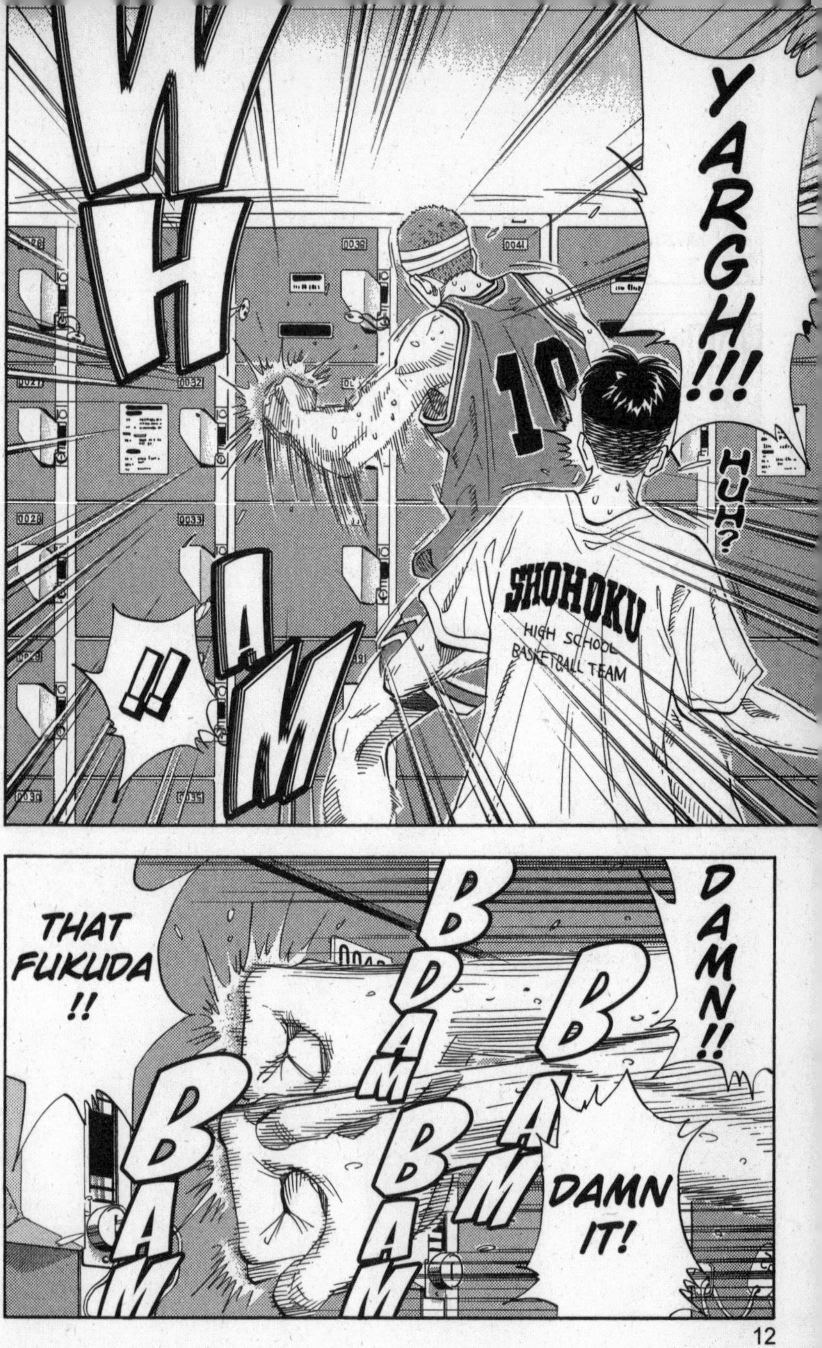
YARGH!!!
HUH?
WHAM
!!
SHOHOKU
HIGH SCHOOL
BASKETBALL TEAM
DAMN!!
BAM
DAMN IT!
BDAM
BAM
THAT FUKUDA!!
BAM

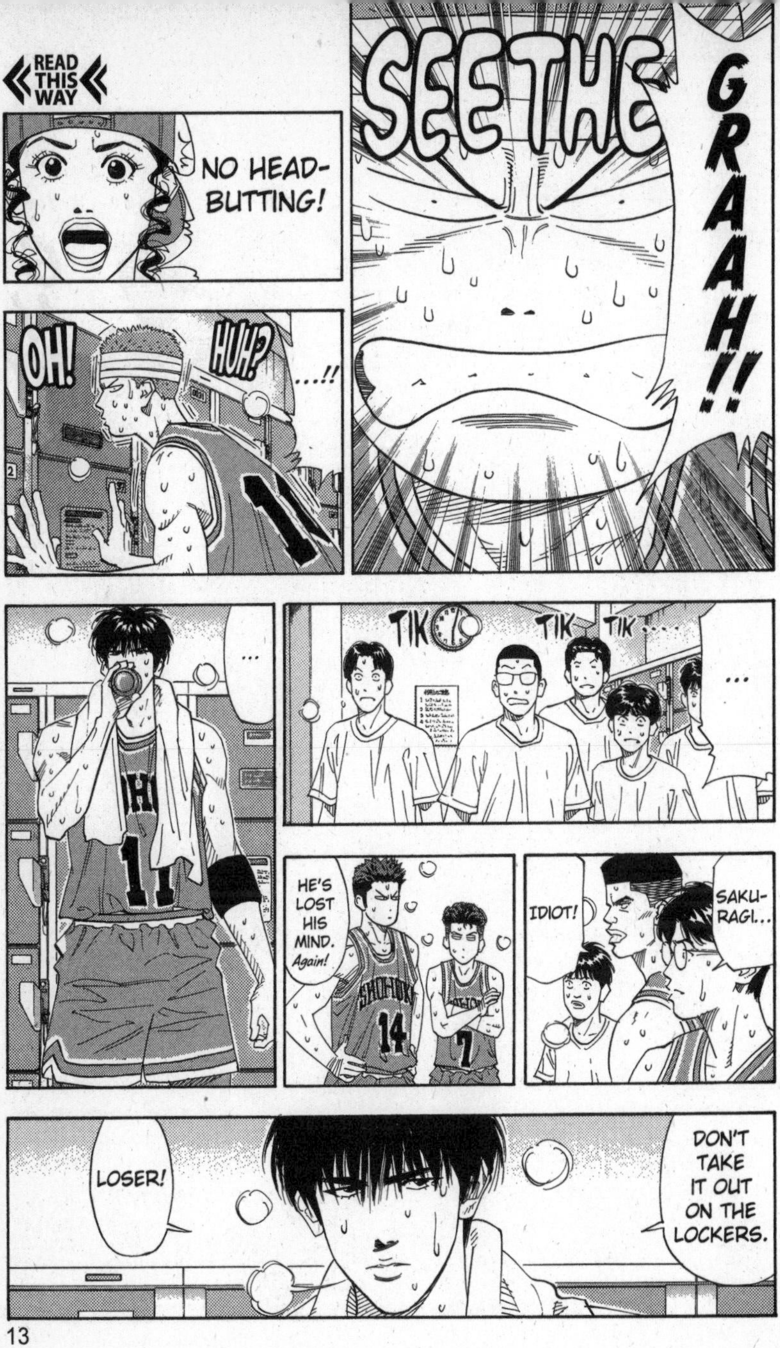

READ THIS WAY
SEETHE
GRAAAH!!
NO HEAD-BUTTING!
...!!
HUH?
OH!
...
TIK TIK TIK...
SAKU-RAGI...
IDIOT!
HE'S LOST HIS MIND. Again!
...
DON'T TAKE IT OUT ON THE LOCKERS.
LOSER!

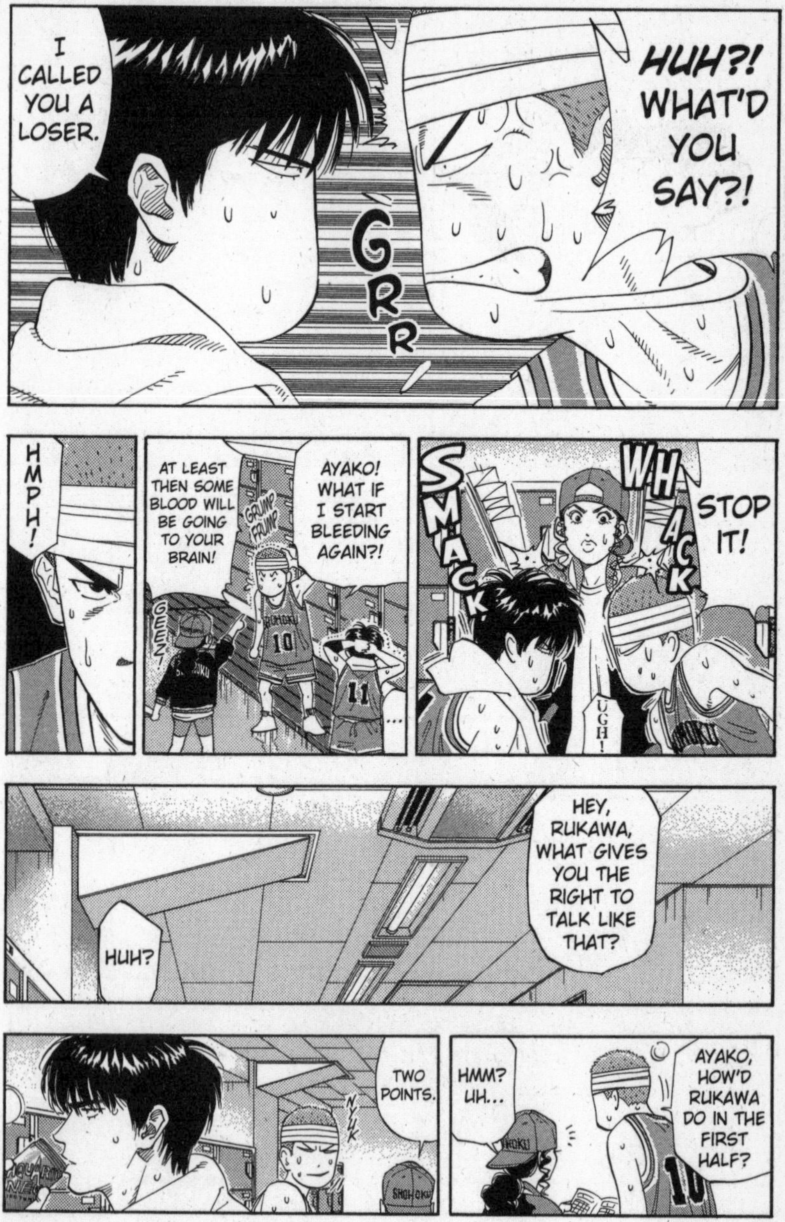
HUH?! WHAT'D YOU SAY?!
I CALLED YOU A LOSER.
GRRR
WHACK
STOP IT!
SMACK
UGH!
AYAKO! WHAT IF I START BLEEDING AGAIN?!
GRUMP FRUMP
AT LEAST THEN SOME BLOOD WILL BE GOING TO YOUR BRAIN!
GEEZ!
...
HMPH!
HEY, RUKAWA, WHAT GIVES YOU THE RIGHT TO TALK LIKE THAT?
HUH?
AYAKO, HOW'D RUKAWA DO IN THE FIRST HALF?
HMM? UH...
TWO POINTS.
NYUK

READ THIS WAY

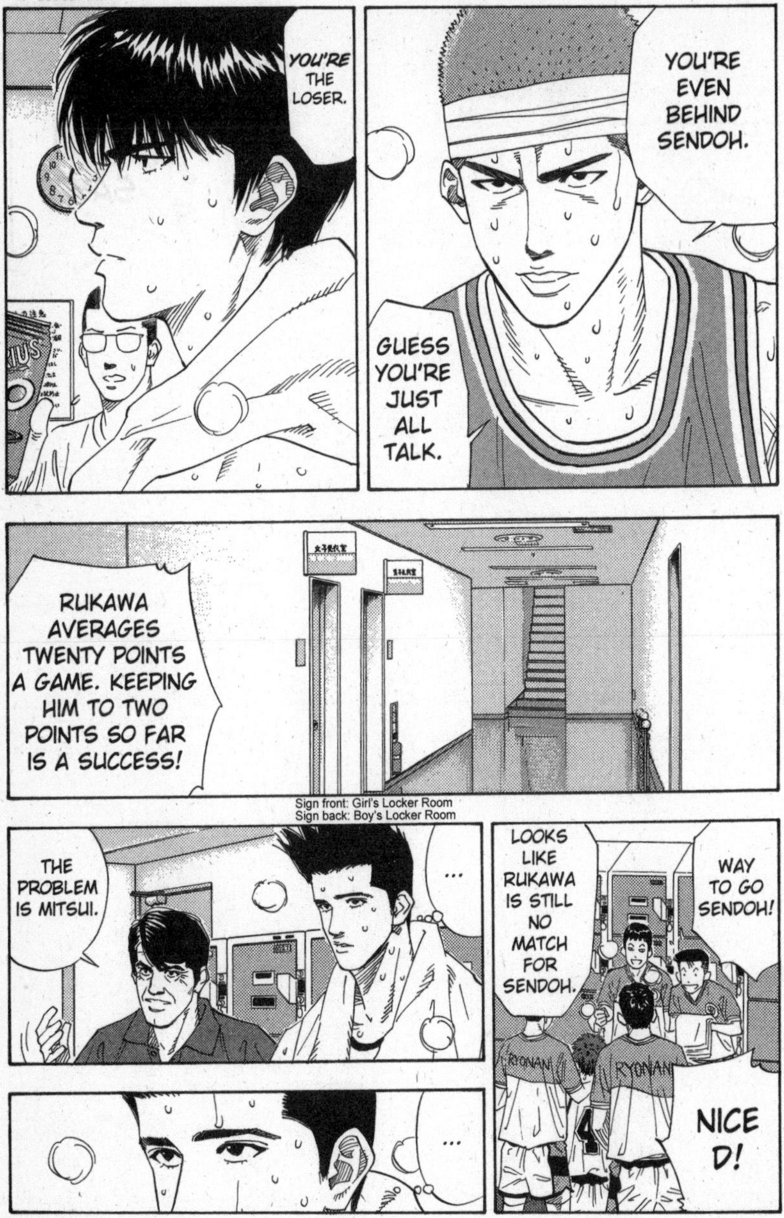
YOU'RE EVEN BEHIND SENDOH.
GUESS YOU'RE JUST ALL TALK.
YOU'RE THE LOSER.
RUKAWA AVERAGES TWENTY POINTS A GAME. KEEPING HIM TO TWO POINTS SO FAR IS A SUCCESS!
Sign front: Girl's Locker Room
Sign back: Boy's Locker Room
WAY TO GO SENDOH!
LOOKS LIKE RUKAWA IS STILL NO MATCH FOR SENDOH.
RYONAN
RYONAN
NICE D!
THE PROBLEM IS MITSUI.
...
...

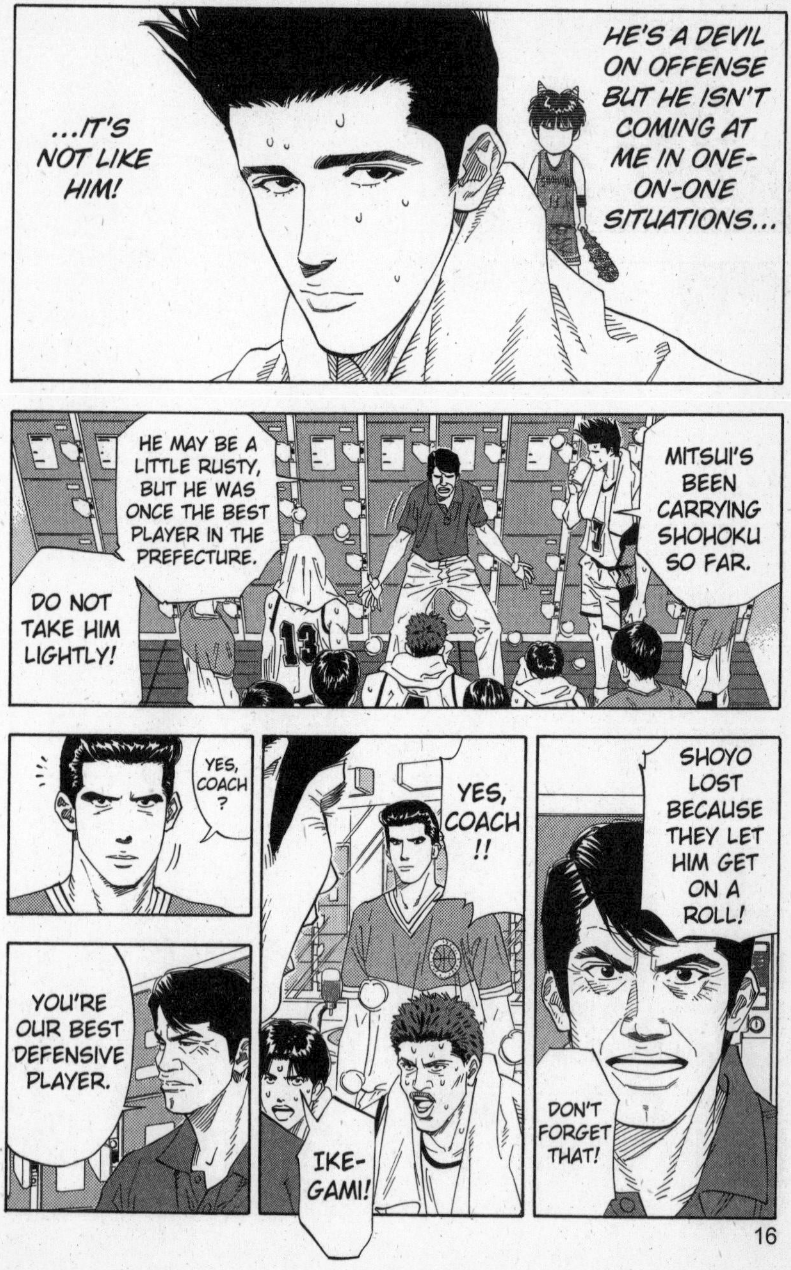
HE'S A DEVIL ON OFFENSE BUT HE ISN'T COMING AT ME IN ONE-ON-ONE SITUATIONS...
...IT'S NOT LIKE HIM!
MITSUI'S BEEN CARRYING SHOHOKU SO FAR.
HE MAY BE A LITTLE RUSTY, BUT HE WAS ONCE THE BEST PLAYER IN THE PREFECTURE.
DO NOT TAKE HIM LIGHTLY!
SHOYO LOST BECAUSE THEY LET HIM GET ON A ROLL!
DON'T FORGET THAT!
YES, COACH!!
IKE-GAMI!
YES, COACH?
YOU'RE OUR BEST DEFENSIVE PLAYER.

READ THIS WAY

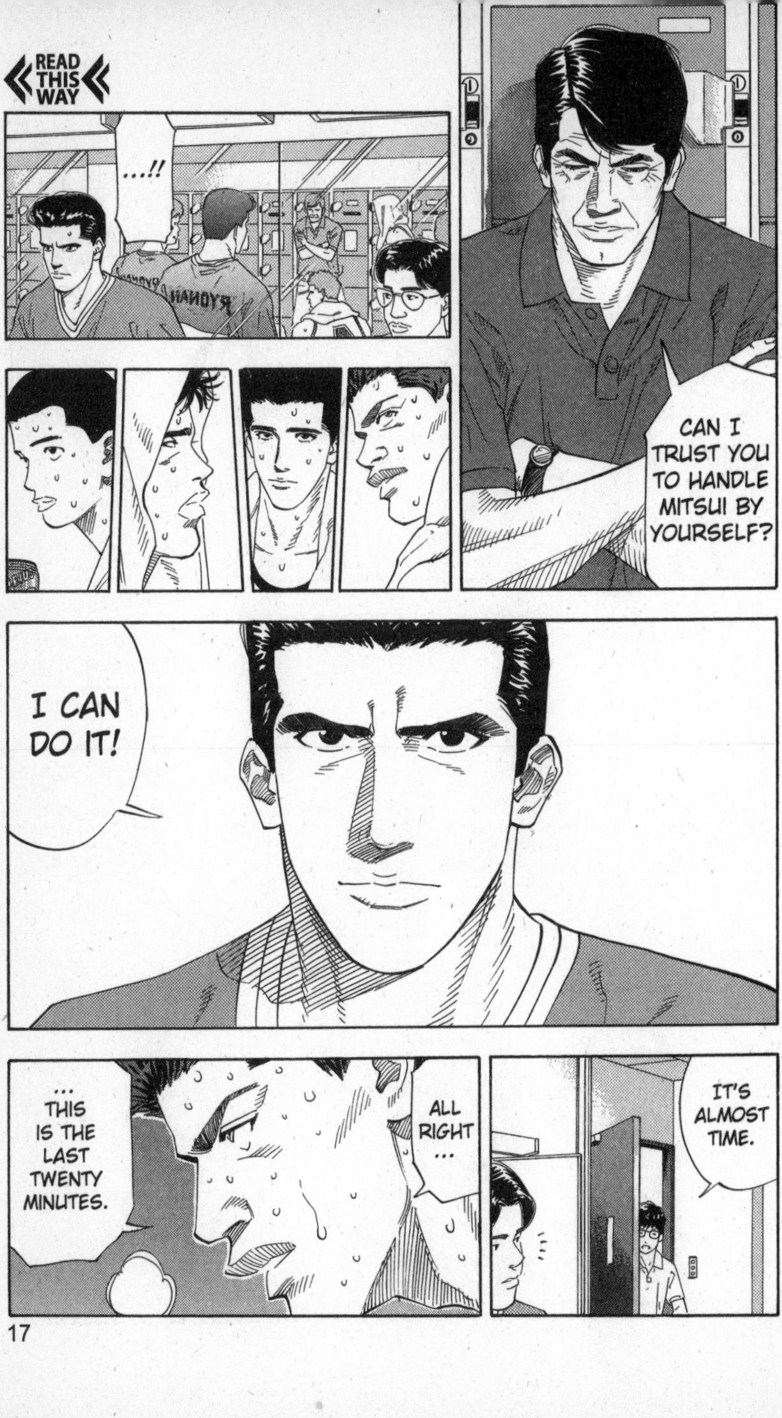
CAN I TRUST YOU TO HANDLE MITSUI BY YOURSELF?
...!!
I CAN DO IT!
IT'S ALMOST TIME.
ALL RIGHT ...
... THIS IS THE LAST TWENTY MINUTES.

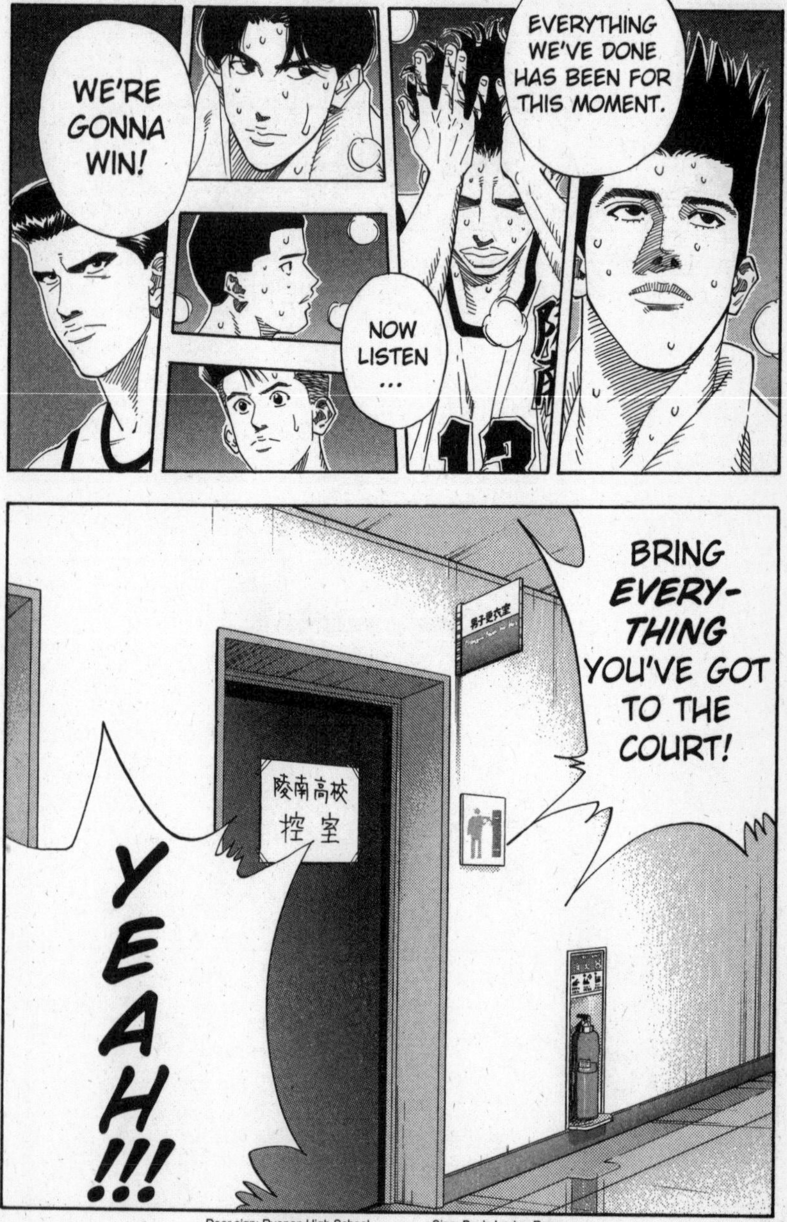
EVERYTHING WE'VE DONE HAS BEEN FOR THIS MOMENT.
NOW LISTEN ...
WE'RE GONNA WIN!
BRING EVERYTHING YOU'VE GOT TO THE COURT!
陵南高校
控室
YEAH!!!

Door sign: Ryonan High School Dressing Room Sign: Boy's Locker Room

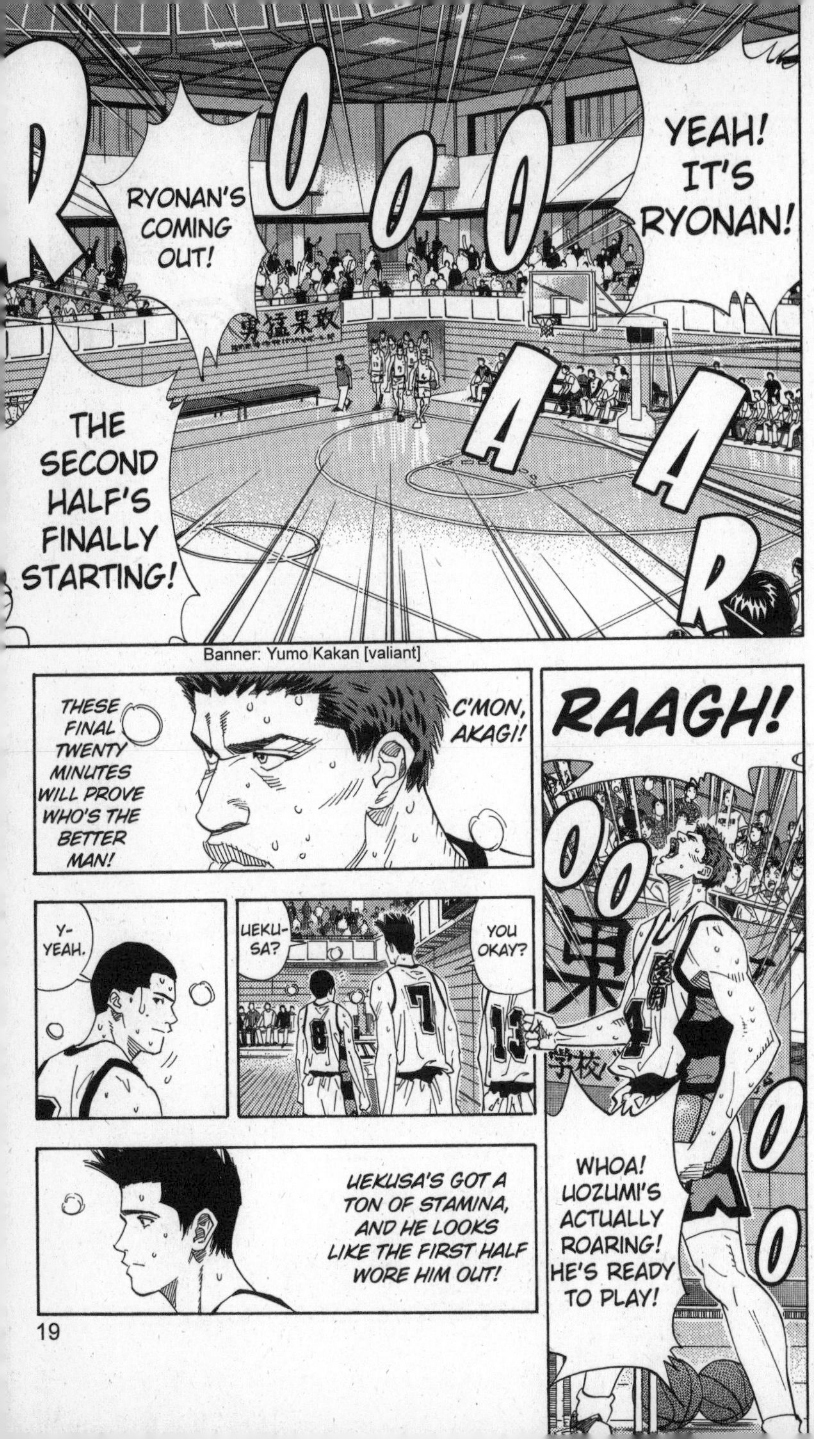
YEAH! IT'S RYONAN!
ROOOOAAAR
RYONAN'S COMING OUT!
THE SECOND HALF'S FINALLY STARTING!
Banner: Yumo Kakan [valiant]
RAAGH!
OOOOO
WHOA! UOZUMI'S ACTUALLY ROARING! HE'S READY TO PLAY!
C'MON, AKAGI!
THESE FINAL TWENTY MINUTES WILL PROVE WHO'S THE BETTER MAN!
YOU OKAY?
UEKU-SA?
Y-YEAH.
UEKUSA'S GOT A TON OF STAMINA, AND HE LOOKS LIKE THE FIRST HALF WORE HIM OUT!

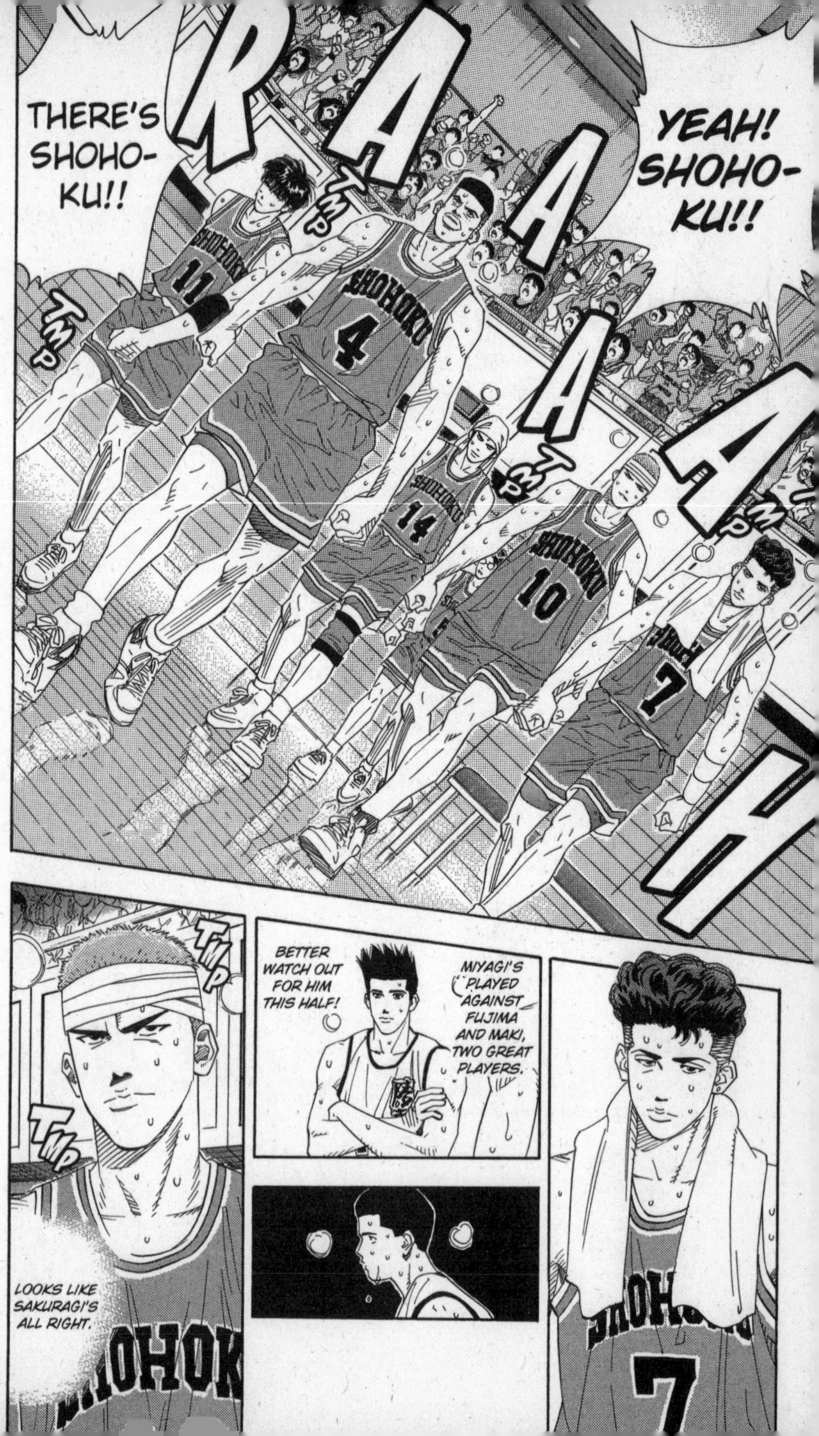
YEAH! SHOHO-KU!!
THERE'S SHOHO-KU!!
RAAAAH
TMP
TMP
TMP
TMP
TMP
MIYAGI'S PLAYED AGAINST FUJIMA AND MAKI, TWO GREAT PLAYERS.
BETTER WATCH OUT FOR HIM THIS HALF!
TMP
TMP
LOOKS LIKE SAKURAGI'S ALL RIGHT.

READ THIS WAY

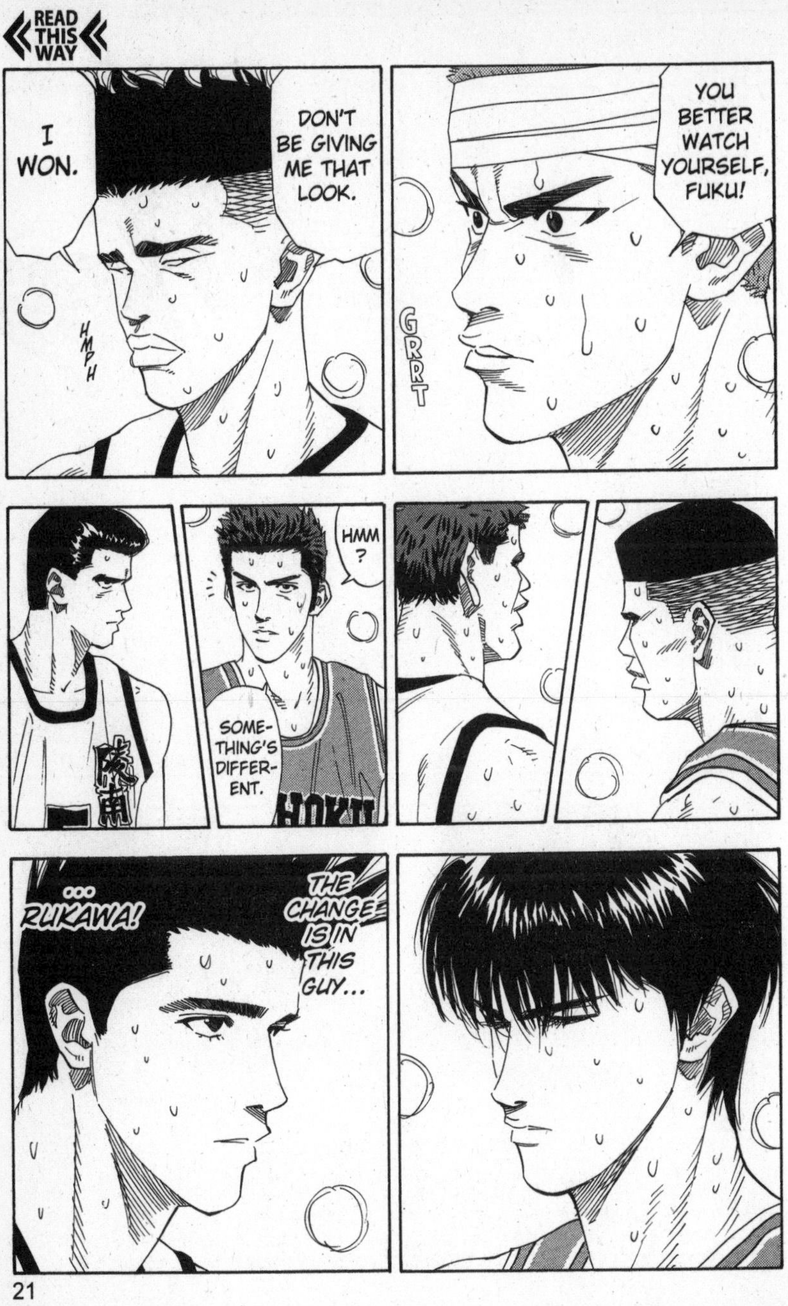

YOU BETTER WATCH YOURSELF, FUKU!
GRRT
DON'T BE GIVING ME THAT LOOK.
I WON.
HMPH
HMM?
SOME-THING'S DIFFER-ENT.
THE CHANGE IS IN THIS GUY...
... RUKAWA!

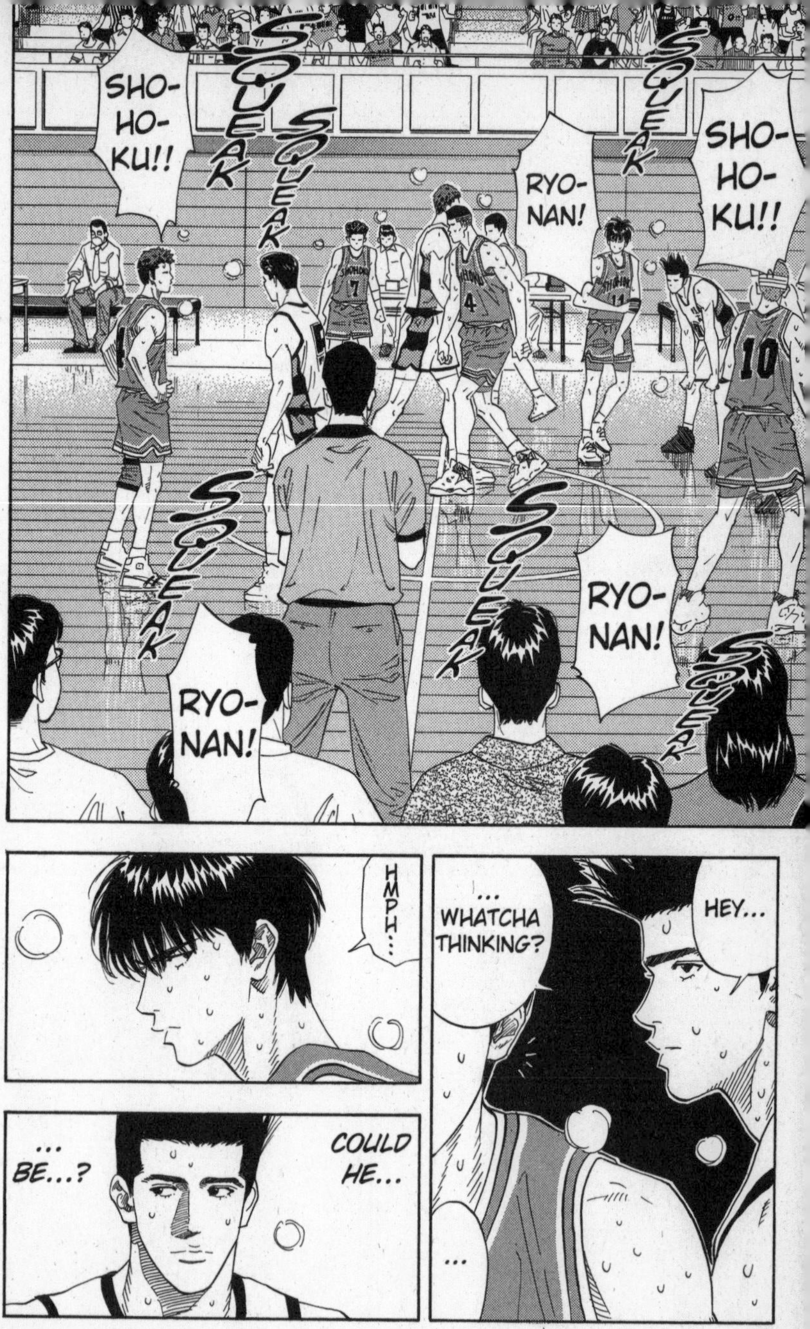
SHO-HO-KU!!
SQUEAK
RYO-NAN!
SQUEAK
SQUEAK
SQUEAK
SHO-HO-KU!!
SQUEAK
RYO-NAN!
SQUEAK
SQUEAK
RYO-NAN!
HEY...
... WHATCHA THINKING?
...
HMPH...
COULD HE...
... BE...?

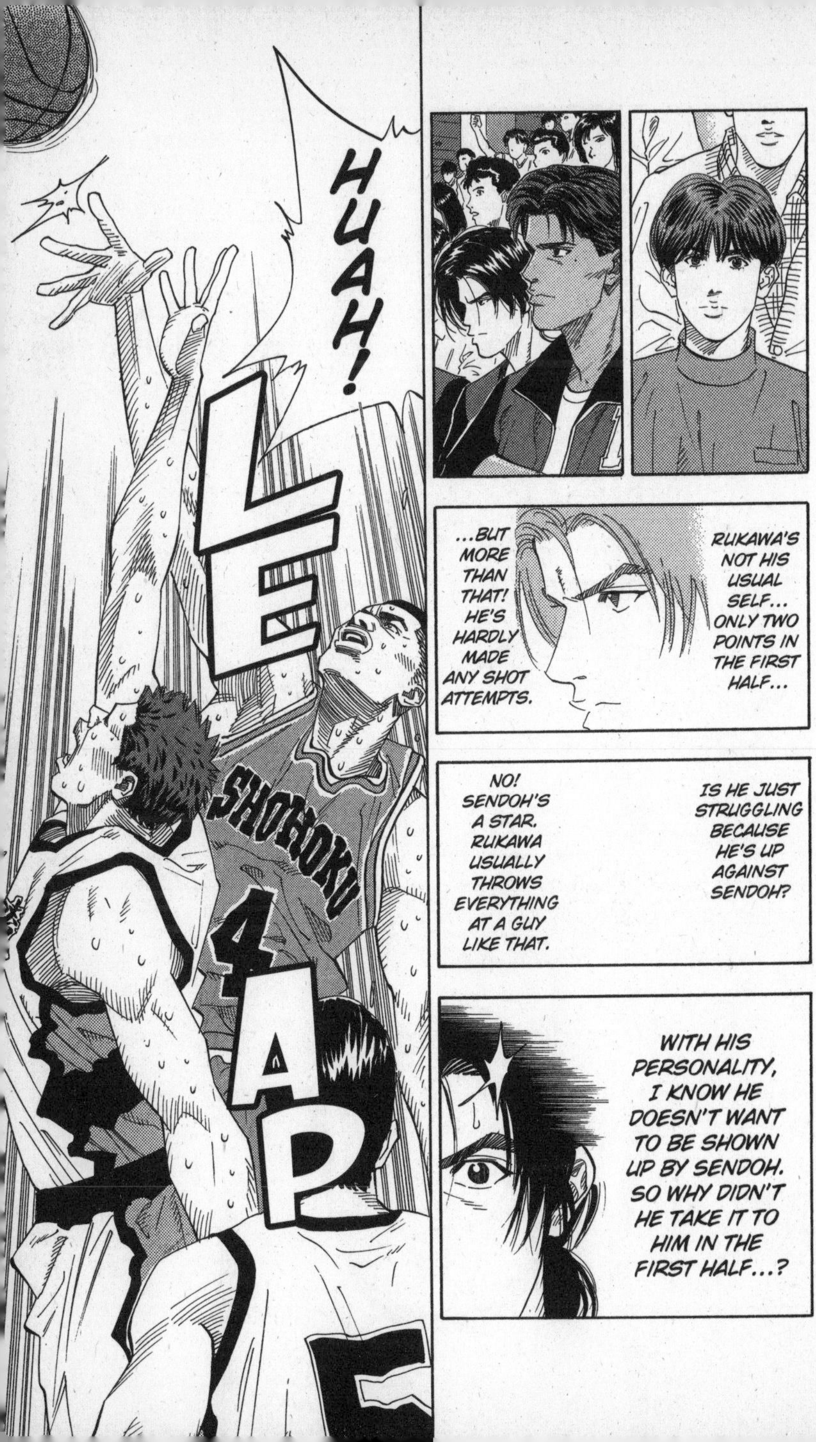
RUKAWA'S NOT HIS USUAL SELF... ONLY TWO POINTS IN THE FIRST HALF...
...BUT MORE THAN THAT! HE'S HARDLY MADE ANY SHOT ATTEMPTS.
IS HE JUST STRUGGLING BECAUSE HE'S UP AGAINST SENDOH?
NO! SENDOH'S A STAR. RUKAWA USUALLY THROWS EVERYTHING AT A GUY LIKE THAT.
WITH HIS PERSONALITY, I KNOW HE DOESN'T WANT TO BE SHOWN UP BY SENDOH. SO WHY DIDN'T HE TAKE IT TO HIM IN THE FIRST HALF...?
HUAH!
LEAP
SHOHOKU
4

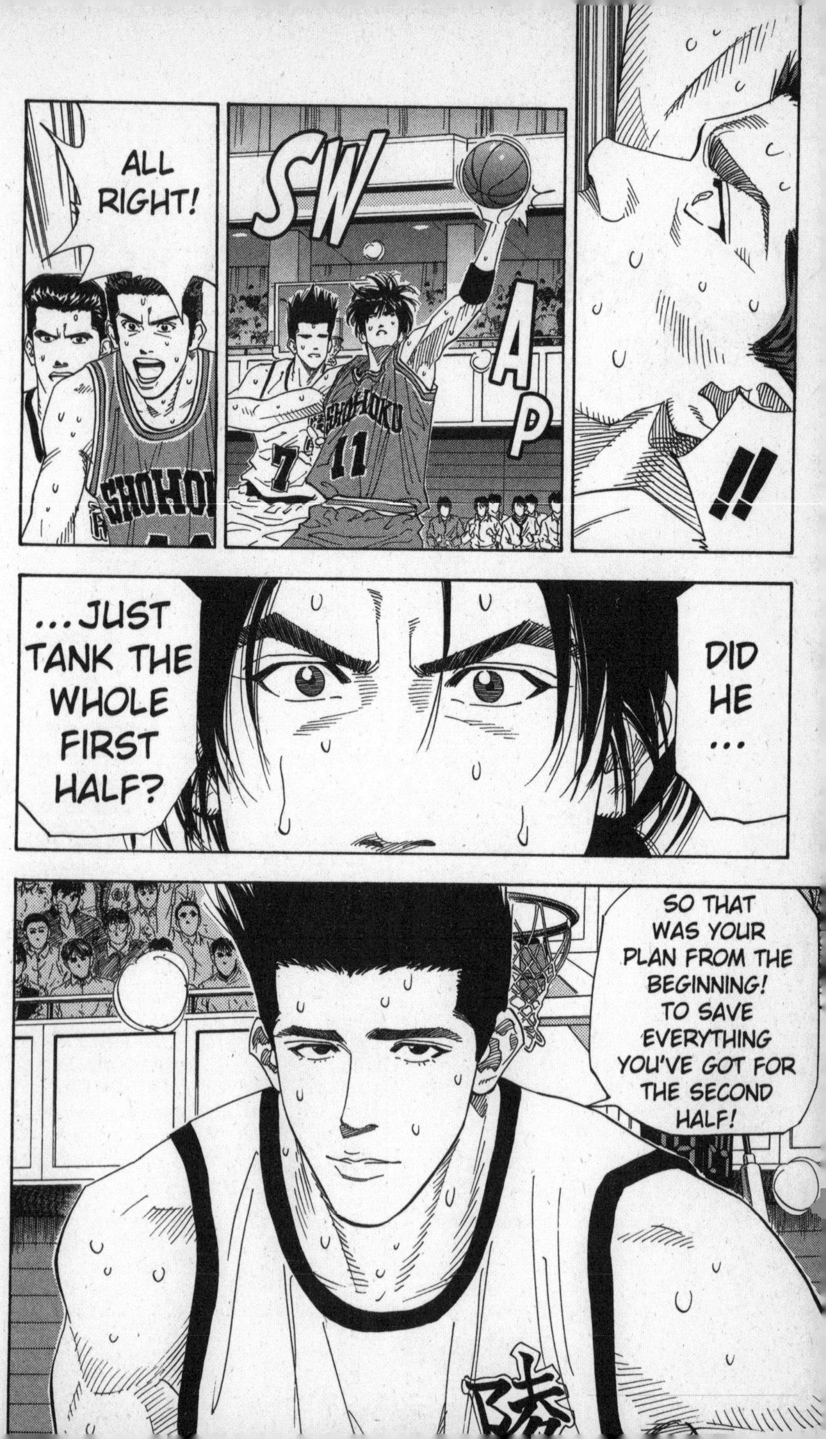
!!
SWAP
ALL RIGHT!
DID HE ...
...JUST TANK THE WHOLE FIRST HALF?
SO THAT WAS YOUR PLAN FROM THE BEGINNING! TO SAVE EVERYTHING YOU'VE GOT FOR THE SECOND HALF!

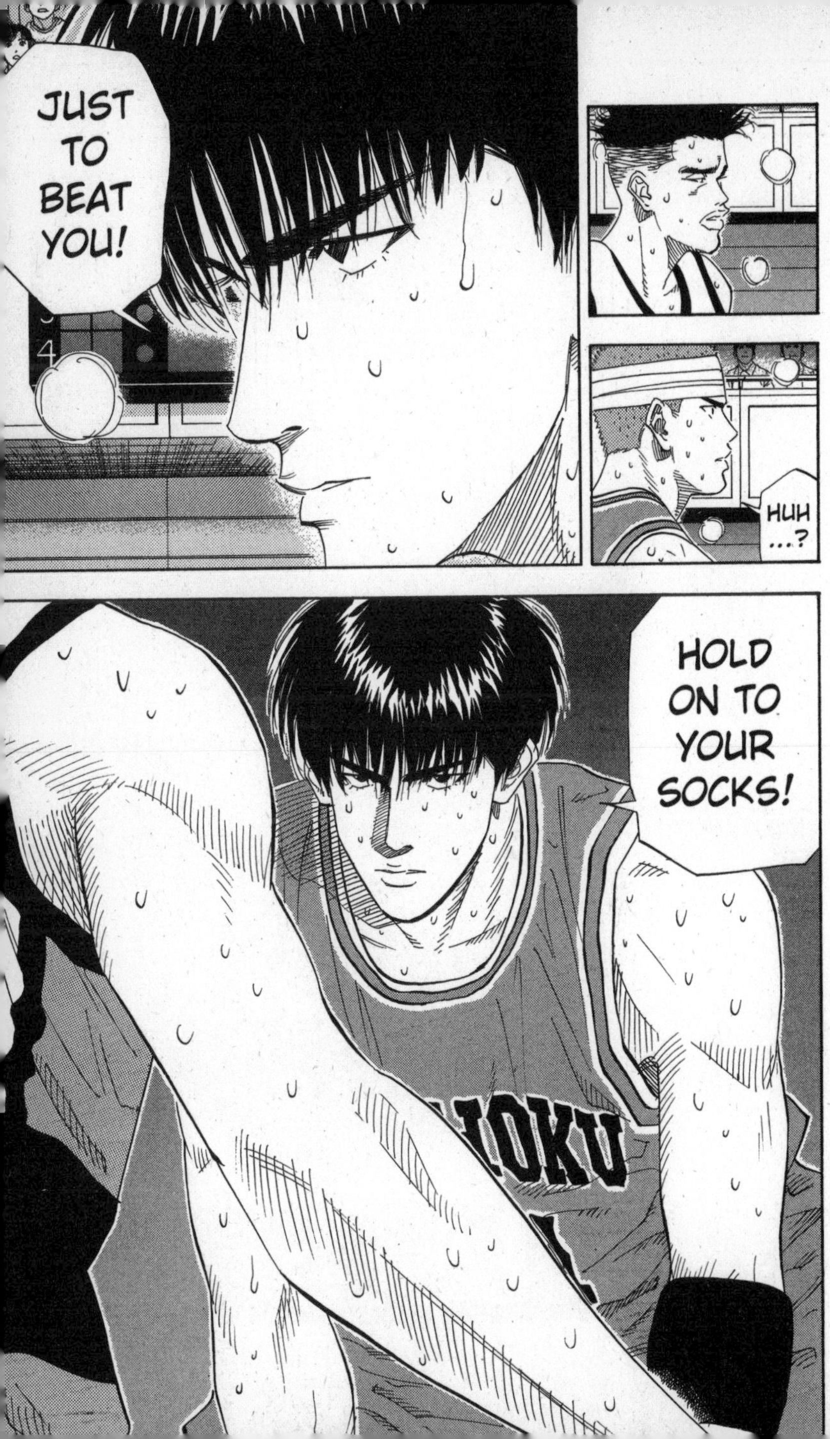
HUH ...?
JUST TO BEAT YOU!
HOLD ON TO YOUR SOCKS!

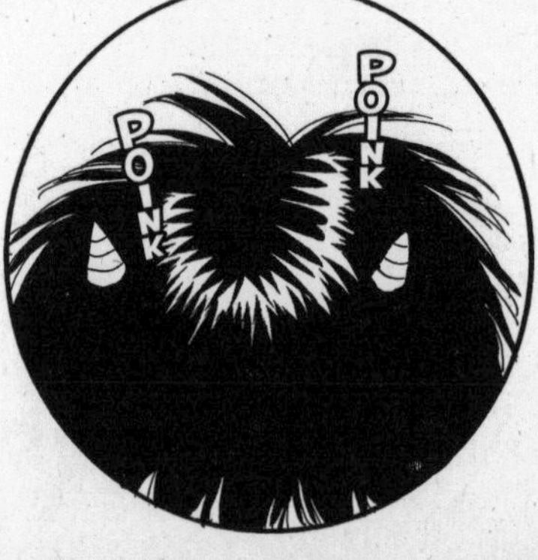
POINK
POINK

SLAM DUNK

SILENT FIRST HALF

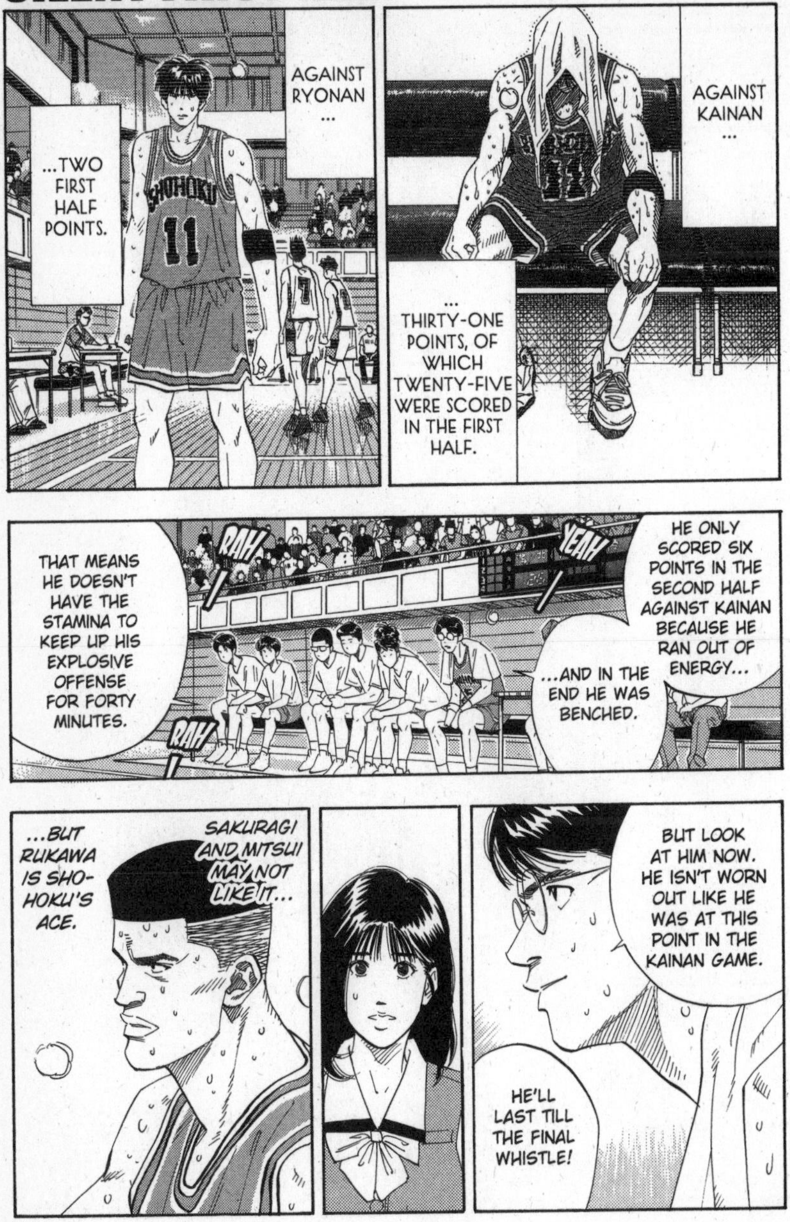

AGAINST KAINAN ...
... THIRTY-ONE POINTS, OF WHICH TWENTY-FIVE WERE SCORED IN THE FIRST HALF.
AGAINST RYONAN ...
...TWO FIRST HALF POINTS.
HE ONLY SCORED SIX POINTS IN THE SECOND HALF AGAINST KAINAN BECAUSE HE RAN OUT OF ENERGY...
...AND IN THE END HE WAS BENCHED.
YEAH
RAH
THAT MEANS HE DOESN'T HAVE THE STAMINA TO KEEP UP HIS EXPLOSIVE OFFENSE FOR FORTY MINUTES.
RAH
BUT LOOK AT HIM NOW. HE ISN'T WORN OUT LIKE HE WAS AT THIS POINT IN THE KAINAN GAME.
HE'LL LAST TILL THE FINAL WHISTLE!
SAKURAGI AND MITSUI MAY NOT LIKE IT...
...BUT RUKAWA IS SHO-HOKU'S ACE.

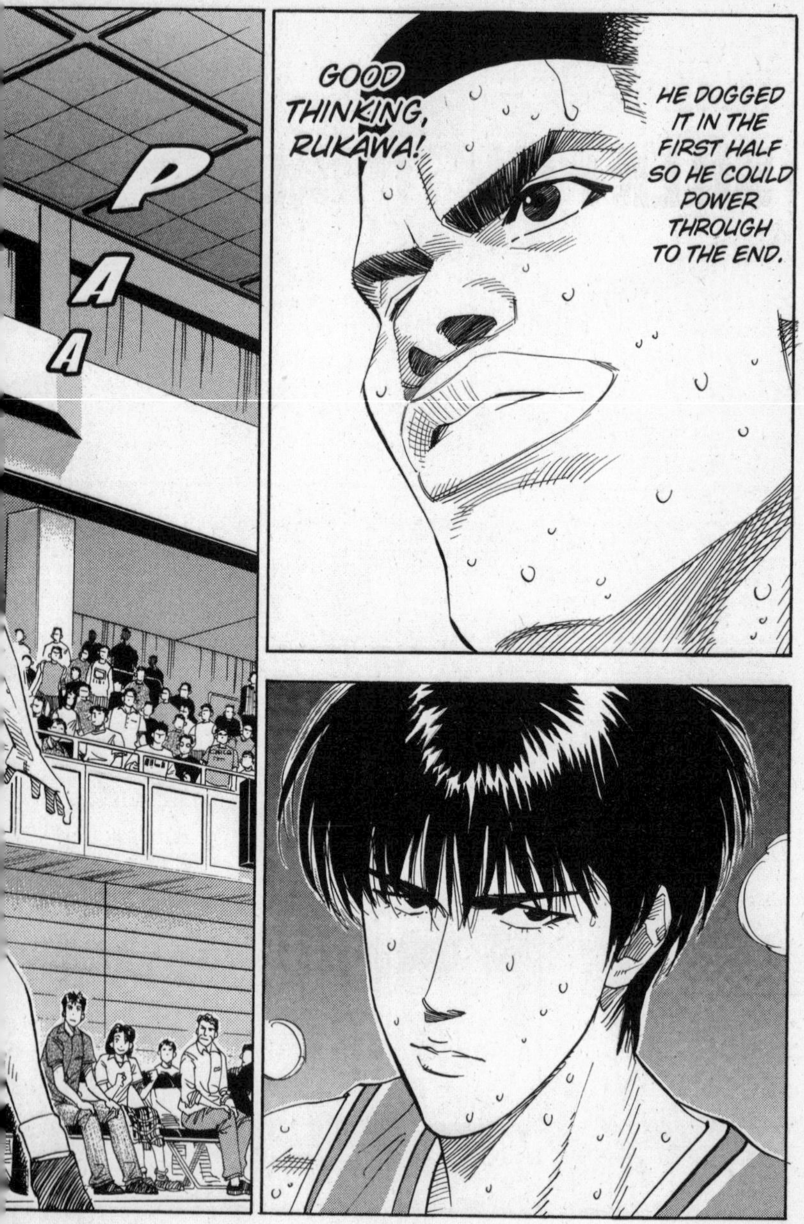
HE DOGGED IT IN THE FIRST HALF SO HE COULD POWER THROUGH TO THE END.
GOOD THINKING, RUKAWA!
PAAA

#163 SILENT FIRST HALF

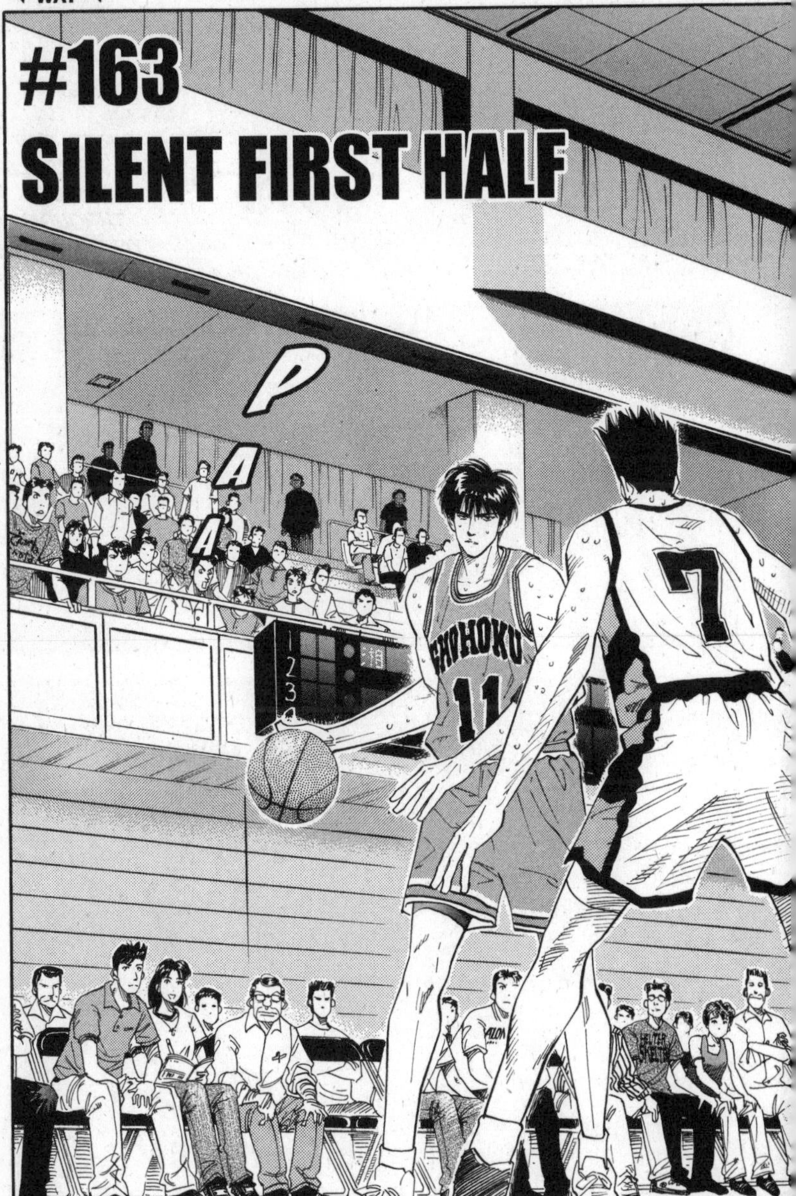
READ THIS WAY
PAAP
SHOHOKU
11
7

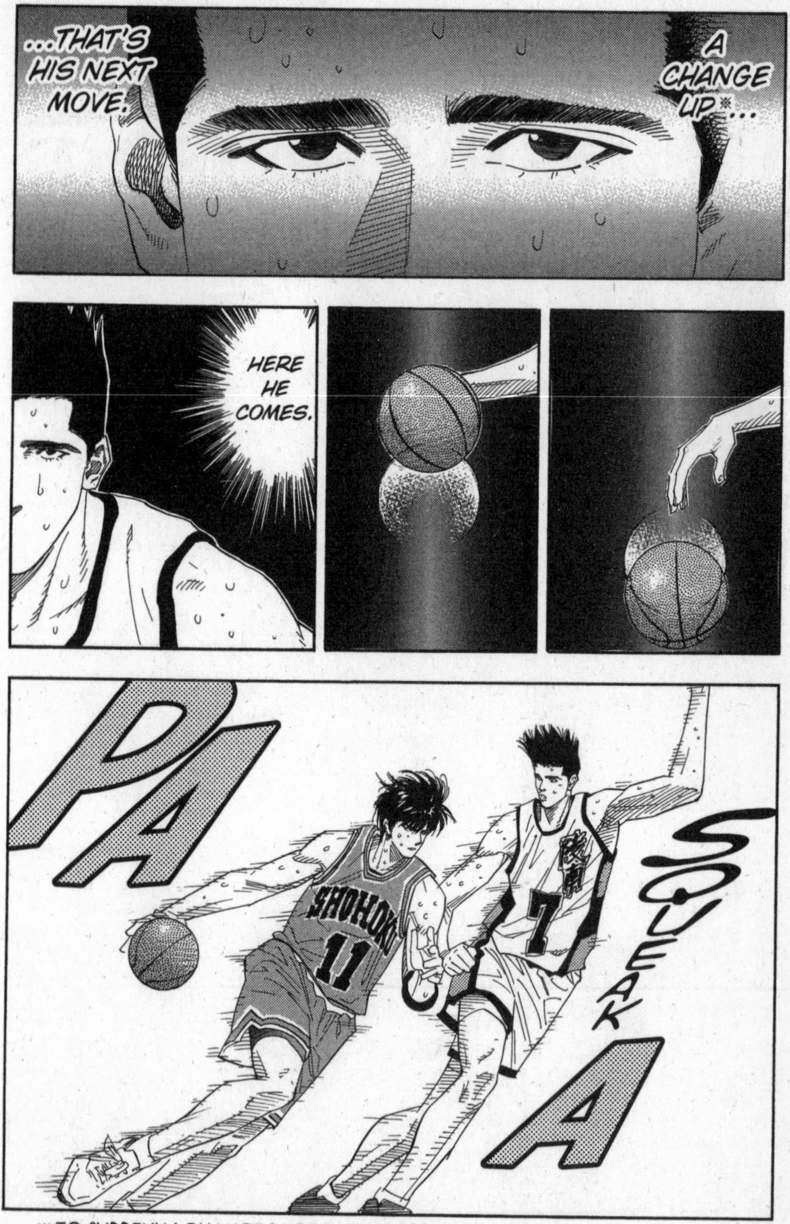
A CHANGE UP※...
...THAT'S HIS NEXT MOVE.
HERE HE COMES.
SQUEAK
PA
A

※ TO SUDDENLY CHANGE PACE IN THE MIDDLE OF A DRIBBLE.
A TECHNIQUE USED TO DRIVE PAST A PLAYER.

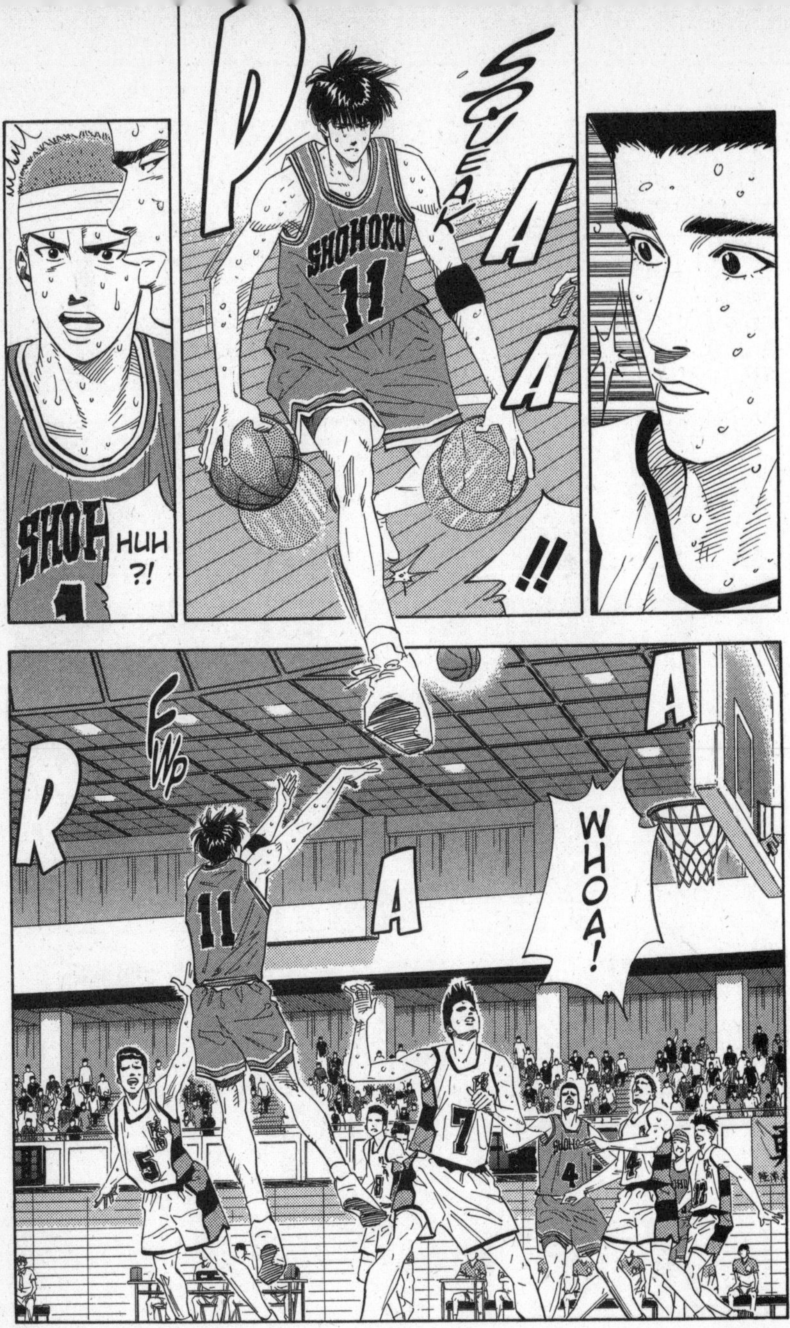
P
SQUEAK
A
A
!!
HUH ?!
A
FWP
R
A
WHOA!

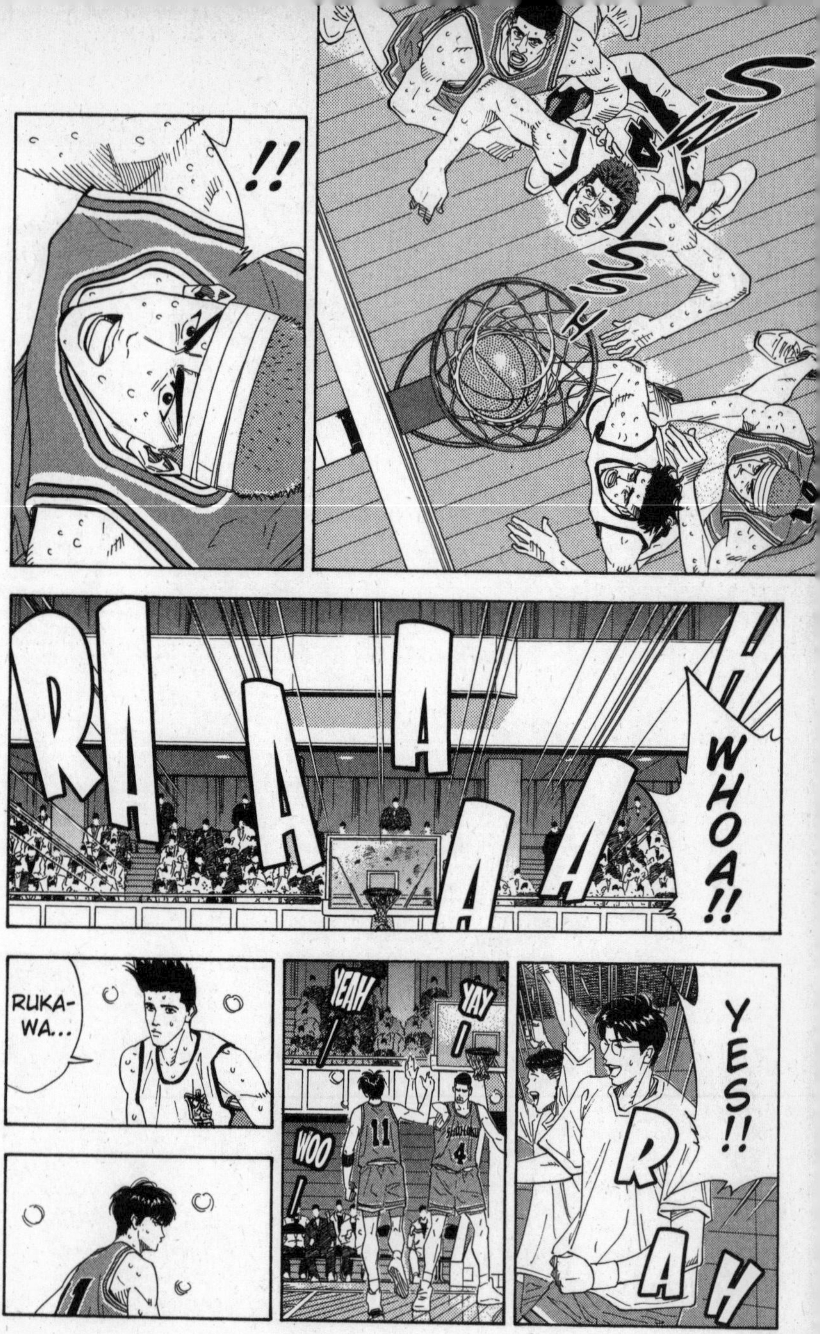
SWSSH
!!
WHOA!!
RAAAAAAH
YES!!
RAH
YEAH
YAY
WOO
RUKA-WA...

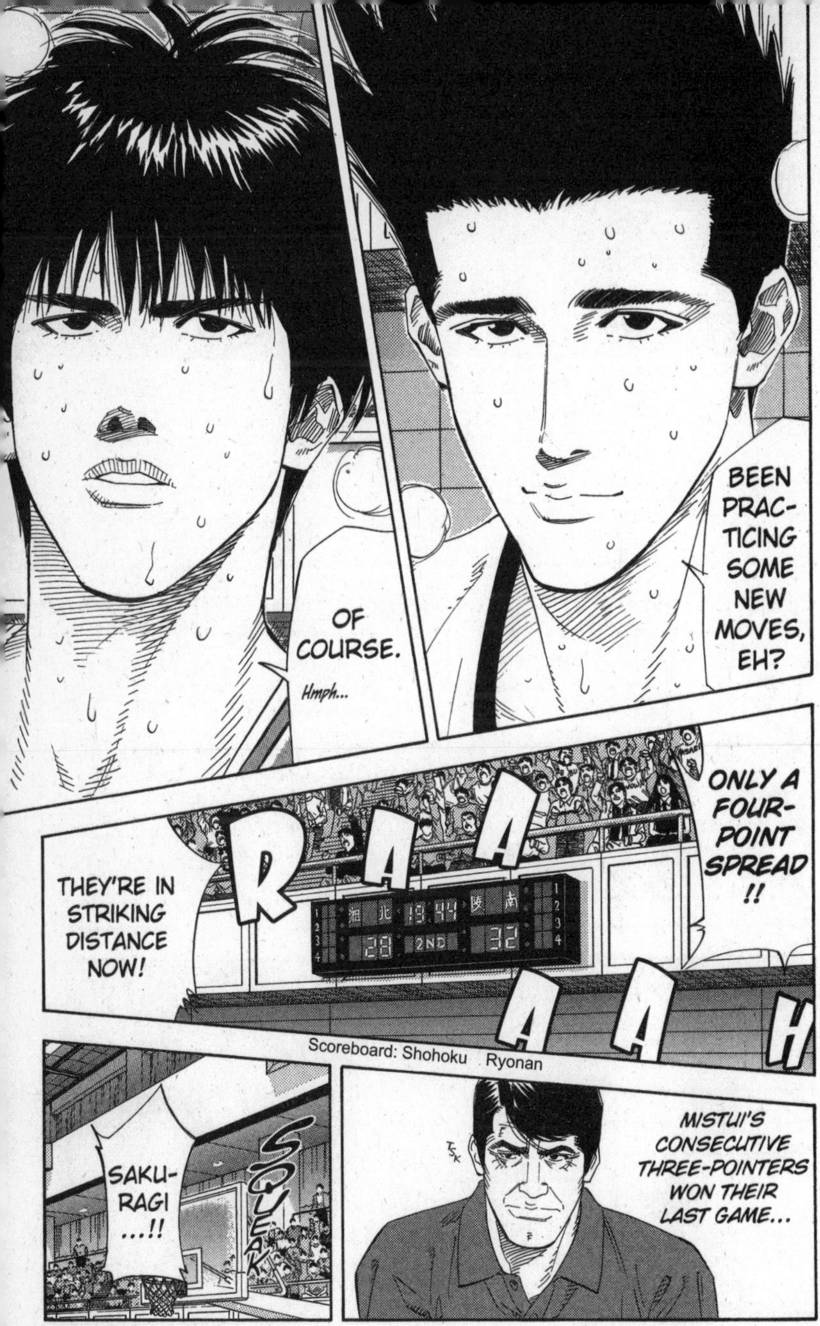
BEEN PRAC-TICING SOME NEW MOVES, EH?
OF COURSE.
Hmph...
ONLY A FOUR-POINT SPREAD!!
THEY'RE IN STRIKING DISTANCE NOW!
RAAAAAH
19:44
28
2ND
32
Scoreboard: Shohoku Ryonan
TSK
MISTUI'S CONSECUTIVE THREE-POINTERS WON THEIR LAST GAME...
SQUEAK
SAKU-RAGI ...!!

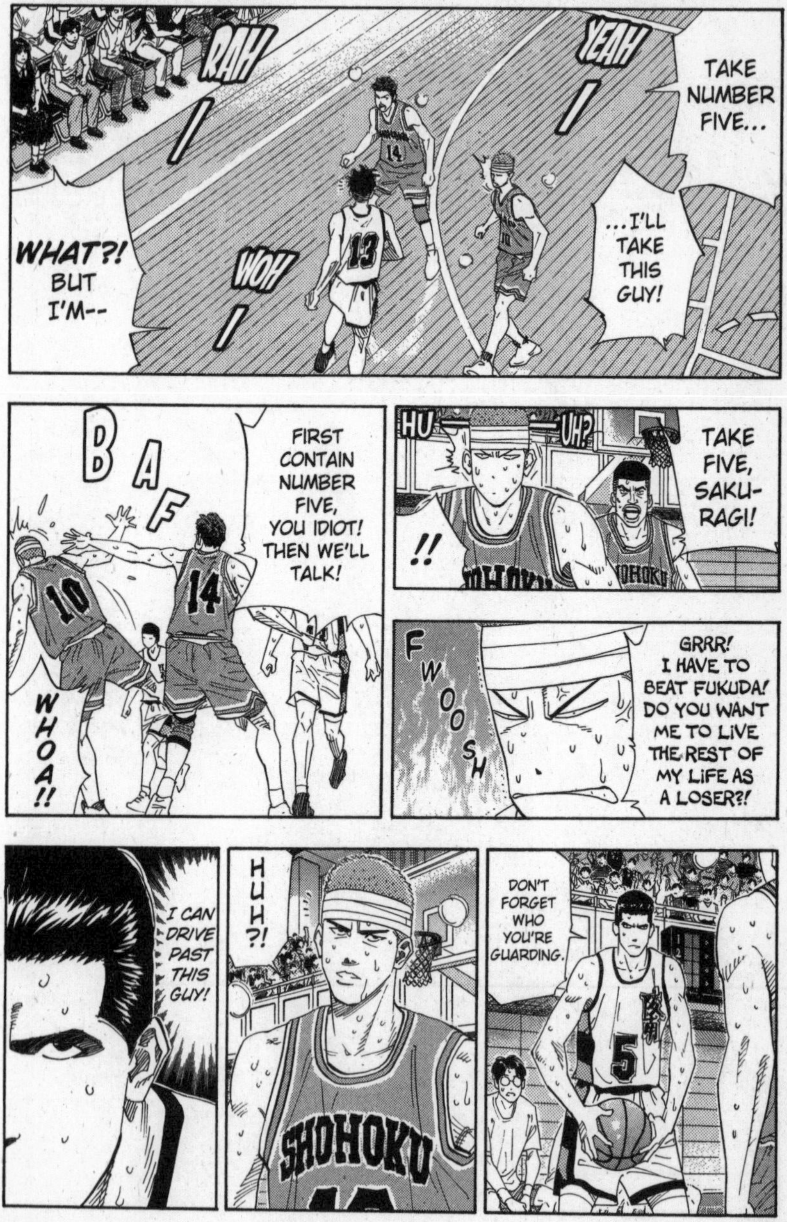
TAKE NUMBER FIVE...
YEAH
RAH
...I'LL TAKE THIS GUY!
WOH
WHAT?! BUT I'M--
TAKE FIVE, SAKU-RAGI!
HU— —UH?
!!
GRRR! I HAVE TO BEAT FUKUDA! DO YOU WANT ME TO LIVE THE REST OF MY LIFE AS A LOSER?!
FWOOSH
FIRST CONTAIN NUMBER FIVE, YOU IDIOT! THEN WE'LL TALK!
BAF
WHOA!!
DON'T FORGET WHO YOU'RE GUARDING.
HUH?!
I CAN DRIVE PAST THIS GUY!

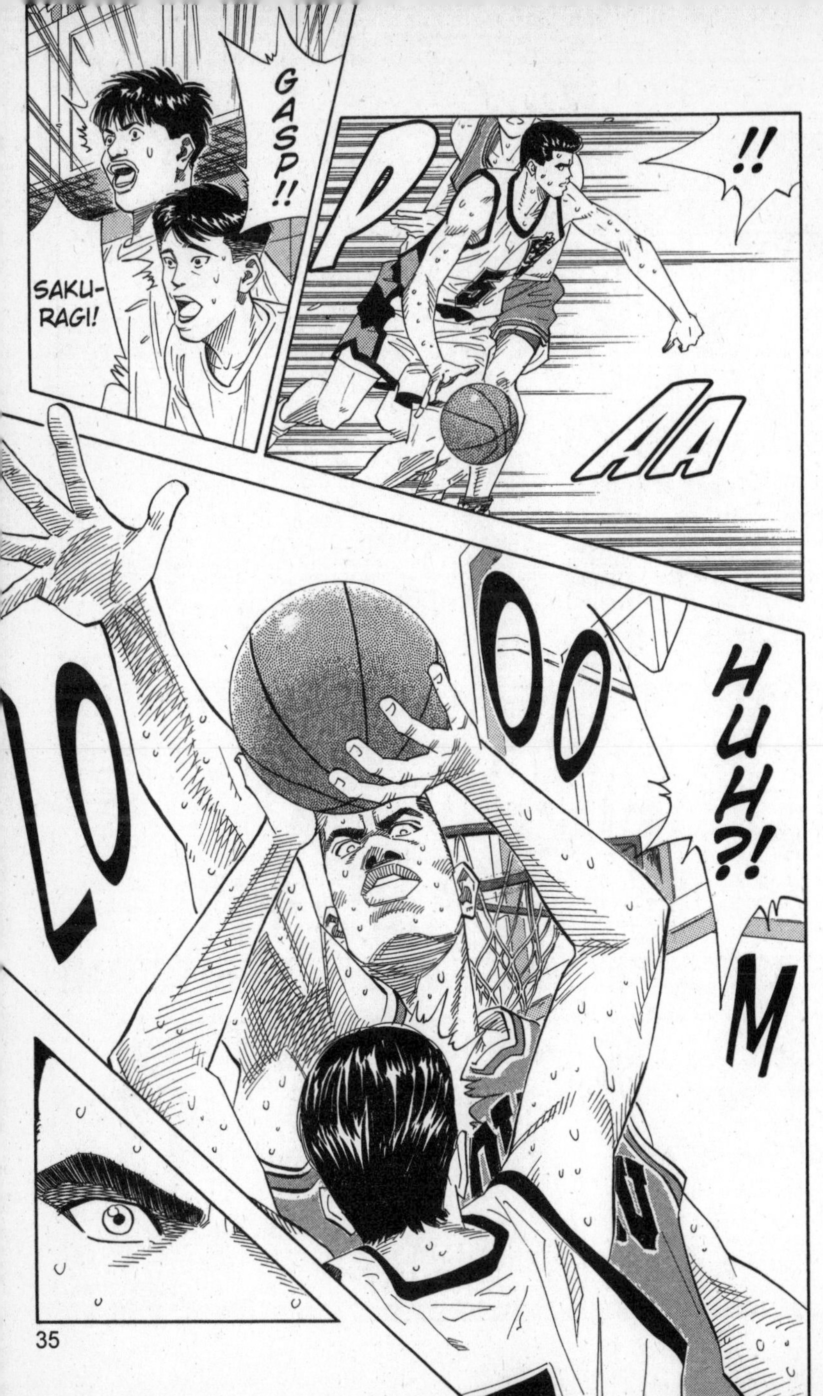
!!
PAA
GASP!!
SAKU-RAGI!
HUH?!
ZOOOM

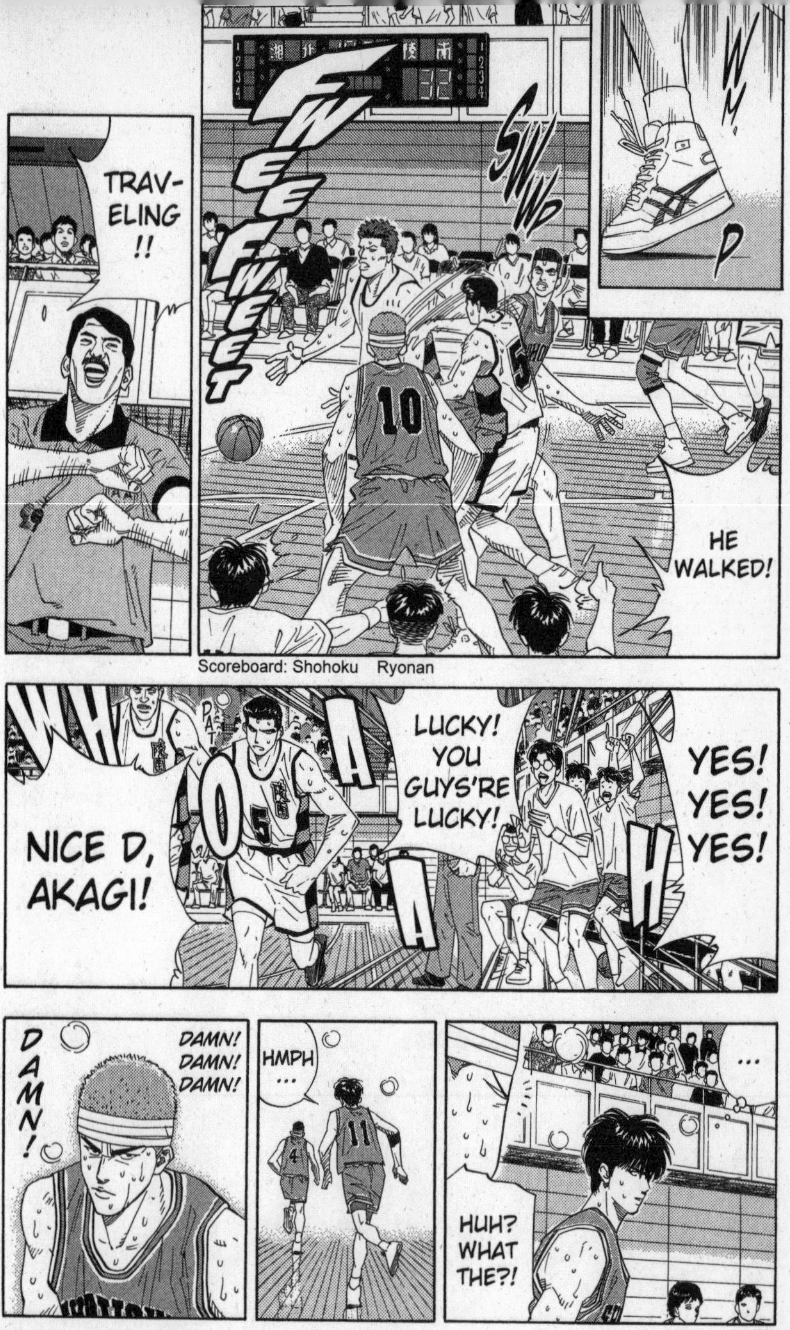
FWEEE
FWEEET
HE WALKED!
TRAV-ELING!!
YES! YES! YES!
LUCKY! YOU GUYS'RE LUCKY!
NICE D, AKAGI!
...
HUH? WHAT THE?!
HMPH ...
DAMN! DAMN! DAMN!
DAMN!
Scoreboard: Shohoku Ryonan

READ THIS WAY

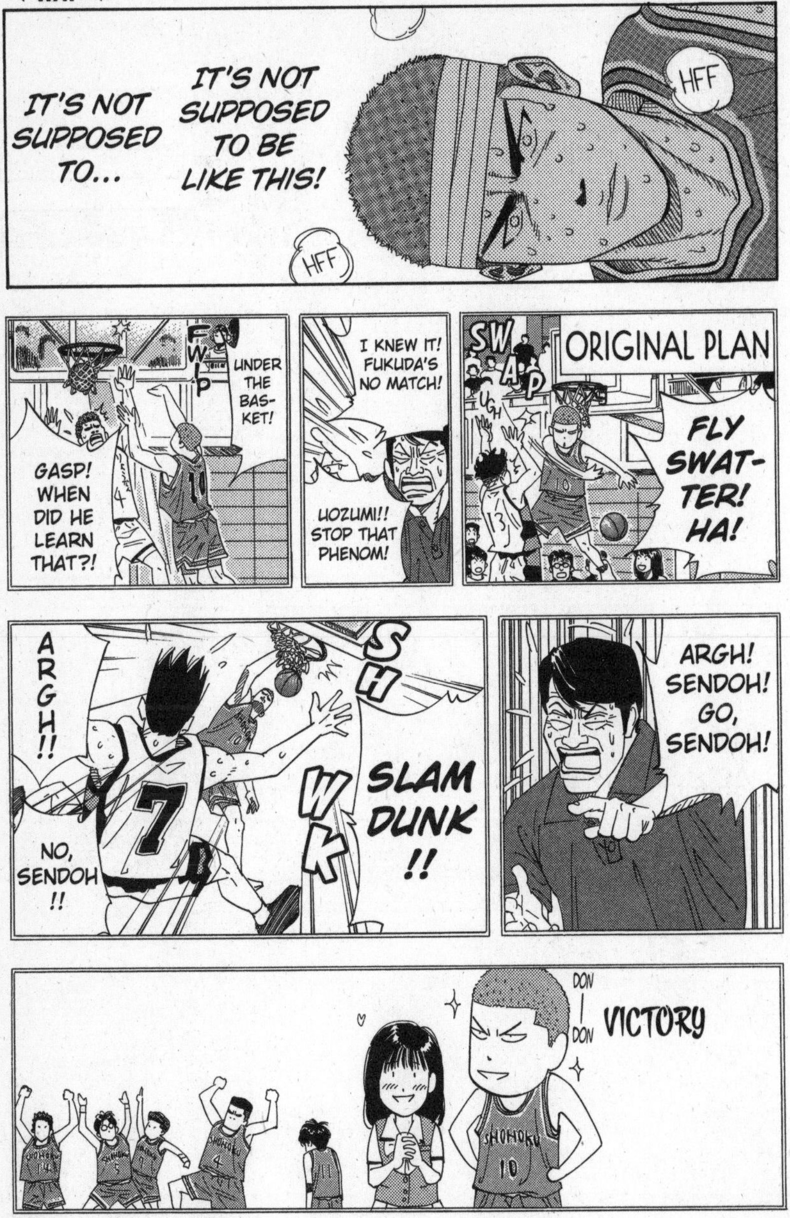

IT'S NOT SUPPOSED TO BE LIKE THIS!
IT'S NOT SUPPOSED TO...
HFF
HFF
ORIGINAL PLAN
SWAP
UGH
FLY SWAT-TER! HA!
I KNEW IT! FUKUDA'S NO MATCH!
UOZUMI!! STOP THAT PHENOM!
FWIP
UNDER THE BAS-KET!
GASP! WHEN DID HE LEARN THAT?!
ARGH! SENDOH! GO, SENDOH!
SH
WK
SLAM DUNK !!
ARGH!!
NO, SENDOH !!
DON DON
VICTORY

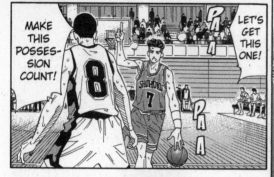

READ THIS WAY

NOW LOOK AT ME!
BURNED NOT ONLY BY SENDOH, BUT ALSO BY FUKUDA, AND NOW HIS GUY!
TWITCH
QUAKE
FUME
PAA
LET'S GET THIS ONE!
PAA
MAKE THIS POSSES-SION COUNT!
MIYAGI'S RIGHT. THIS POSSES-SION IS HUGE!
TAKE ADVANTAGE OF THAT TURNOVER AND SHRINK THE LEAD TO A BASKET... THEN WE'LL HAVE THE MOMENTUM!!
GASP! LOOK!
ROAR
SQUEAK
UGH ...!
SQUEAK

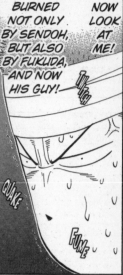

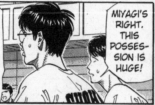

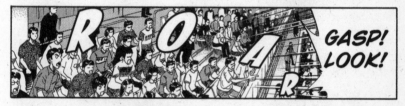

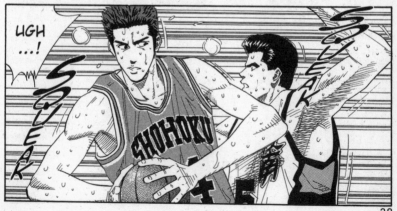

READ THIS WAY

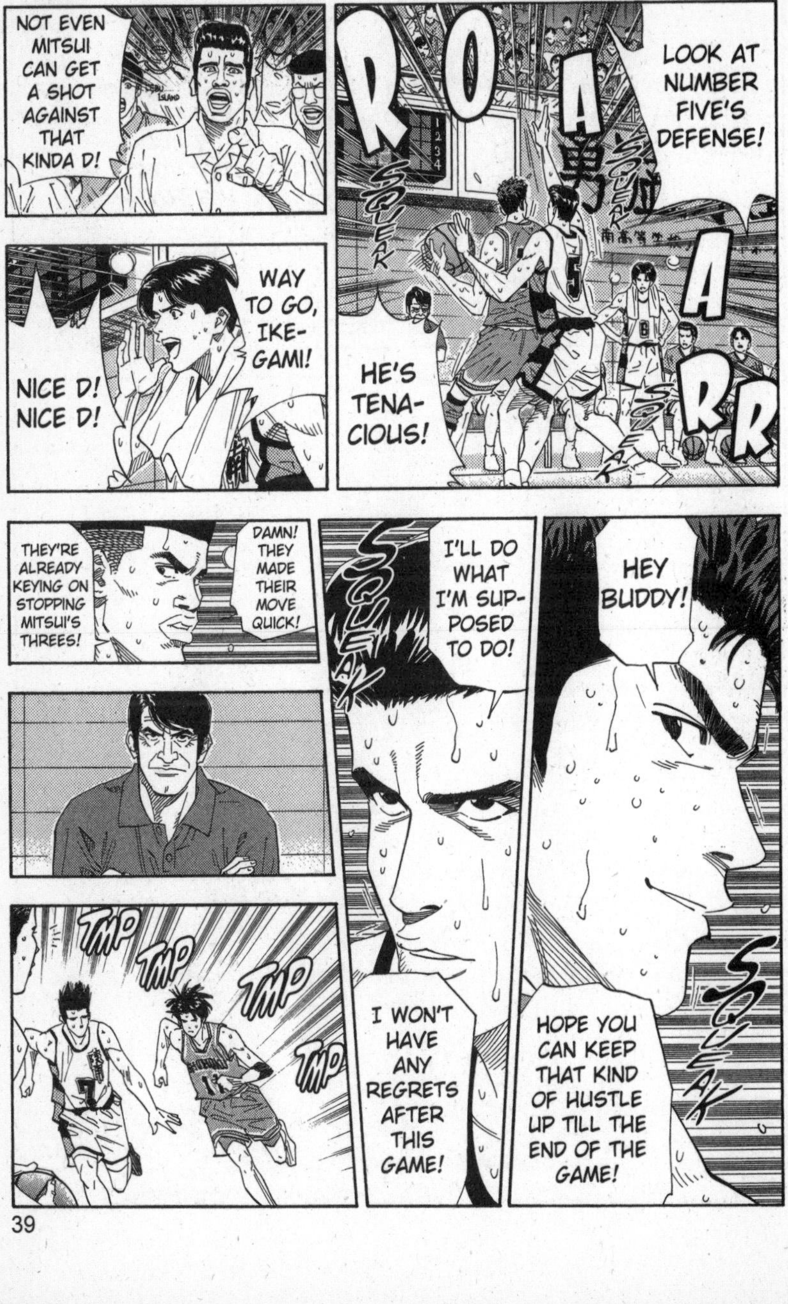
ROAAARR
SQUEAK
SQUEAK
LOOK AT NUMBER FIVE'S DEFENSE!
SQUEAK
HE'S TENACIOUS!
NOT EVEN MITSUI CAN GET A SHOT AGAINST THAT KINDA D!
WAY TO GO, IKE-GAMI!
NICE D! NICE D!
HEY BUDDY!
HOPE YOU CAN KEEP THAT KIND OF HUSTLE UP TILL THE END OF THE GAME!
SQUEAK
I'LL DO WHAT I'M SUP-POSED TO DO!
SQUEAK
I WON'T HAVE ANY REGRETS AFTER THIS GAME!
DAMN! THEY MADE THEIR MOVE QUICK!
THEY'RE ALREADY KEYING ON STOPPING MITSUI'S THREES!
TMP
TMP
TMP
TMP

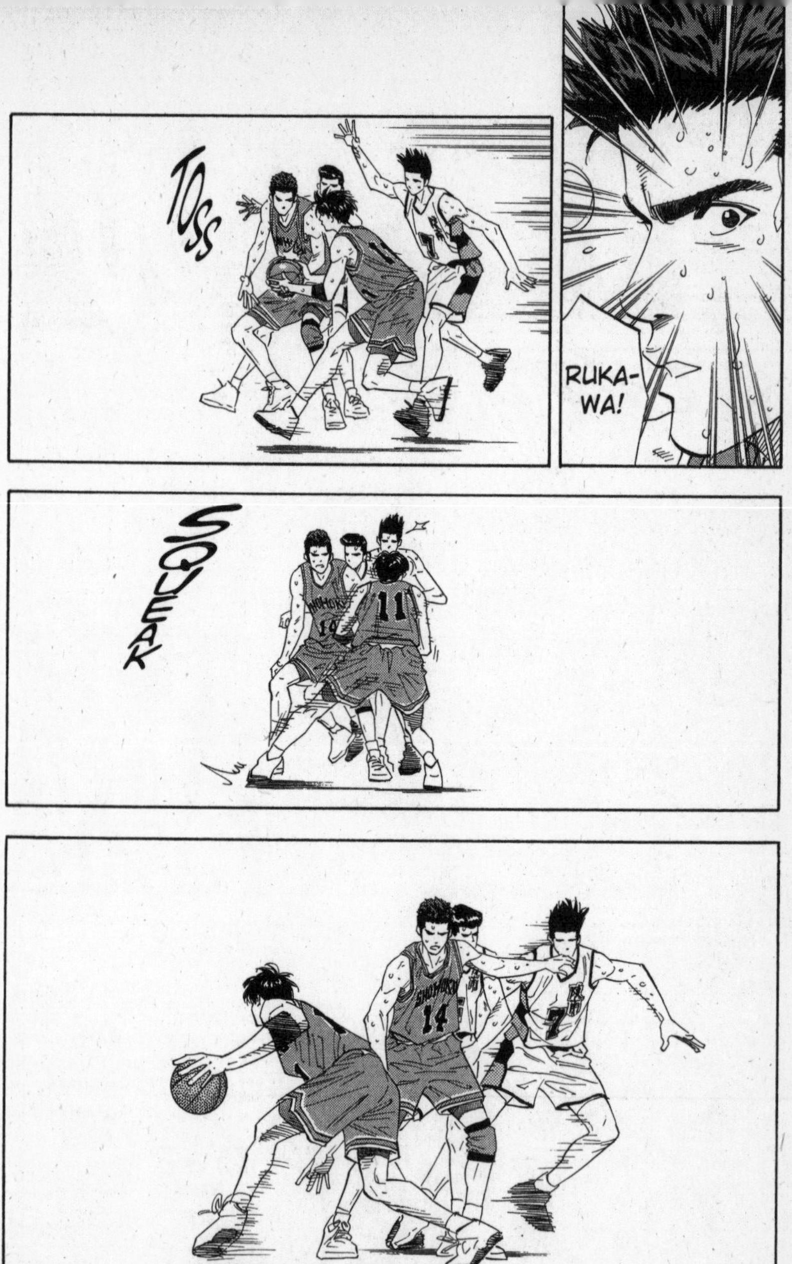
RUKA-
WA!
TOSS
SQUEAK

READ THIS WAY

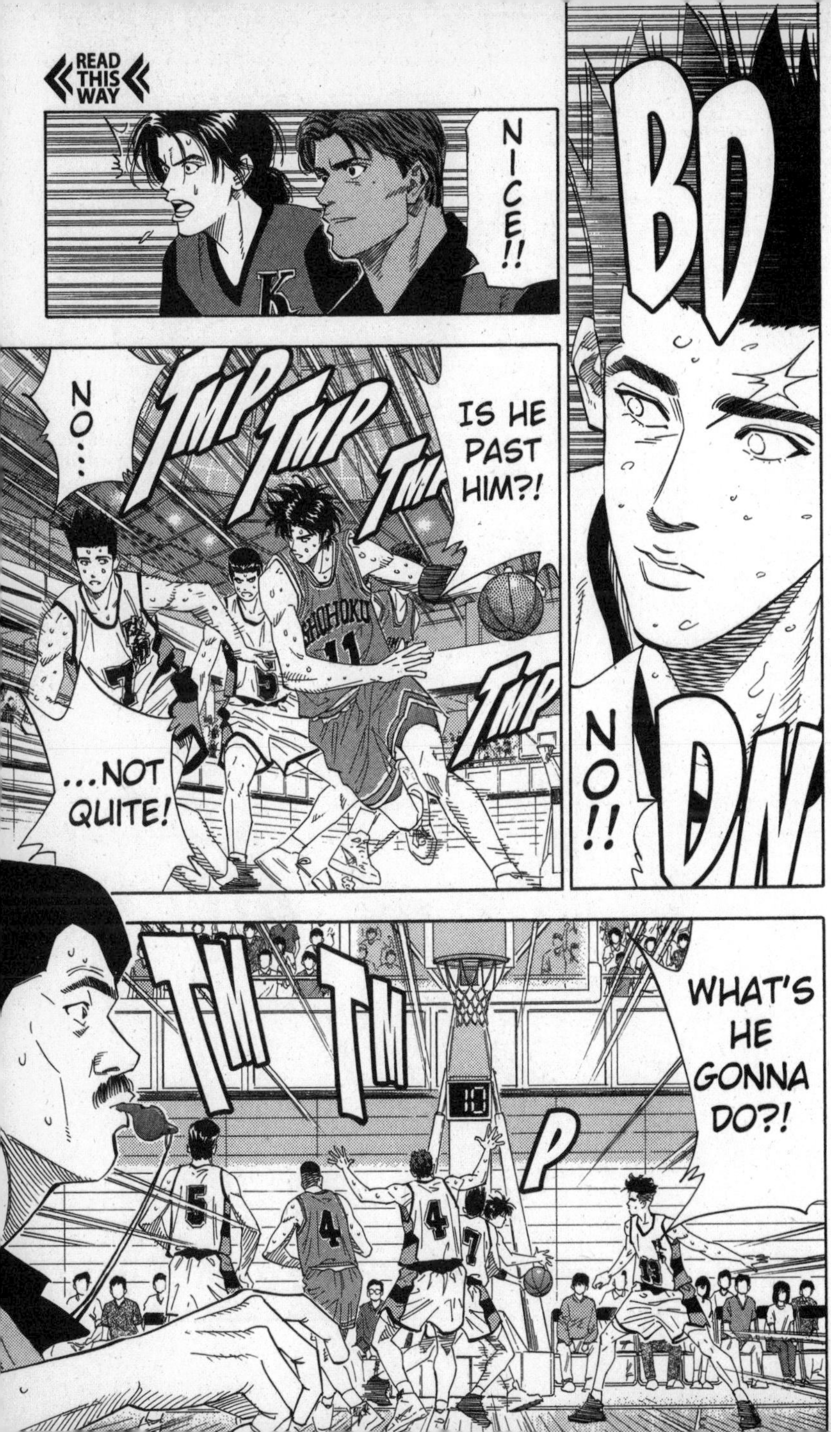
BD
NO!!
DN
NICE!!
IS HE PAST HIM?!
TMP TMP TMP
NO...
...NOT QUITE!
TMP
WHAT'S HE GONNA DO?!
P
TM TM

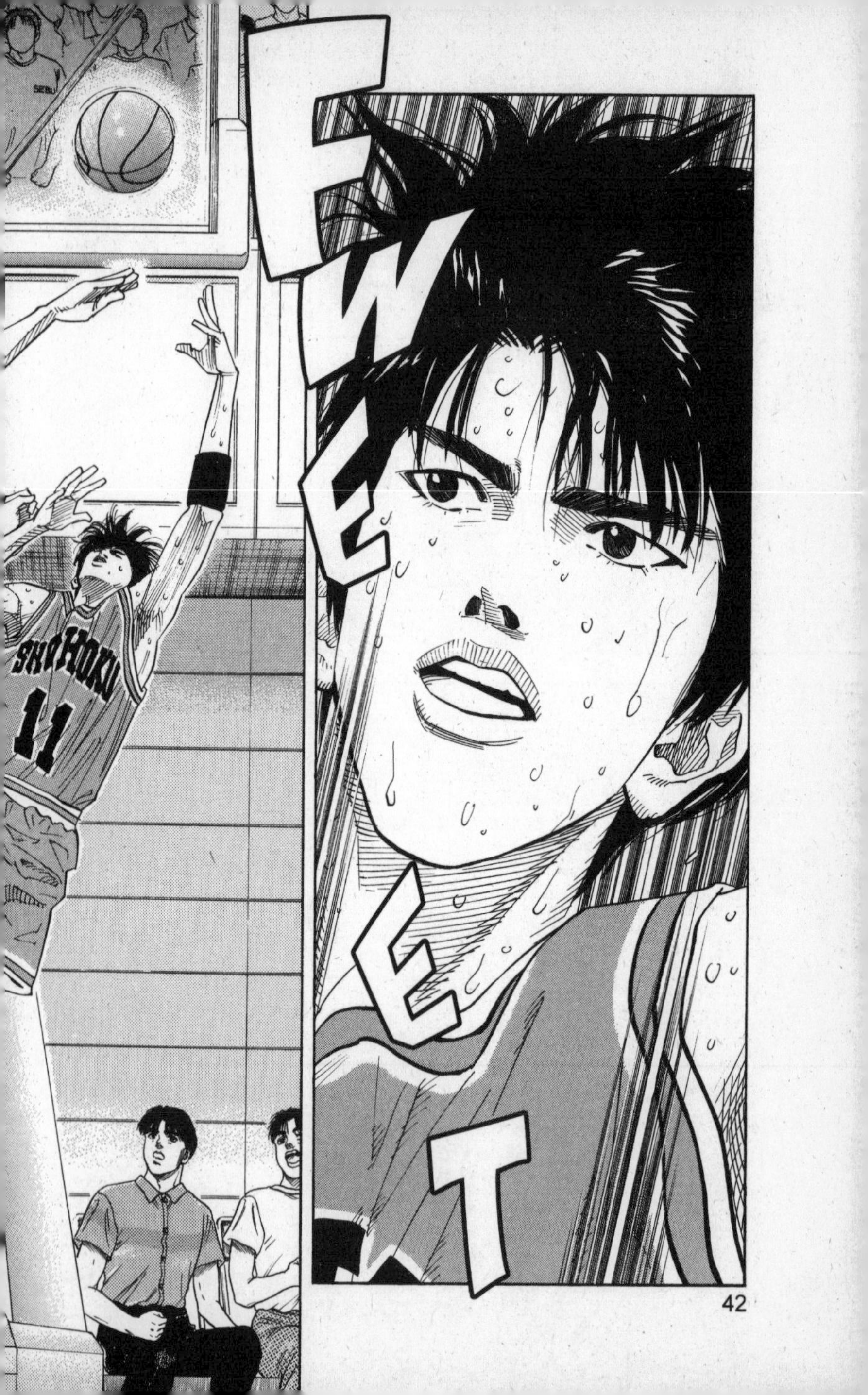
SHOHOKU
11

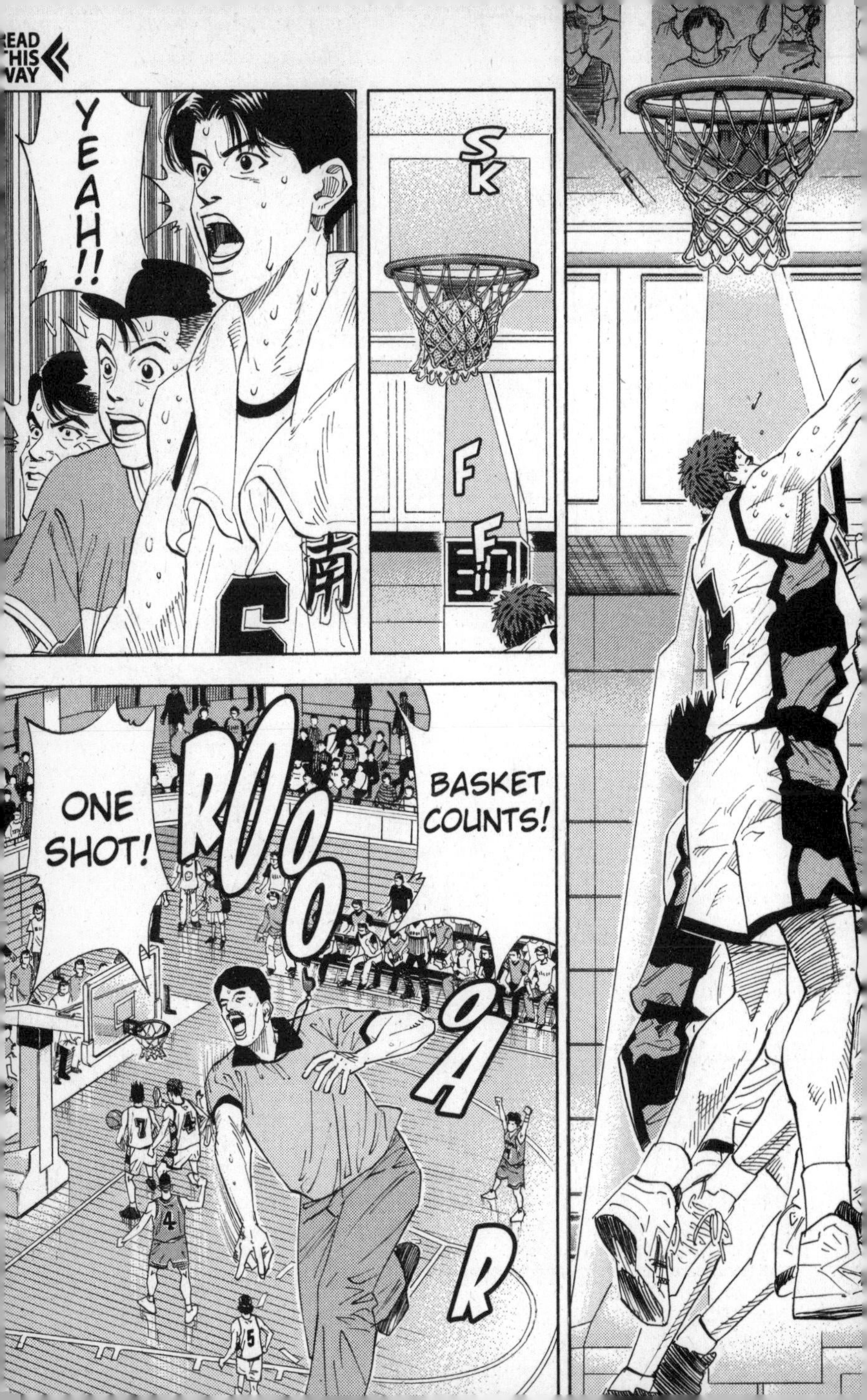
READ THIS WAY
SK
FF
YEAH!!
BASKET COUNTS!
ROOOOOAR
ONE SHOT!

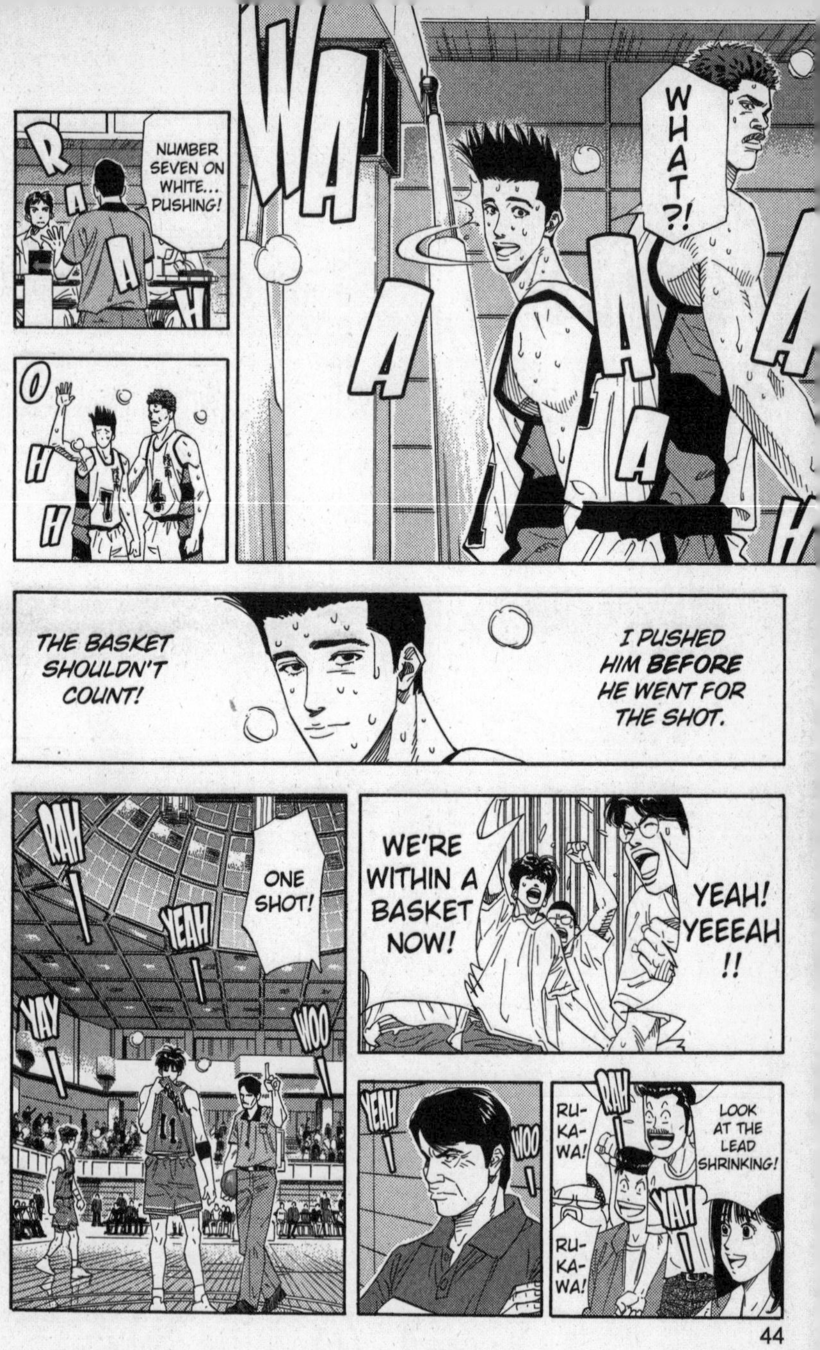
WAAAAAH
WHAT?!
NUMBER SEVEN ON WHITE... PUSHING!
RAAAH
OHH
I PUSHED HIM BEFORE HE WENT FOR THE SHOT.
THE BASKET SHOULDN'T COUNT!
YEAH! YEEEAH !!
WE'RE WITHIN A BASKET NOW!
LOOK AT THE LEAD SHRINKING!
RAH
RU-KA-WA!
YAH
RU-KA-WA!
YEAH
WOO
ONE SHOT!
RAH
YEAH
YAY
WOO

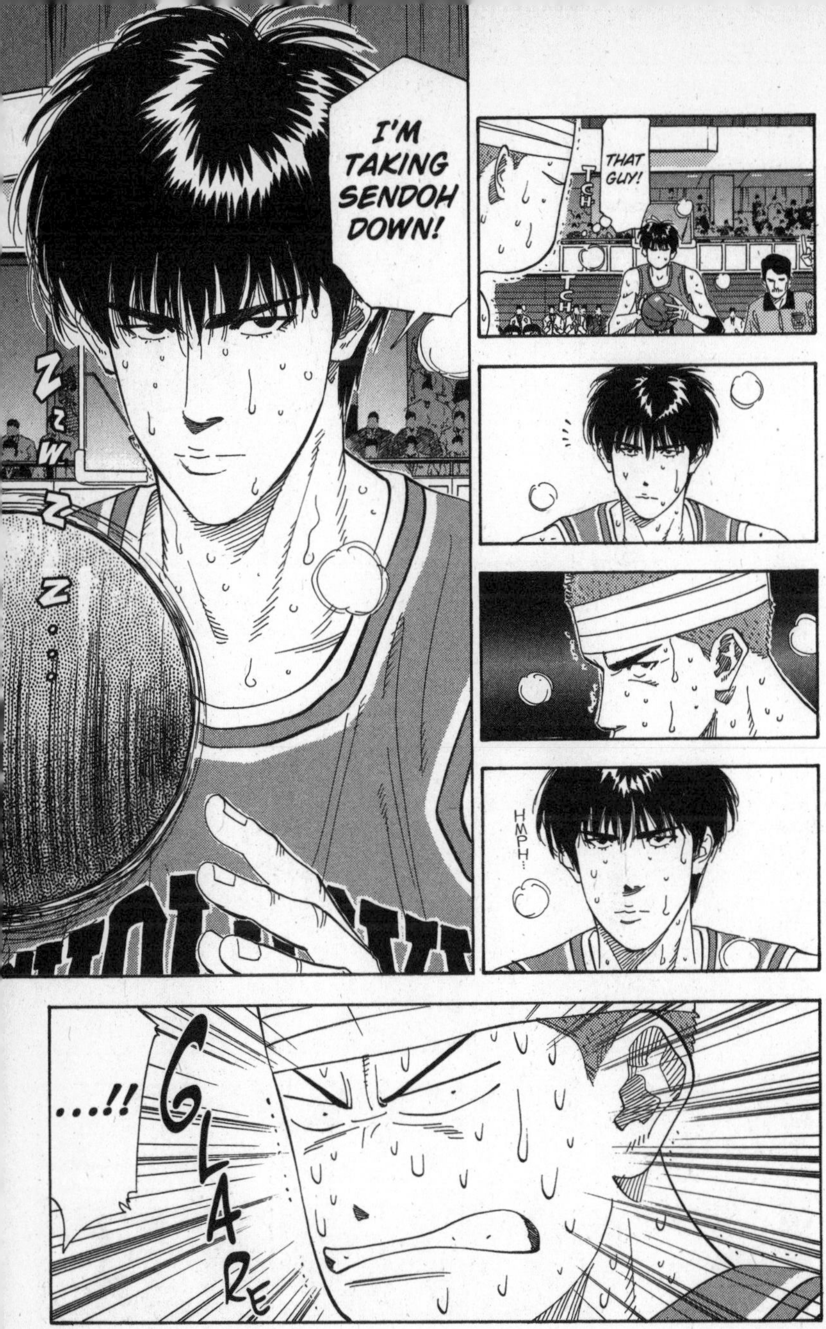
THAT GUY!
HMPH...
I'M TAKING SENDOH DOWN!
ZZWZZ...
GLARE
...!!

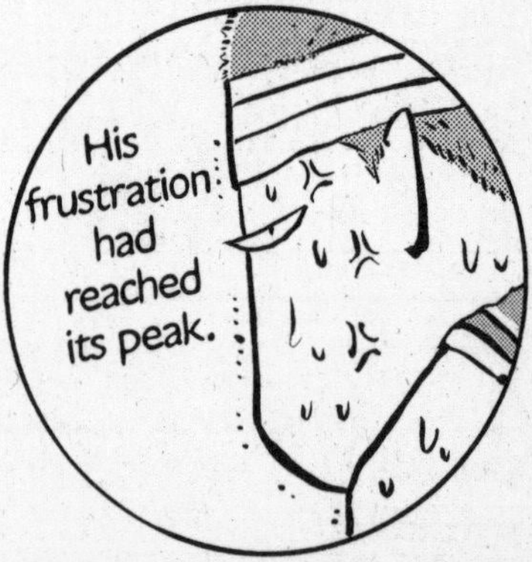
His frustration had reached its peak.

SLAM DUNK

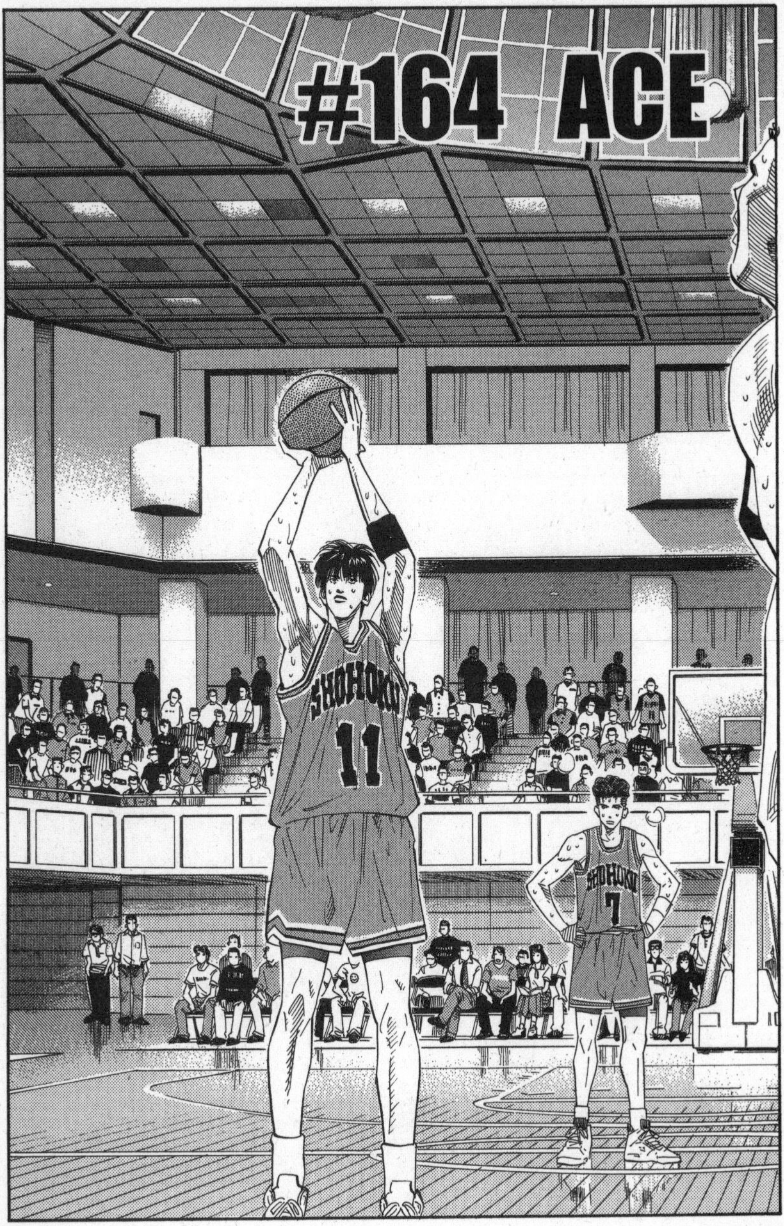
#164 ACE
SHOHOKU
11
SHOHOKU
7

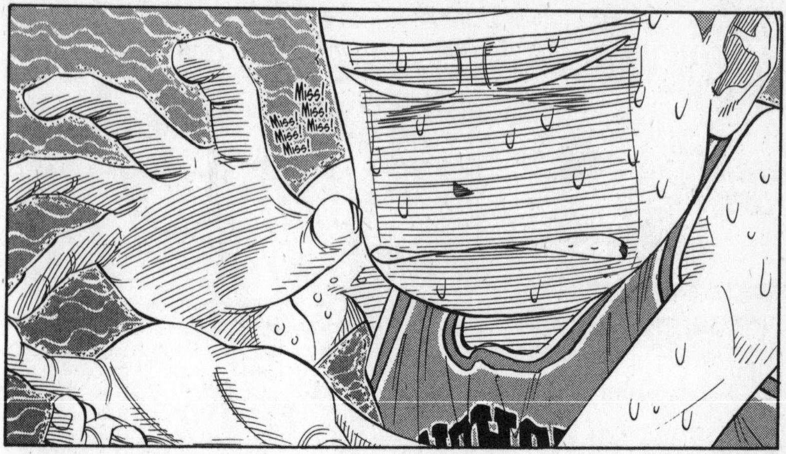
Miss! Miss! Miss! Miss! Miss! Miss!

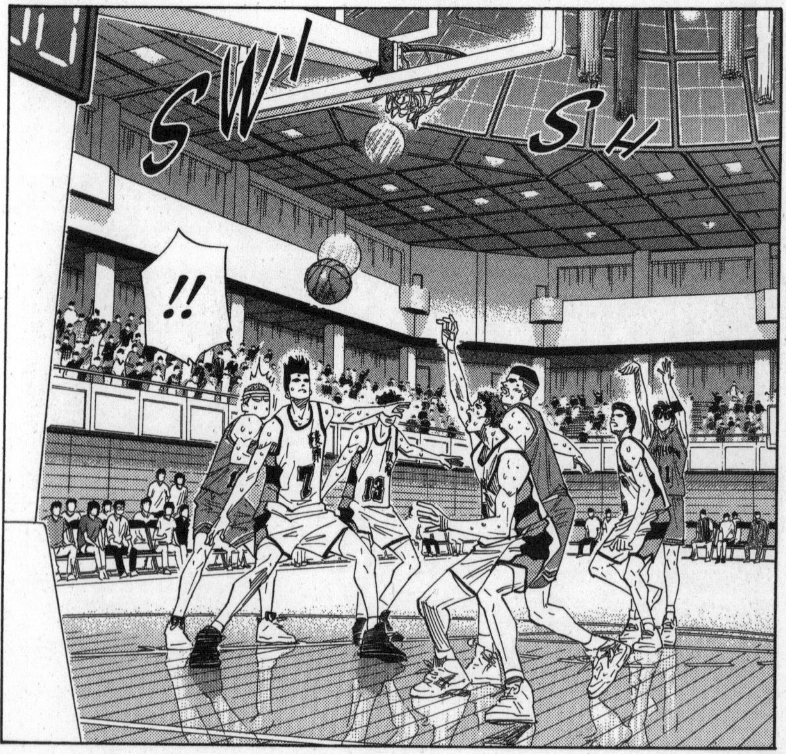
SWISH
!!

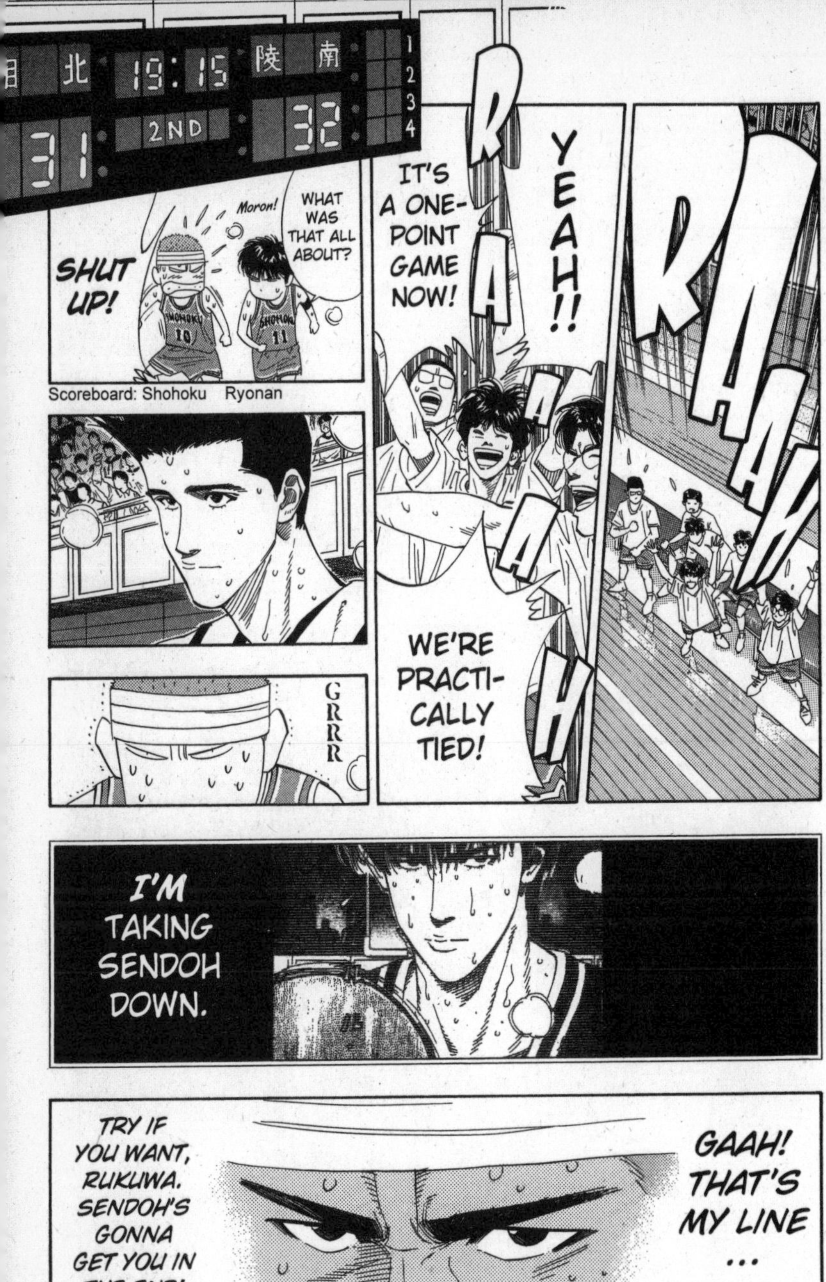
RAAAAH
IT'S A ONE-POINT GAME NOW!
YEAH!!
RAAAH
WE'RE PRACTICALLY TIED!
北
19:15
陵南
31
2ND
32
1
2
3
4
WHAT WAS THAT ALL ABOUT?
Moron!
SHUT UP!
GRRR
I'M TAKING SENDOH DOWN.
GAAH! THAT'S MY LINE...
TRY IF YOU WANT, RUKUWA. SENDOH'S GONNA GET YOU IN THE END!
Scoreboard: Shohoku Ryonan

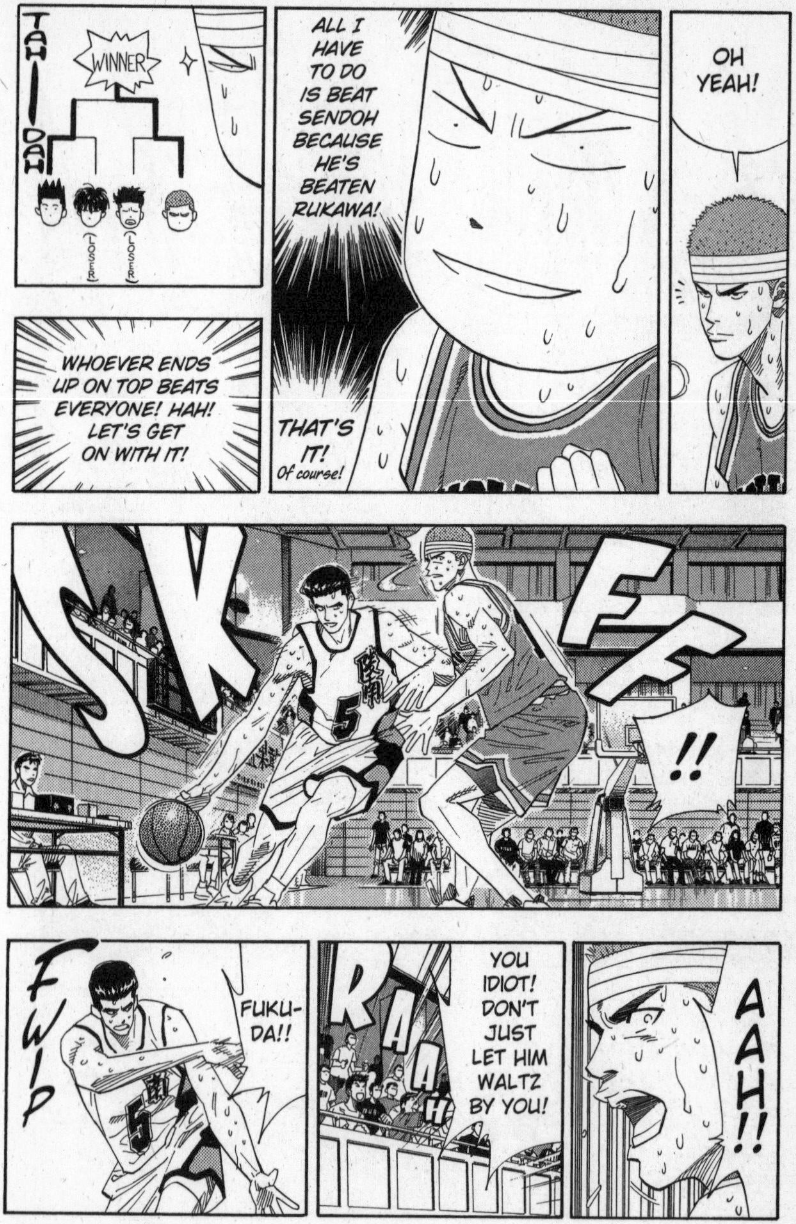
OH YEAH!
ALL I HAVE TO DO IS BEAT SENDOH BECAUSE HE'S BEATEN RUKAWA!
THAT'S IT!
Of course!
TAH-DAH
WINNER
LOSER
LOSER
WHOEVER ENDS UP ON TOP BEATS EVERYONE! HAH! LET'S GET ON WITH IT!
FF
!!
SK
AAH!!
YOU IDIOT! DON'T JUST LET HIM WALTZ BY YOU!
RAAAH
FUKU-DA!!
FWIP

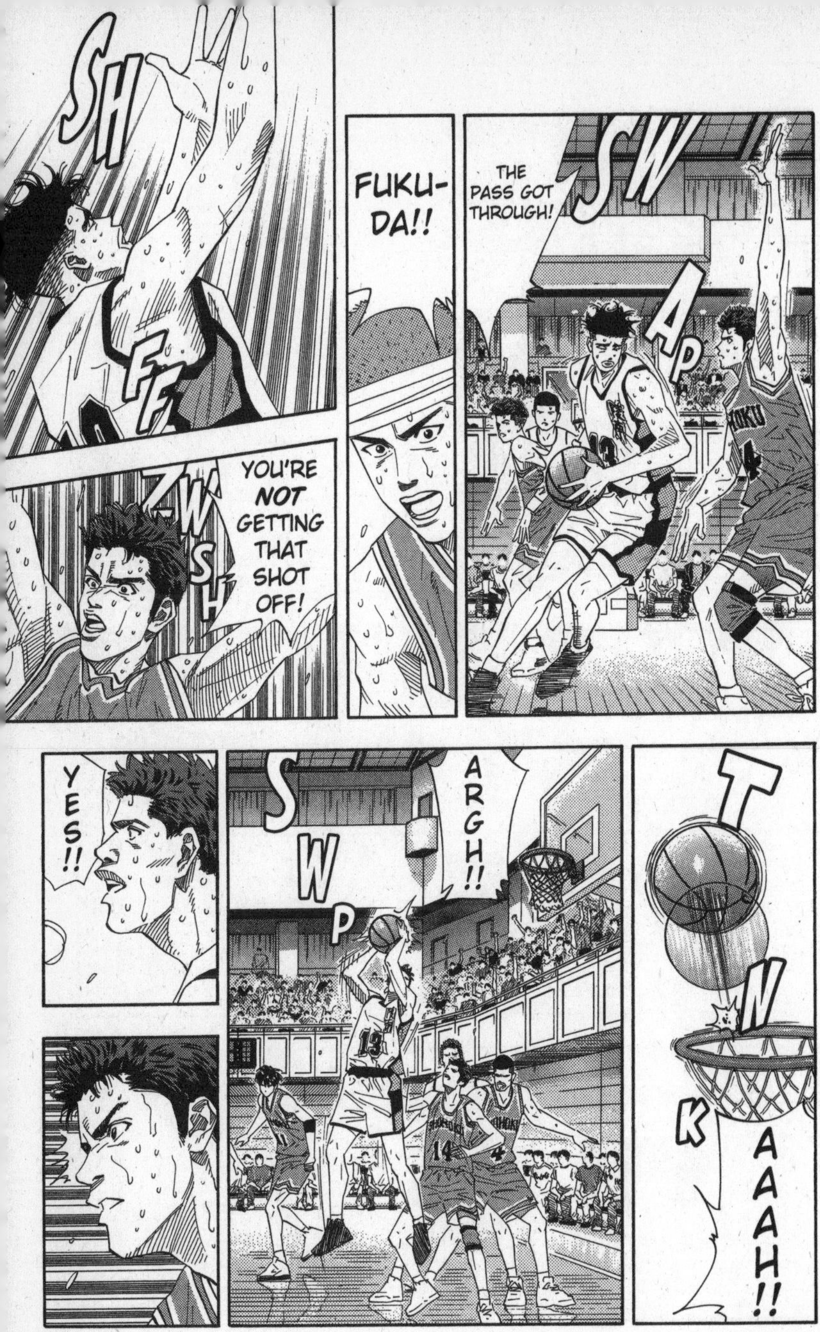
SW
AP
THE PASS GOT THROUGH!
FUKU-DA!!
SH
FF
ZWSH
YOU'RE *NOT* GETTING THAT SHOT OFF!
TNK
AAAH!!
SWP
ARGH!!
YES!!

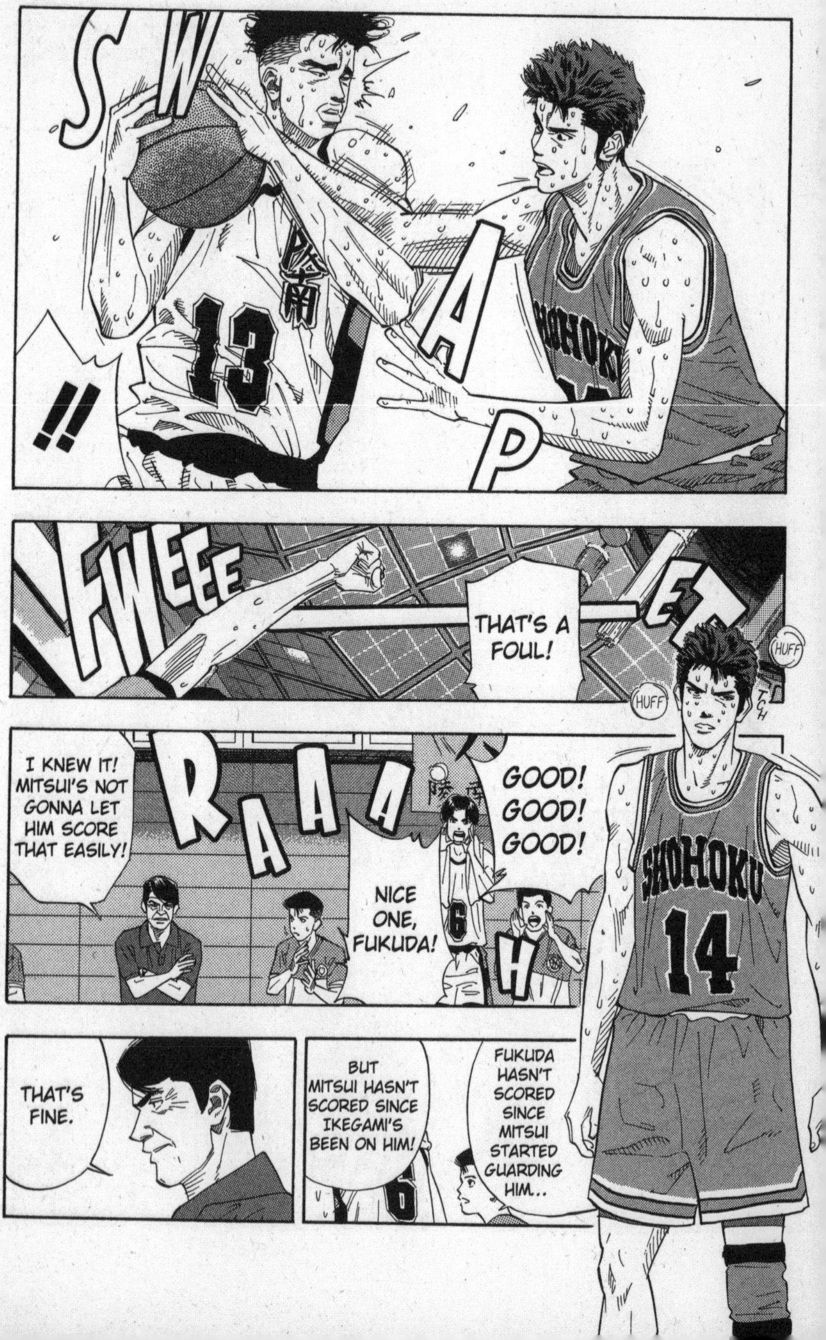
!!
SWAP
EWEEEET
THAT'S A FOUL!
HUFF
HUFF
TCH
GOOD! GOOD! GOOD!
NICE ONE, FUKUDA!
H
RAAA
I KNEW IT! MITSUI'S NOT GONNA LET HIM SCORE THAT EASILY!
FUKUDA HASN'T SCORED SINCE MITSUI STARTED GUARDING HIM...
BUT MITSUI HASN'T SCORED SINCE IKEGAMI'S BEEN ON HIM!
THAT'S FINE.

READ THIS WAY

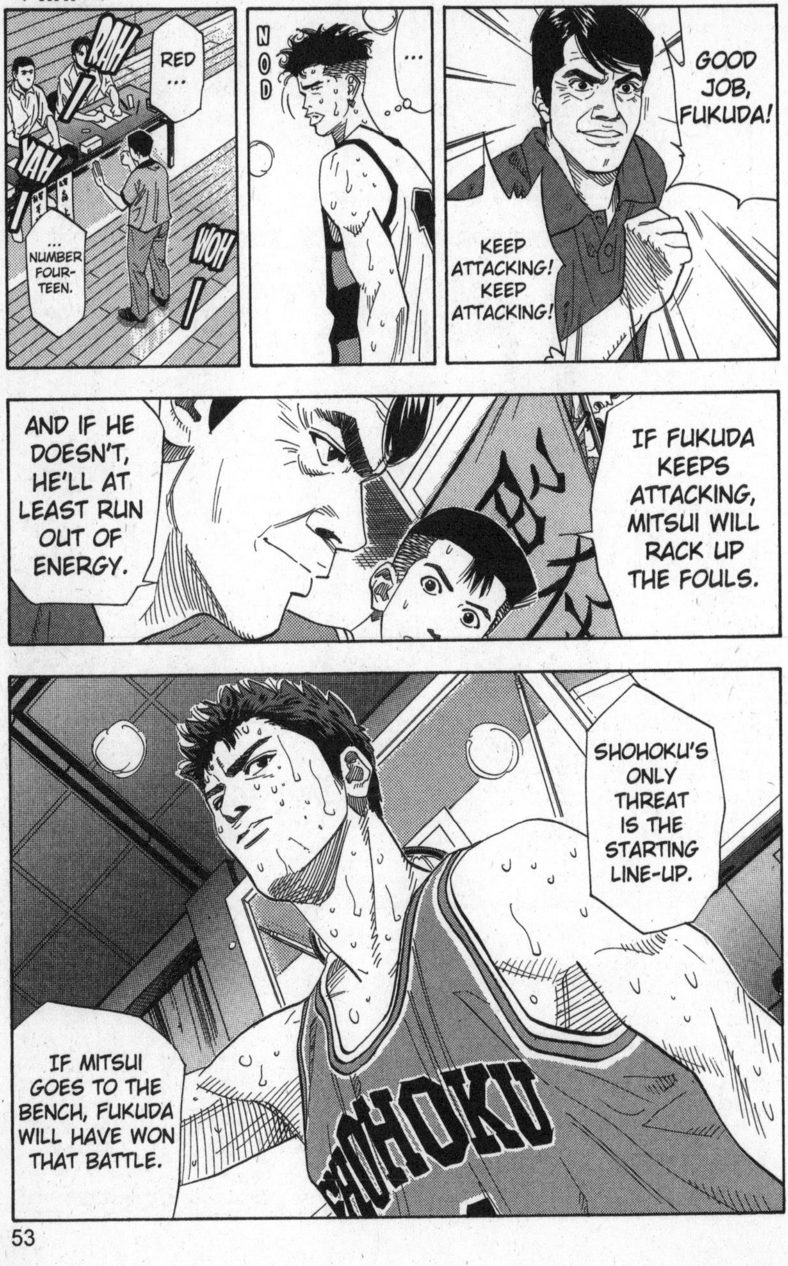

GOOD JOB, FUKUDA!
KEEP ATTACKING! KEEP ATTACKING!
NOD
...
RED ...
RAH
YAH
... NUMBER FOUR-TEEN.
WOH
IF FUKUDA KEEPS ATTACKING, MITSUI WILL RACK UP THE FOULS.
AND IF HE DOESN'T, HE'LL AT LEAST RUN OUT OF ENERGY.
SHOHOKU'S ONLY THREAT IS THE STARTING LINE-UP.
IF MITSUI GOES TO THE BENCH, FUKUDA WILL HAVE WON THAT BATTLE.
SHOHOKU

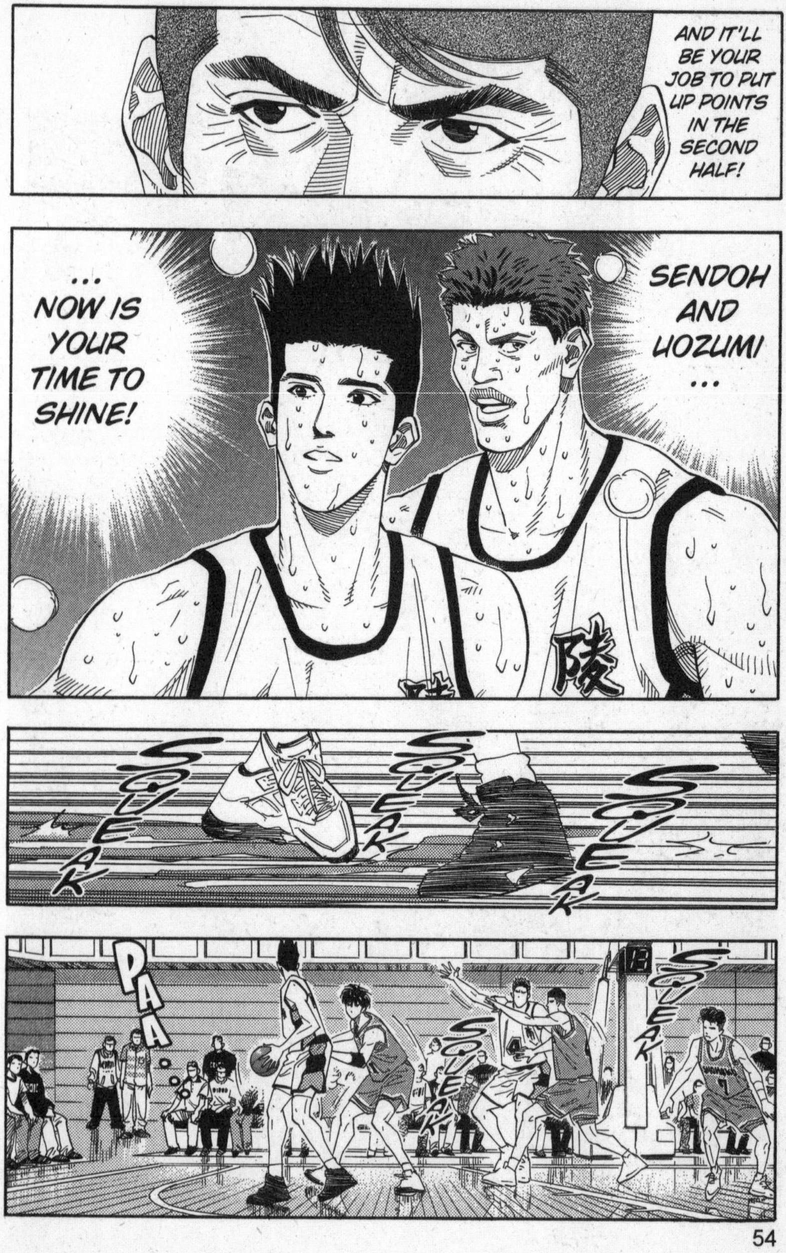
AND IT'LL BE YOUR JOB TO PUT UP POINTS IN THE SECOND HALF!
SENDOH AND UOZUMI ...
... NOW IS YOUR TIME TO SHINE!
SQUEAK
SQUEAK
SQUEAK
SQUEAK
SQUEAK
PAA

READ THIS WAY

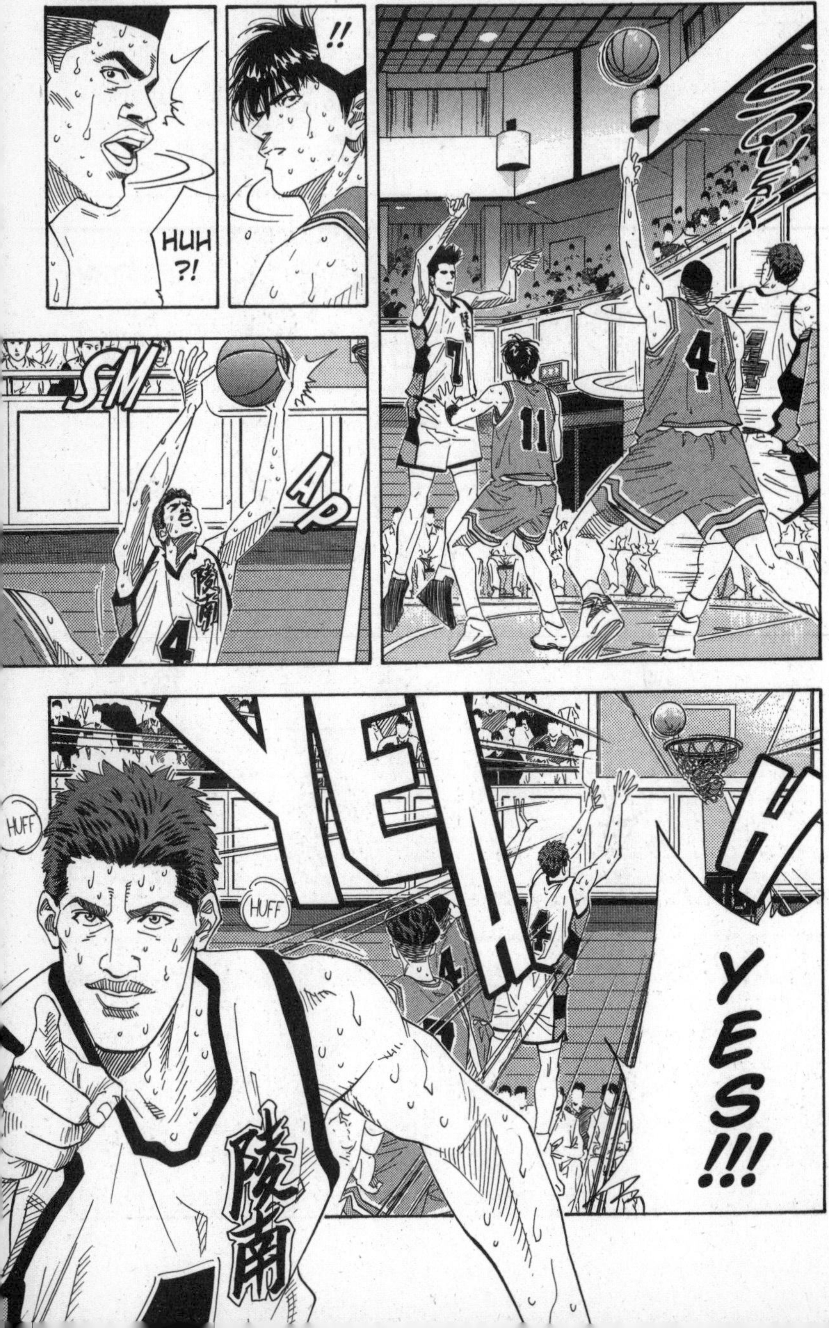
SQUEAK
!!
HUH ?!
SMAP
HUFF
HUFF
YEAHH
YES!!!

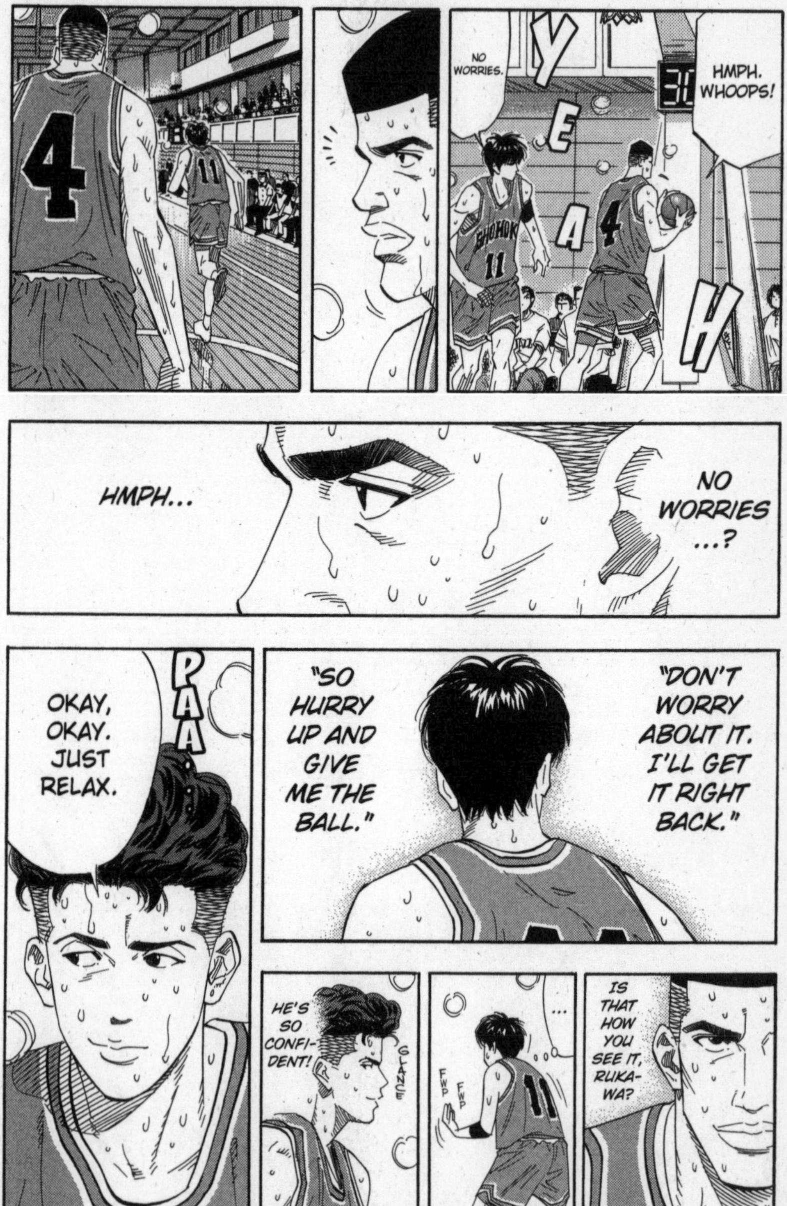

HMPH. WHOOPS!
NO WORRIES.
YEAH
NO WORRIES ...?
HMPH...
"DON'T WORRY ABOUT IT. I'LL GET IT RIGHT BACK."
"SO HURRY UP AND GIVE ME THE BALL."
IS THAT HOW YOU SEE IT, RUKAWA?
...
FWP FWP
HE'S SO CONFIDENT!
GLANCE
PAA
OKAY, OKAY. JUST RELAX.

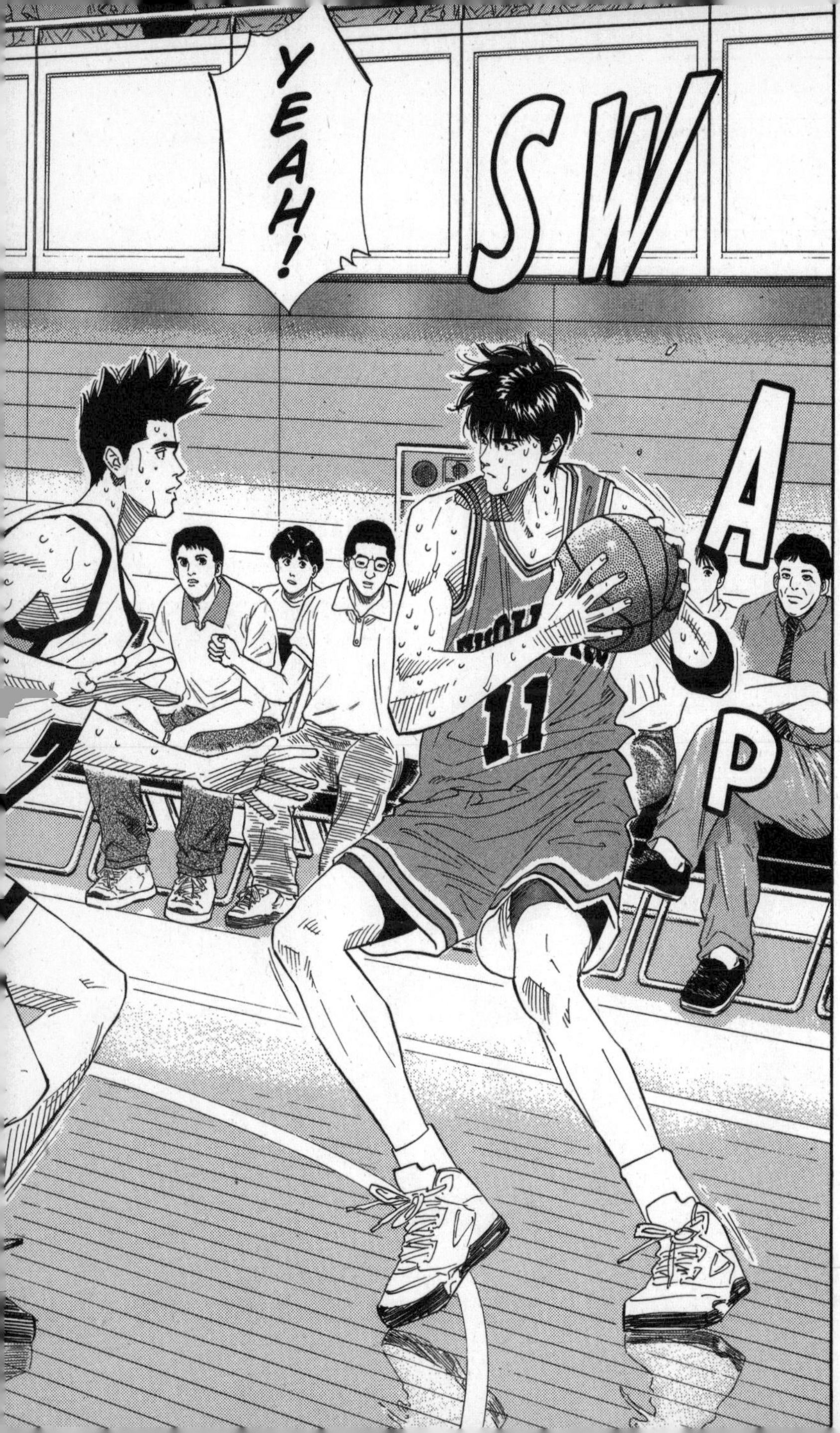
YEAH!
SWAP

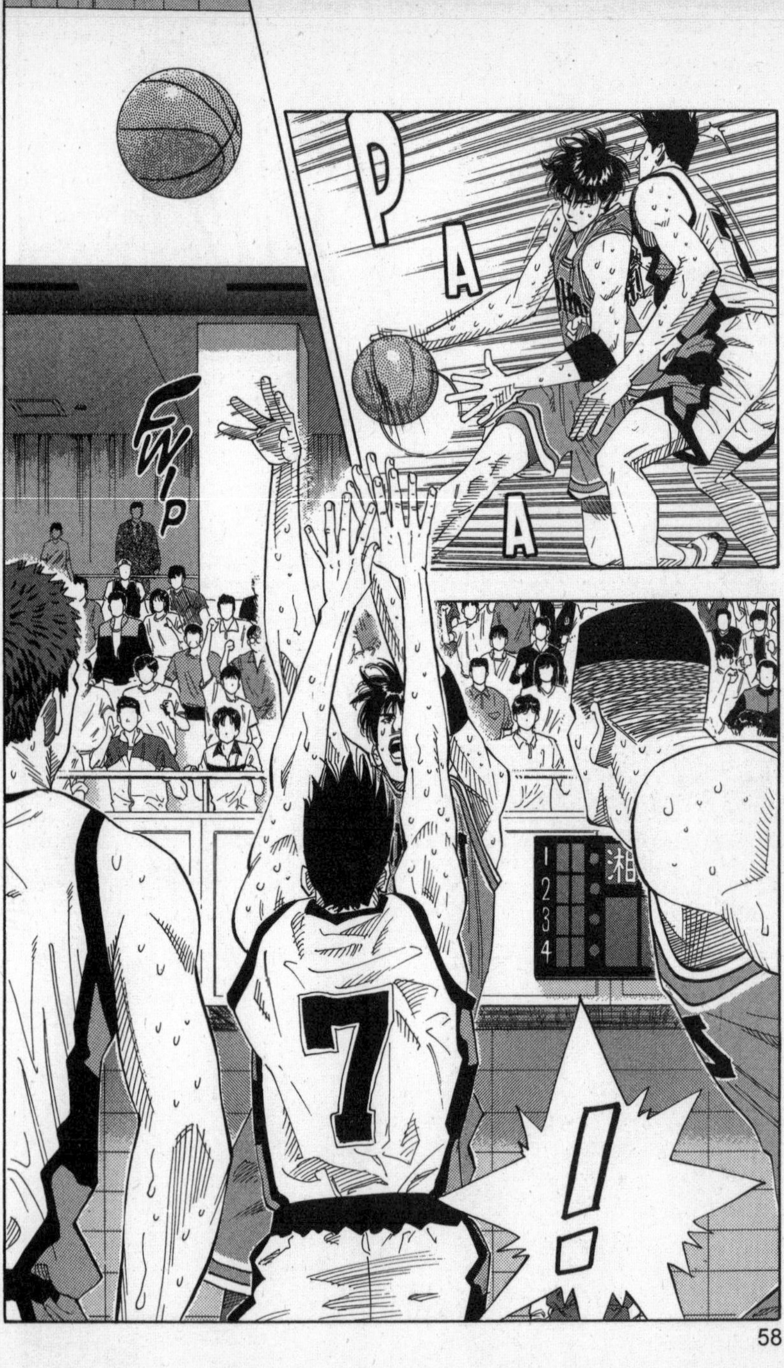
PAA
FWIP
湘
1
2
3
4
!

READ THIS WAY

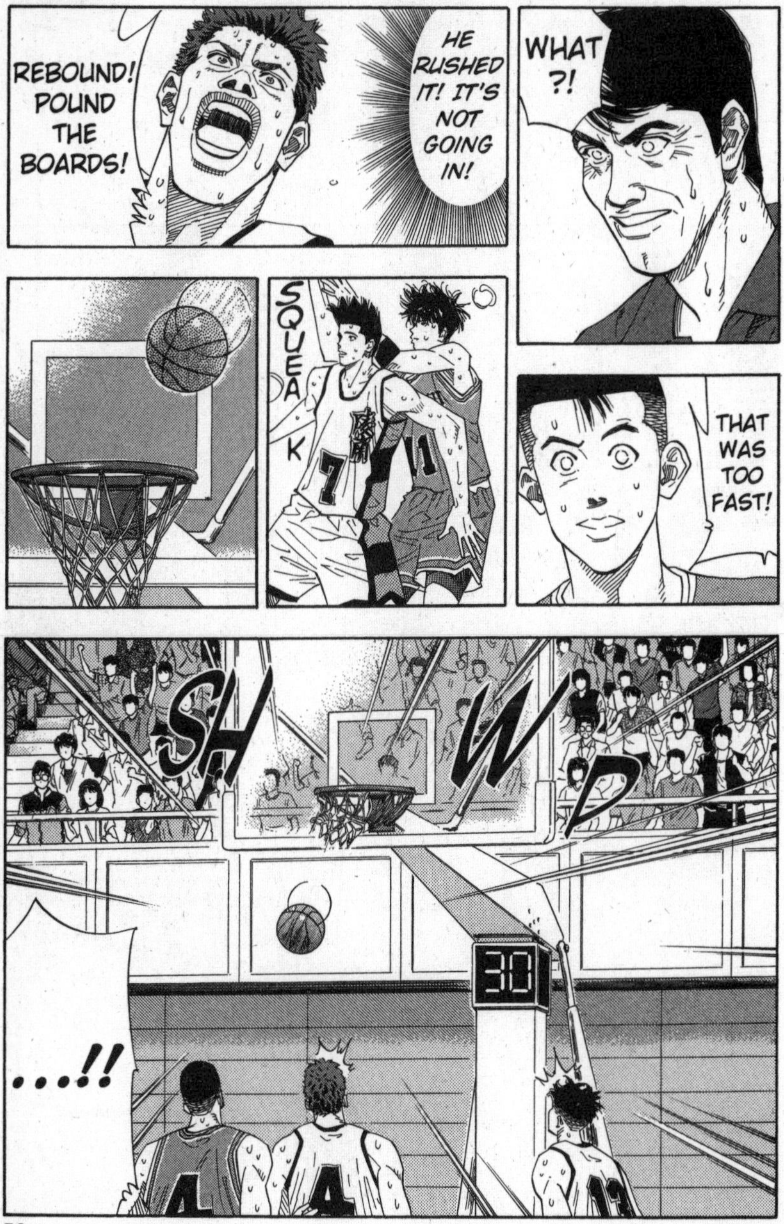
WHAT ?!
HE RUSHED IT! IT'S NOT GOING IN!
REBOUND! POUND THE BOARDS!
THAT WAS TOO FAST!
SQUEAK
SHWD
....!!

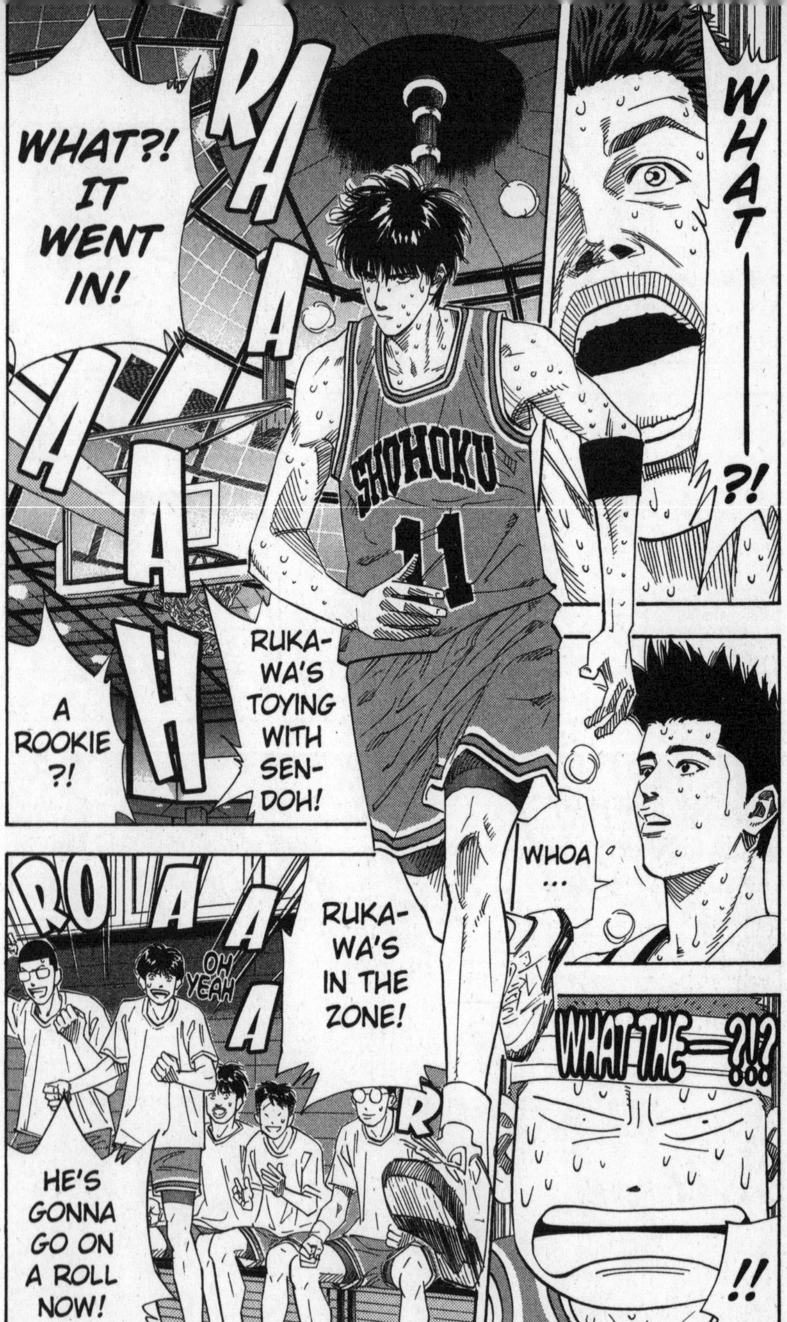
WHAT——?!
WHAT?! IT WENT IN!
RAAAAAH
RUKA-WA'S TOYING WITH SEN-DOH!
A ROOKIE?!
WHOA...
ROAAAAR
RUKA-WA'S IN THE ZONE!
OH YEAH
HE'S GONNA GO ON A ROLL NOW!
WHAT THE——?!?
!!

READ THIS WAY

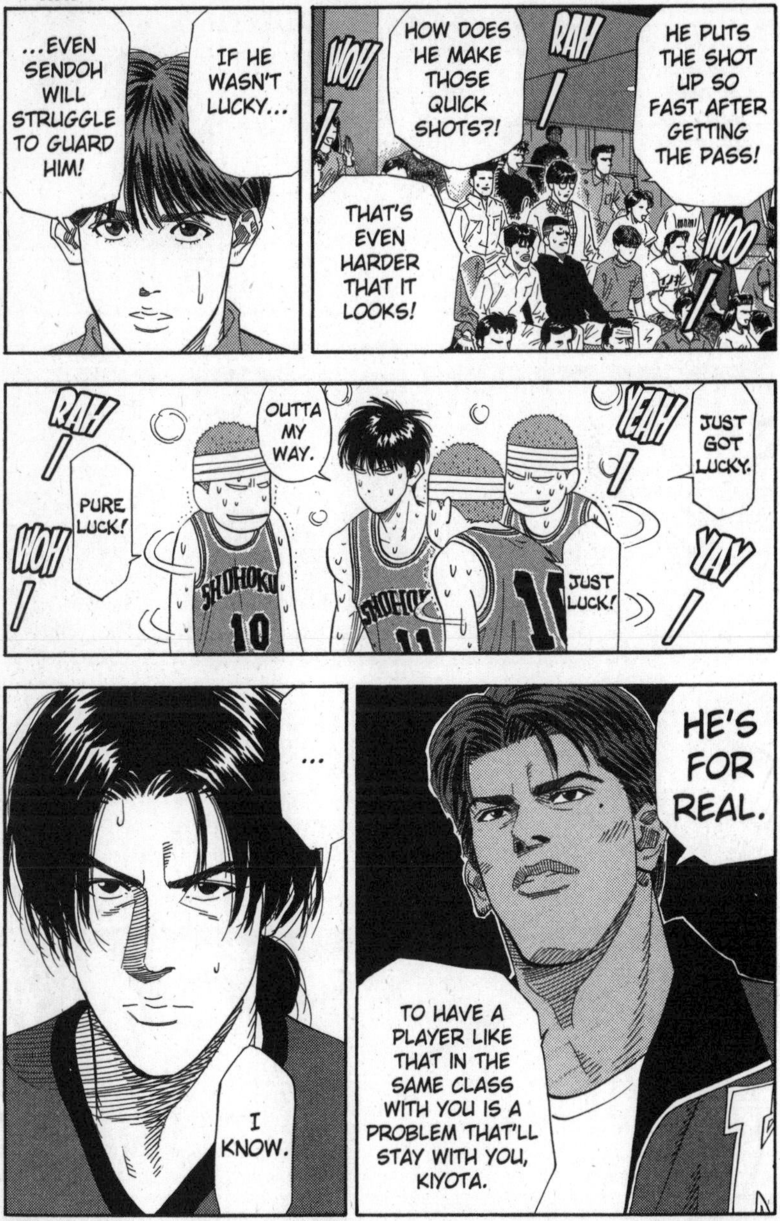
HE PUTS THE SHOT UP SO FAST AFTER GETTING THE PASS!
RAH
HOW DOES HE MAKE THOSE QUICK SHOTS?!
WOH
THAT'S EVEN HARDER THAT IT LOOKS!
WOO
IF HE WASN'T LUCKY...
...EVEN SENDOH WILL STRUGGLE TO GUARD HIM!
JUST GOT LUCKY.
YEAH
YAY
JUST LUCK!
OUTTA MY WAY.
RAH
PURE LUCK!
WOH
HE'S FOR REAL.
TO HAVE A PLAYER LIKE THAT IN THE SAME CLASS WITH YOU IS A PROBLEM THAT'LL STAY WITH YOU, KIYOTA.
...
I KNOW.

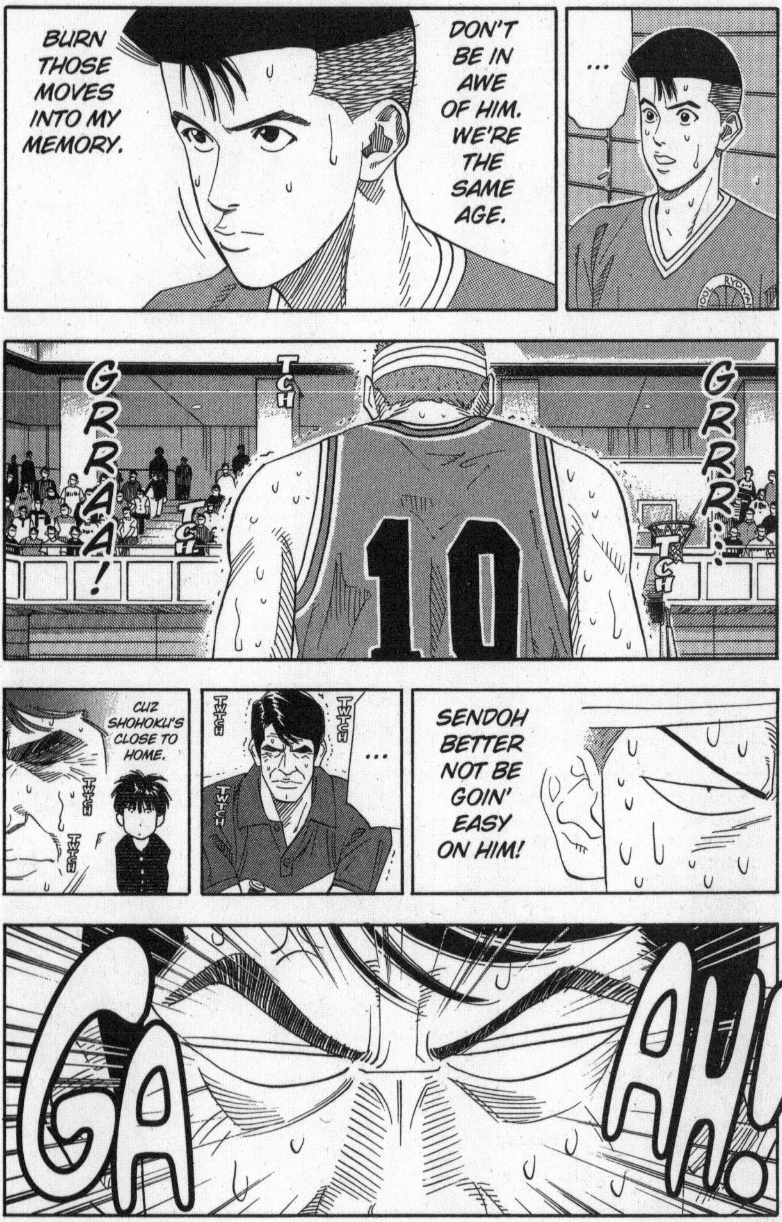
...
DON'T BE IN AWE OF HIM. WE'RE THE SAME AGE.
BURN THOSE MOVES INTO MY MEMORY.
GRRRR...
TCH
TCH
GRRAAA!
TCH
TCH
SENDOH BETTER NOT BE GOIN' EASY ON HIM!
TWTCH
...
TWTCH
CUZ SHOHOKU'S CLOSE TO HOME.
TWTCH
TWTCH
GAAH!!

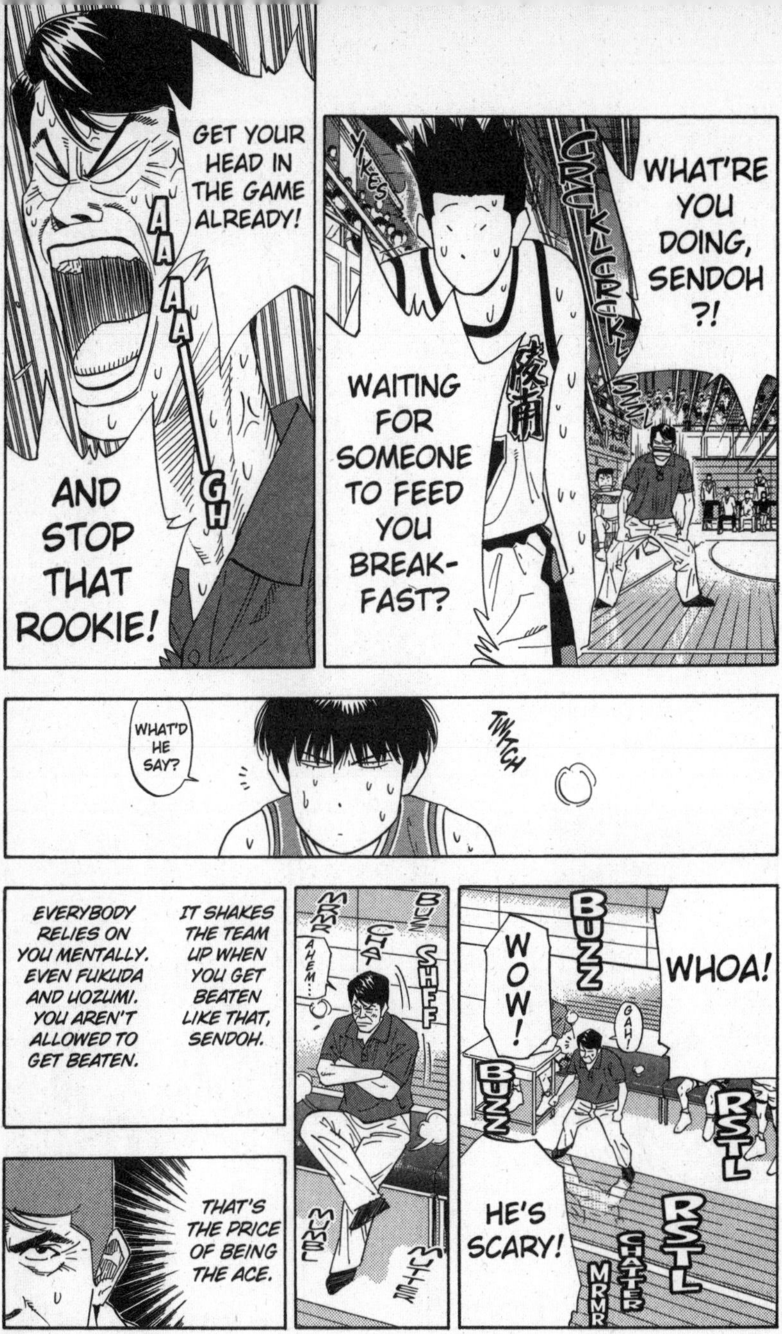
CRICK CRICK CRICK
YIKES
WHAT'RE YOU DOING, SENDOH?!
WAITING FOR SOMEONE TO FEED YOU BREAK-FAST?
SWL
GET YOUR HEAD IN THE GAME ALREADY!
AAAAAGH
AND STOP THAT ROOKIE!
TWITCH
WHAT'D HE SAY?
BUZZ
WHOA!
WOW!
GAH!
BUZZ
RSTL
RSTL
HE'S SCARY!
CHATTER
MRMR
BUZZ SHFF
CHAT
MRMR
AHEM...
MUTTER
MUMBL
IT SHAKES THE TEAM UP WHEN YOU GET BEATEN LIKE THAT, SENDOH.
EVERYBODY RELIES ON YOU MENTALLY. EVEN FUKUDA AND UOZUMI. YOU AREN'T ALLOWED TO GET BEATEN.
THAT'S THE PRICE OF BEING THE ACE.

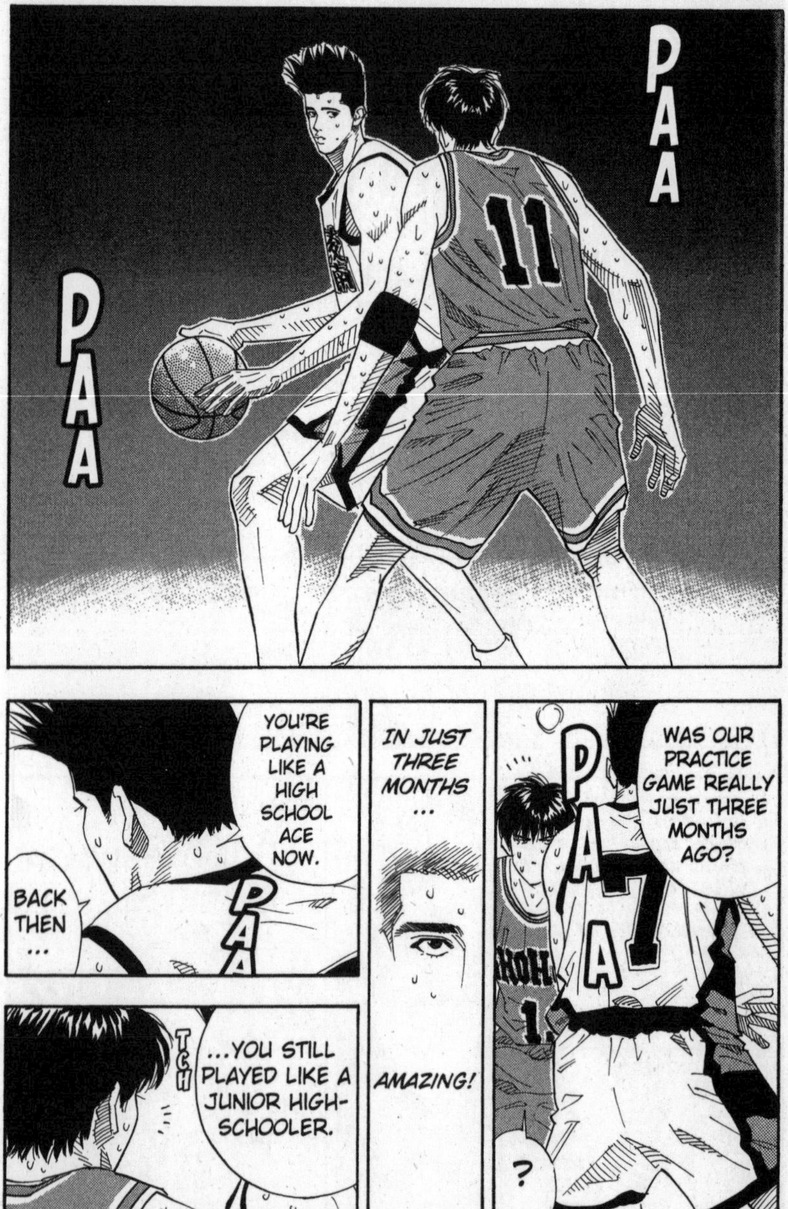
PAA
PAA
WAS OUR PRACTICE GAME REALLY JUST THREE MONTHS AGO?
PAA
?
IN JUST THREE MONTHS ...
AMAZING!
YOU'RE PLAYING LIKE A HIGH SCHOOL ACE NOW.
BACK THEN ...
PAA
TCH
...YOU STILL PLAYED LIKE A JUNIOR HIGH-SCHOOLER.

READ THIS WAY

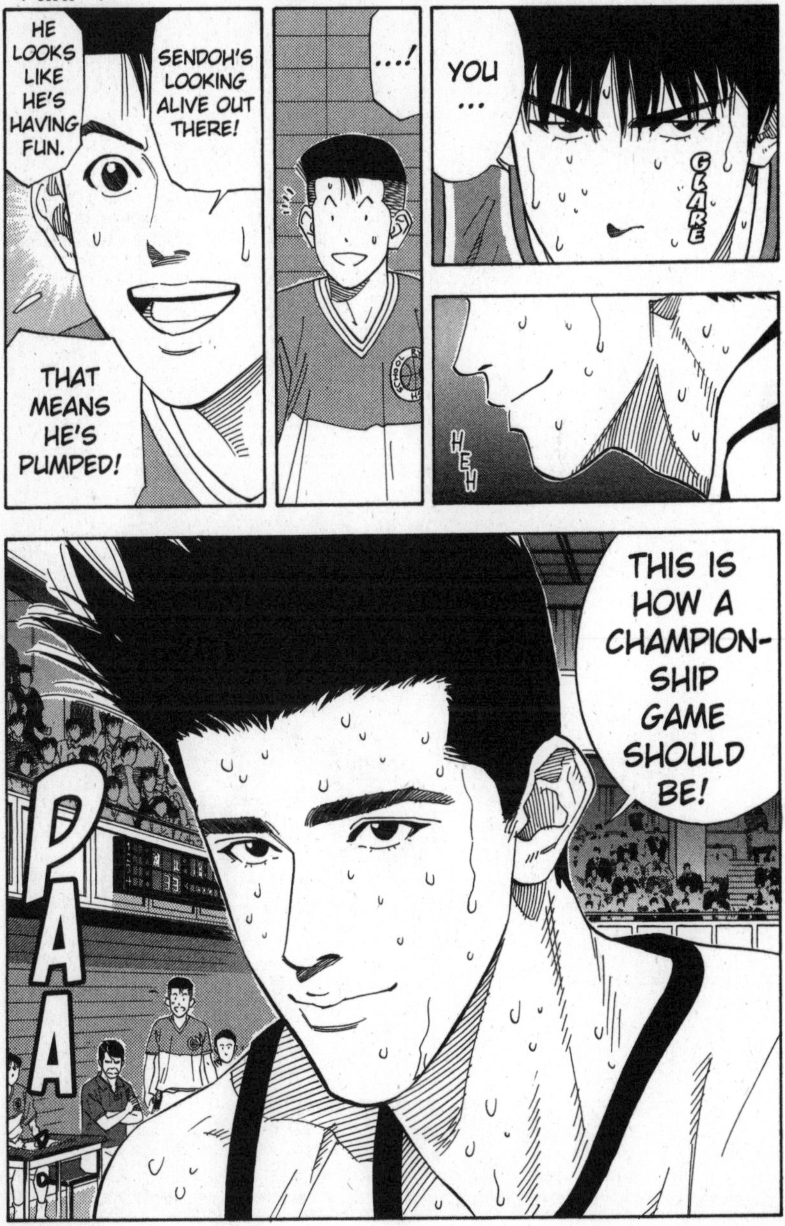
YOU ...
GLARE
HEH
....!
SENDOH'S LOOKING ALIVE OUT THERE!
HE LOOKS LIKE HE'S HAVING FUN.
THAT MEANS HE'S PUMPED!
THIS IS HOW A CHAMPION-SHIP GAME SHOULD BE!
PAA

SPOING
This is how it should be...
SPOING
Hmph!
That all you got?

SLAM DUNK

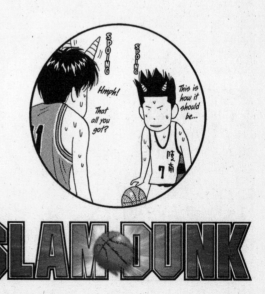

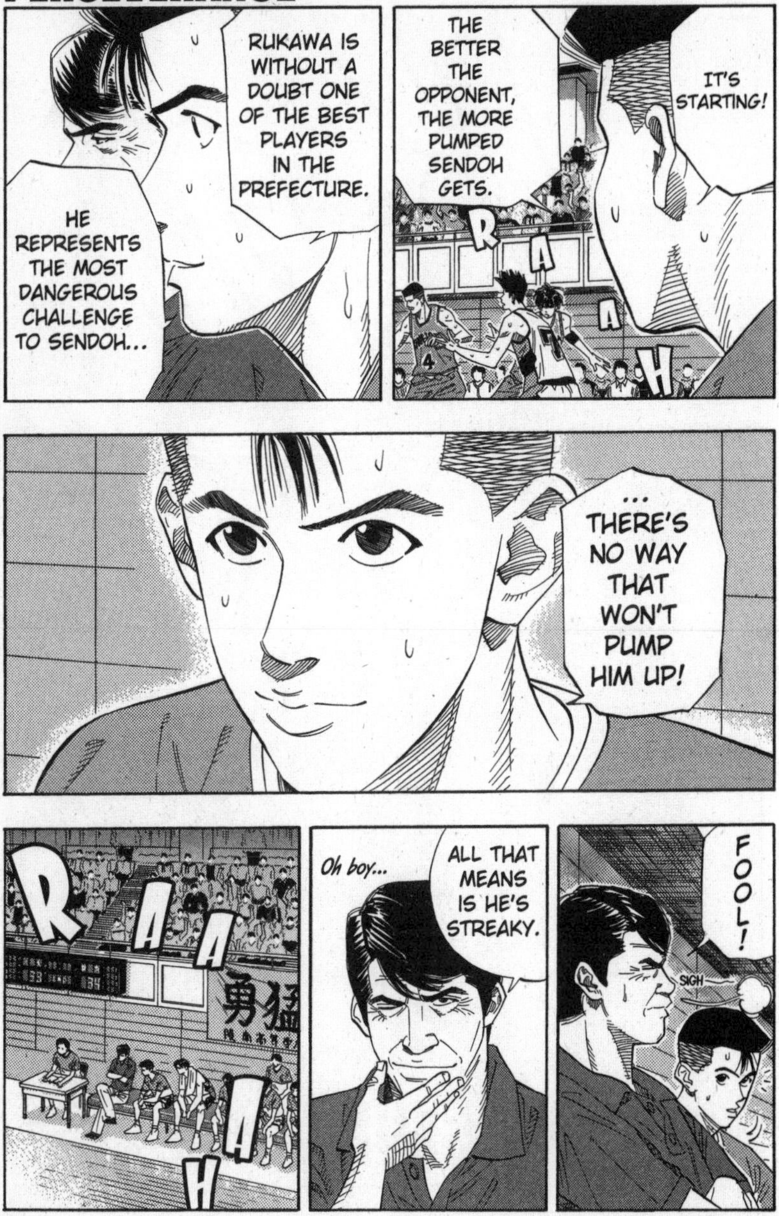
IT'S STARTING!
THE BETTER THE OPPONENT, THE MORE PUMPED SENDOH GETS.
RAAH
RUKAWA IS WITHOUT A DOUBT ONE OF THE BEST PLAYERS IN THE PREFECTURE.
HE REPRESENTS THE MOST DANGEROUS CHALLENGE TO SENDOH...
... THERE'S NO WAY THAT WON'T PUMP HIM UP!
FOOL!
SIGH
ALL THAT MEANS IS HE'S STREAKY.
Oh boy...
RAAAAH
勇猛

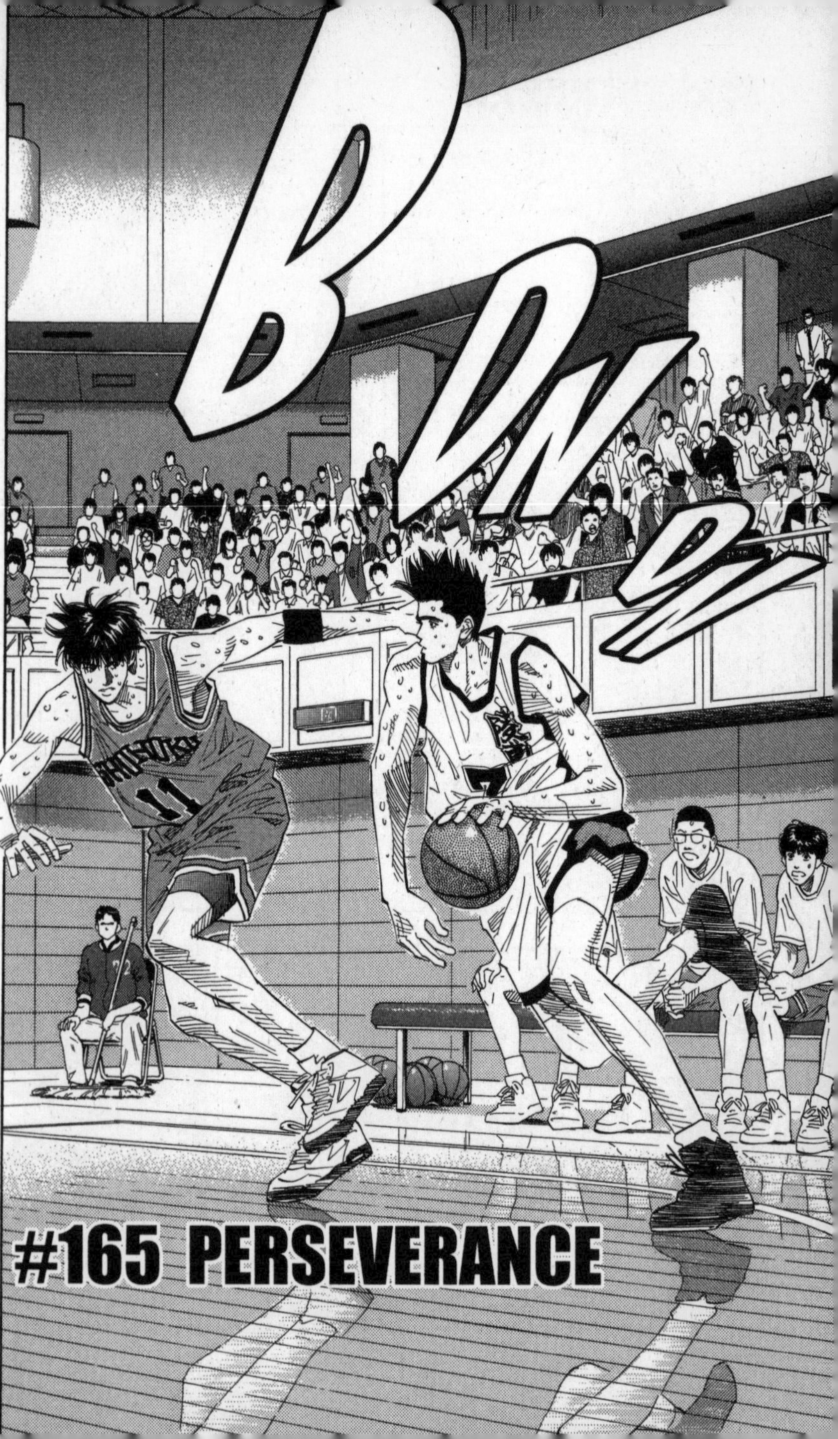
BDNDN
#165 PERSEVERANCE

READ THIS WAY

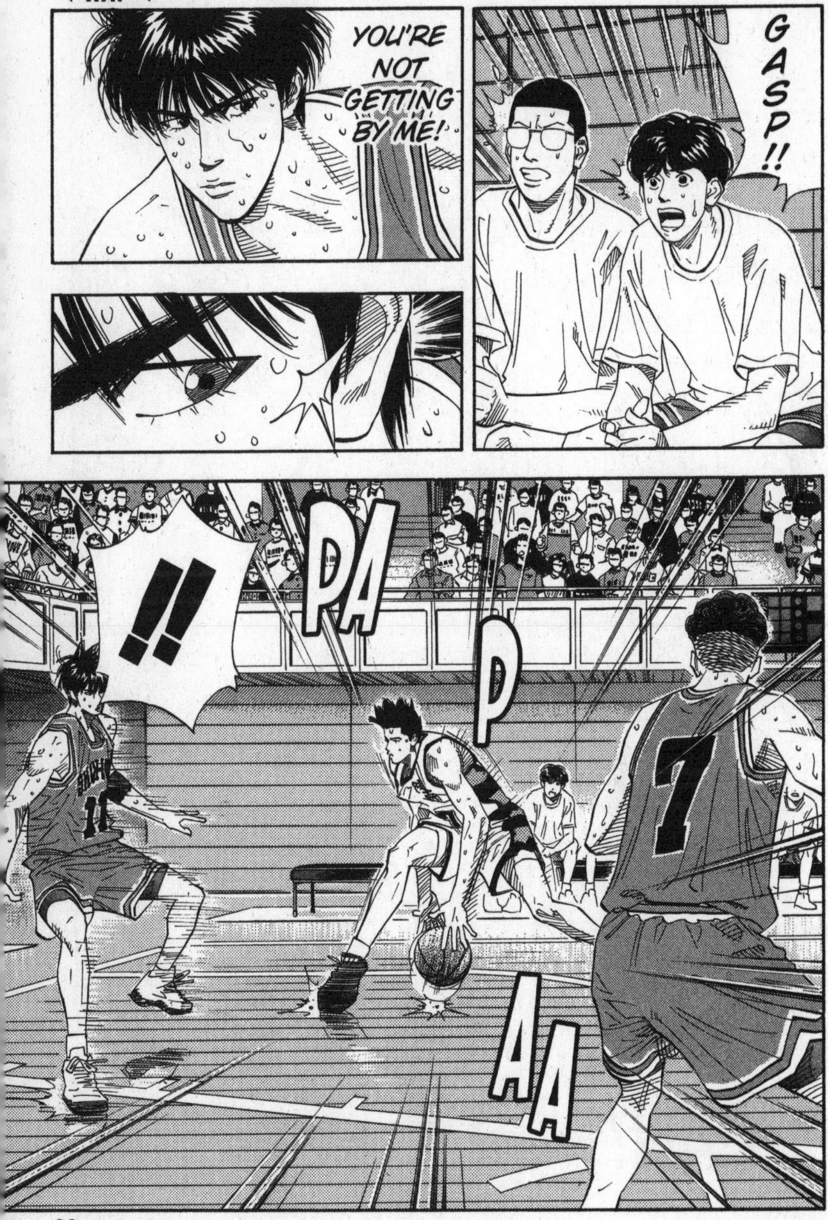
GASP!!
YOU'RE NOT GETTING BY ME!
PA
P
AA
!!

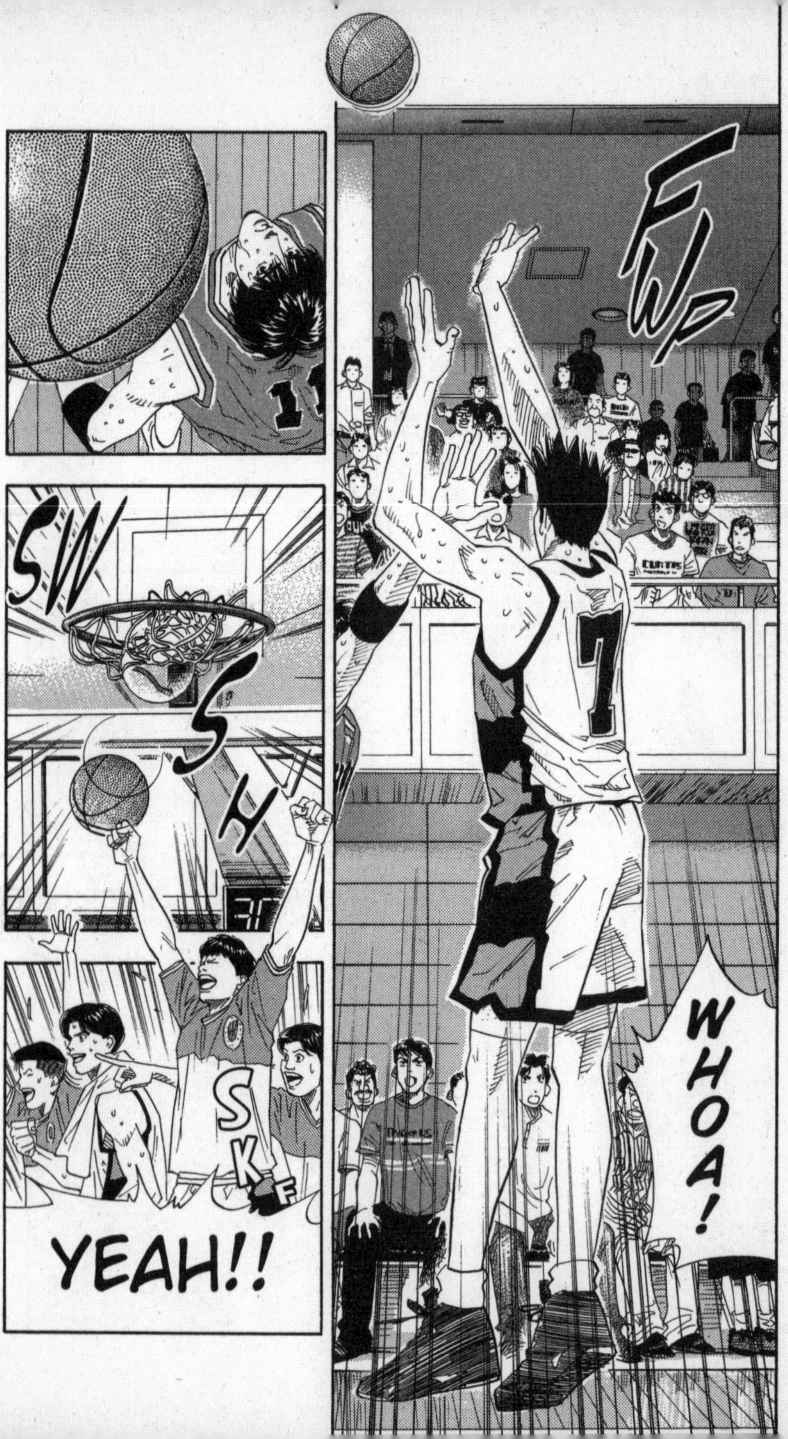
FWP
WHOA!
SWSH
SKF
YEAH!!

READ THIS WAY

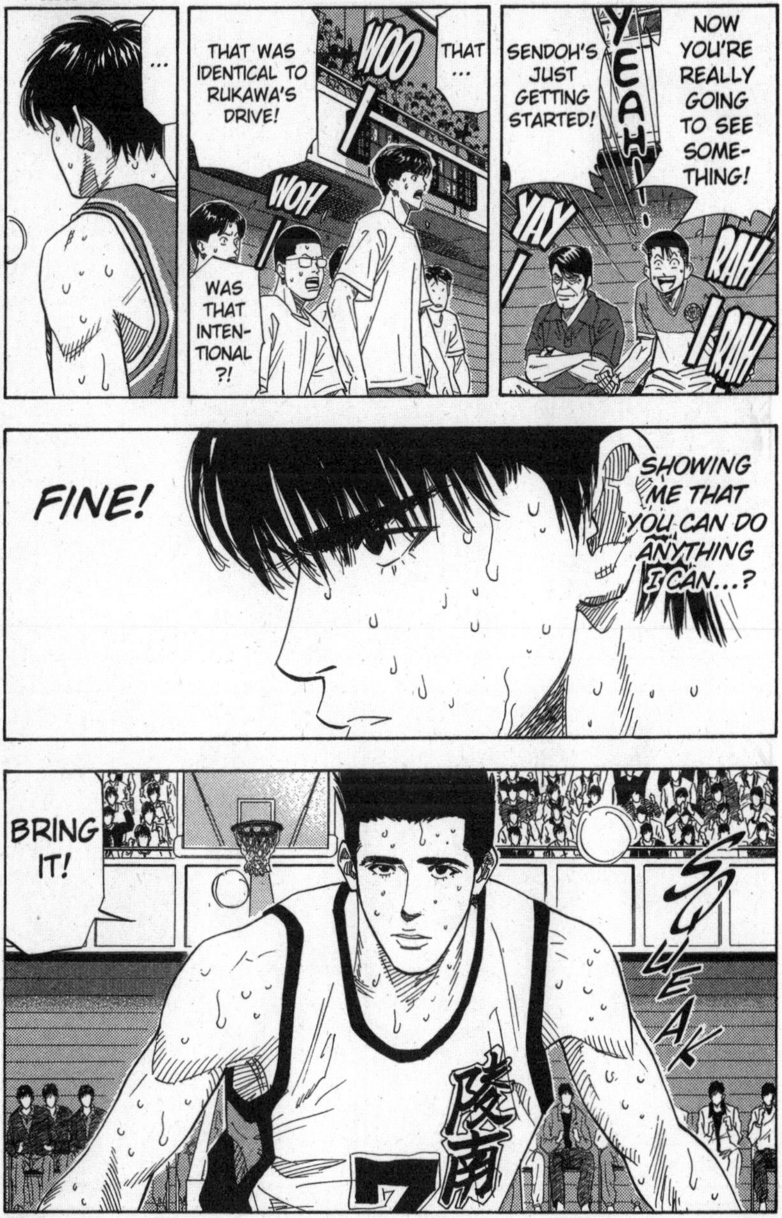
NOW YOU'RE REALLY GOING TO SEE SOME-THING!
YEAH!
SENDOH'S JUST GETTING STARTED!
RAH
RAH
RAH
YAY
THAT ...
WOO
THAT WAS IDENTICAL TO RUKAWA'S DRIVE!
WOH
WAS THAT INTEN-TIONAL ?!
...
SHOWING ME THAT YOU CAN DO ANYTHING I CAN...?
FINE!
SQUEAK
BRING IT!

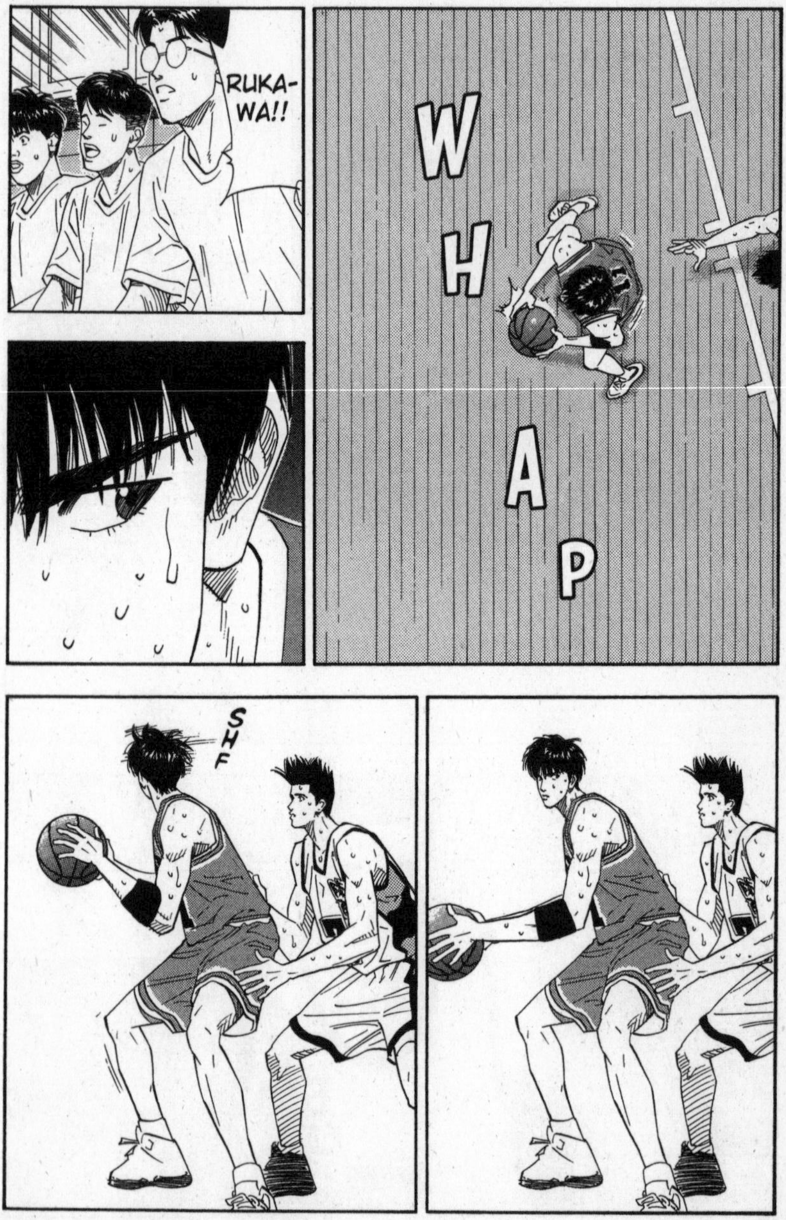
WHAP
RUKA-
WA!!
SHF

READ THIS WAY

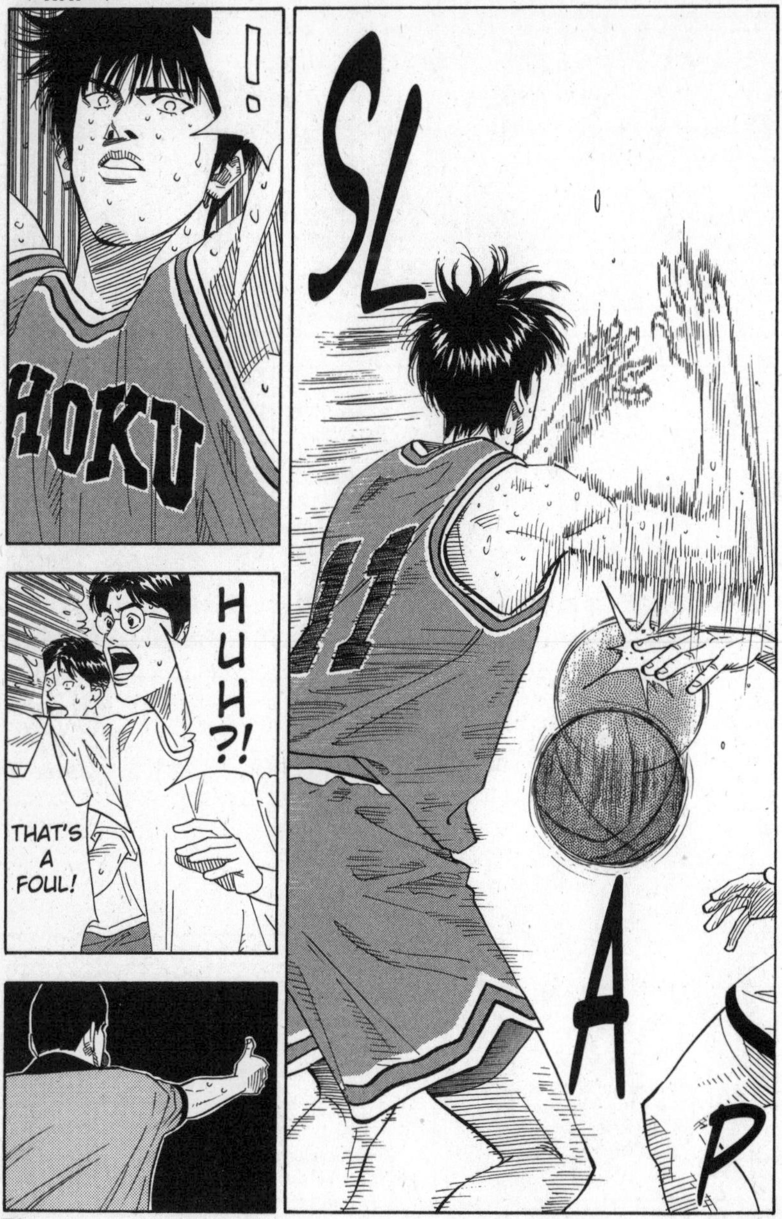
SLAP
!
HUH?!
THAT'S A FOUL!

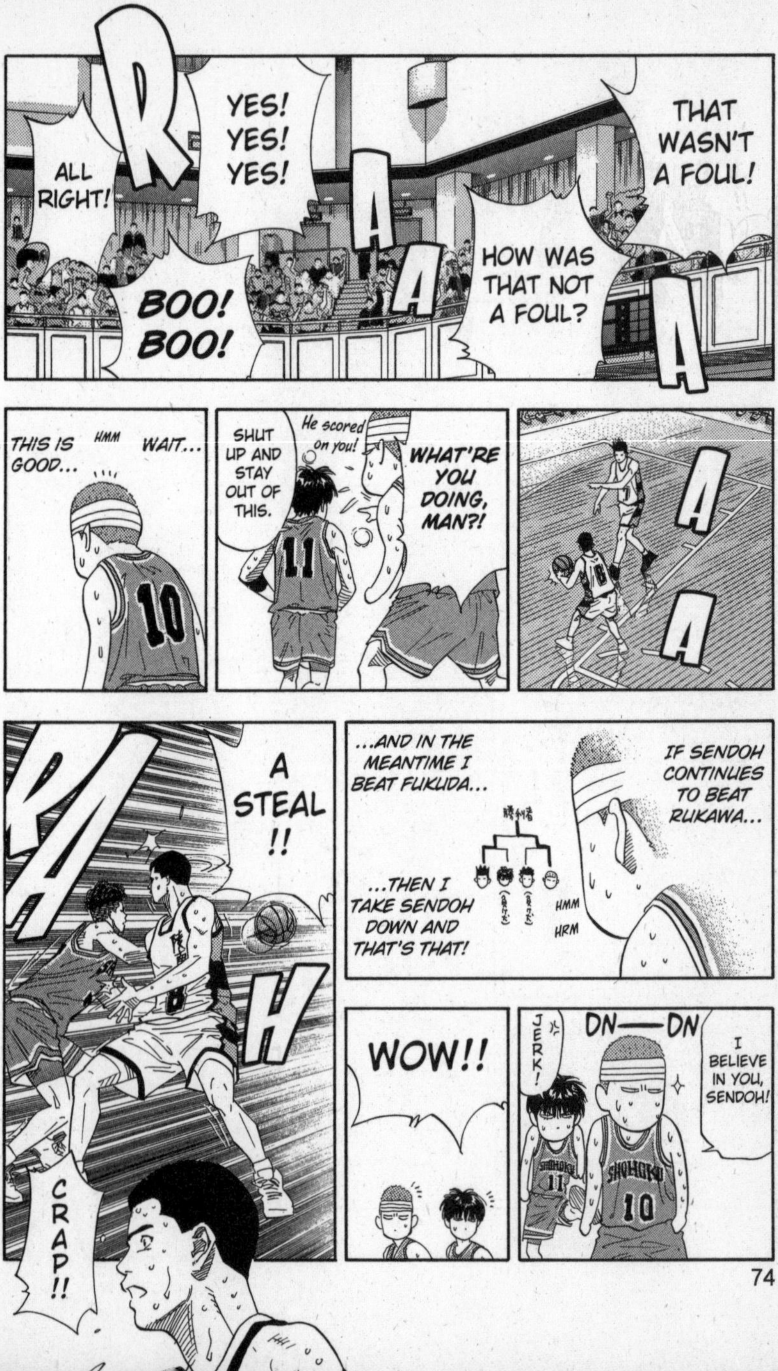
THAT WASN'T A FOUL!
HOW WAS THAT NOT A FOUL?
A
A
A
YES! YES! YES!
R
ALL RIGHT!
BOO! BOO!
A
A
WHAT'RE YOU DOING, MAN?!
He scored on you!
SHUT UP AND STAY OUT OF THIS.
WAIT...
HMM
THIS IS GOOD...
IF SENDOH CONTINUES TO BEAT RUKAWA...
...AND IN THE MEANTIME I BEAT FUKUDA...
勝利者
...THEN I TAKE SENDOH DOWN AND THAT'S THAT!
HMM
HRM
I BELIEVE IN YOU, SENDOH!
DN—DN
JERK!
SHOHOKU
WOW!!
A STEAL!!
H
CRAP!!

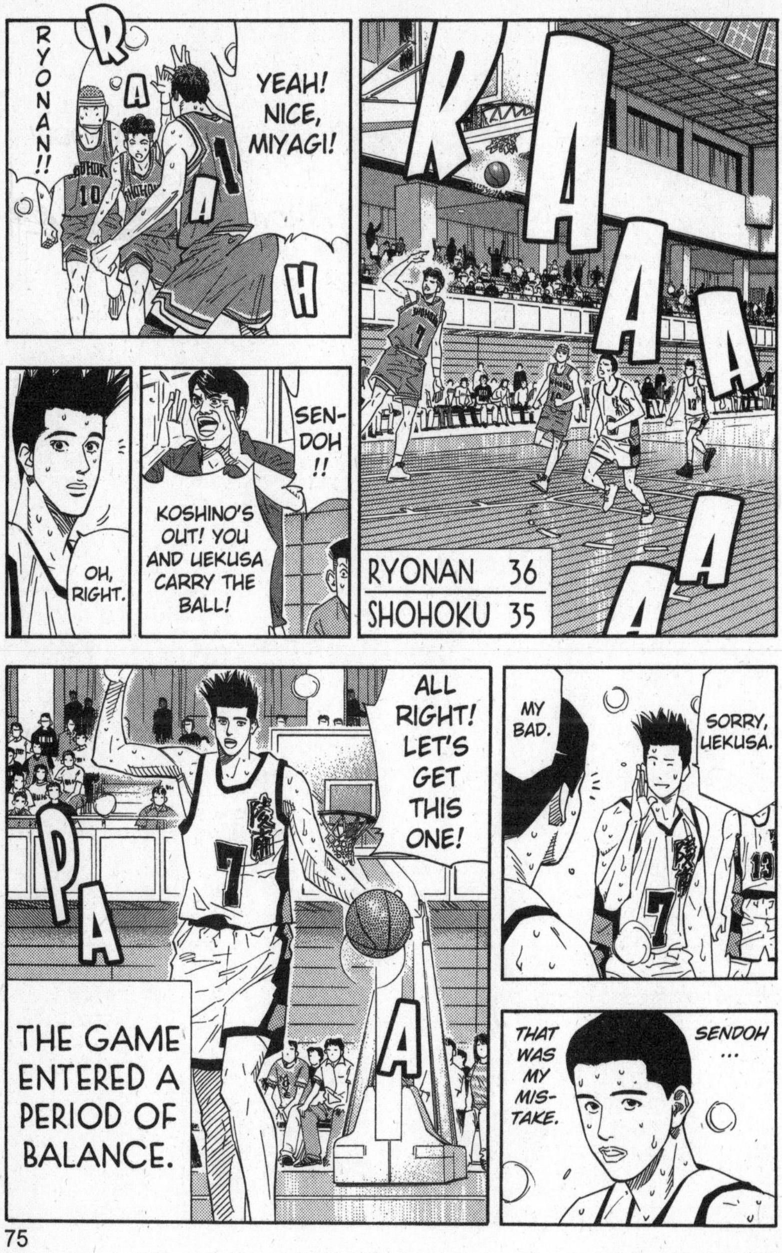
RAAAAAA
RYONAN 36
SHOHOKU 35
YEAH! NICE, MIYAGI!
RYONAN!!
RAAH
SEN-DOH!!
KOSHINO'S OUT! YOU AND UEKUSA CARRY THE BALL!
OH, RIGHT.
SORRY, UEKUSA.
MY BAD.
SENDOH ...
THAT WAS MY MIS-TAKE.
ALL RIGHT! LET'S GET THIS ONE!
PAA
THE GAME ENTERED A PERIOD OF BALANCE.

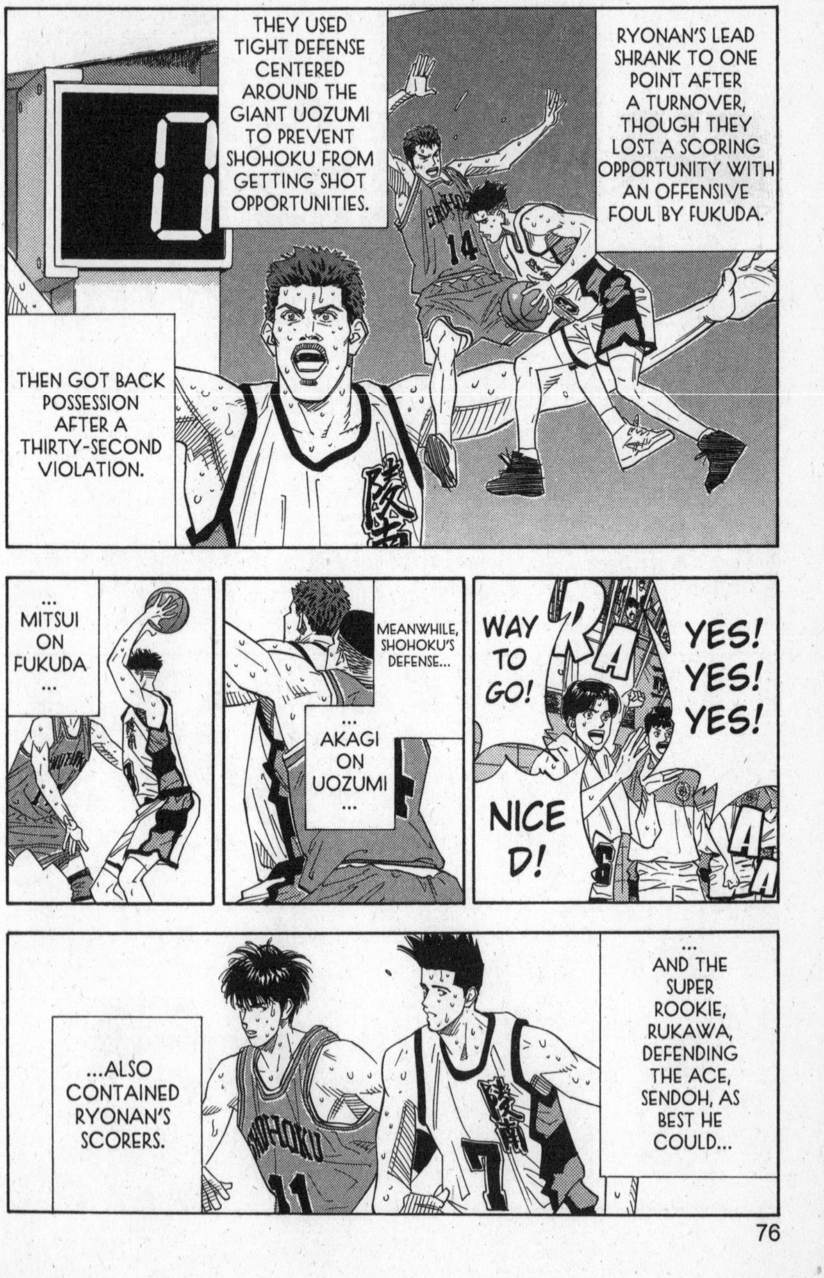
RYONAN'S LEAD SHRANK TO ONE POINT AFTER A TURNOVER, THOUGH THEY LOST A SCORING OPPORTUNITY WITH AN OFFENSIVE FOUL BY FUKUDA.
THEY USED TIGHT DEFENSE CENTERED AROUND THE GIANT UOZUMI TO PREVENT SHOHOKU FROM GETTING SHOT OPPORTUNITIES.
THEN GOT BACK POSSESSION AFTER A THIRTY-SECOND VIOLATION.
YES! YES! YES!
RA
WAY TO GO!
A
A
NICE D!
MEANWHILE, SHOHOKU'S DEFENSE...
...AKAGI ON UOZUMI...
...MITSUI ON FUKUDA...
...AND THE SUPER ROOKIE, RUKAWA, DEFENDING THE ACE, SENDOH, AS BEST HE COULD...
...ALSO CONTAINED RYONAN'S SCORERS.

READ THIS WAY

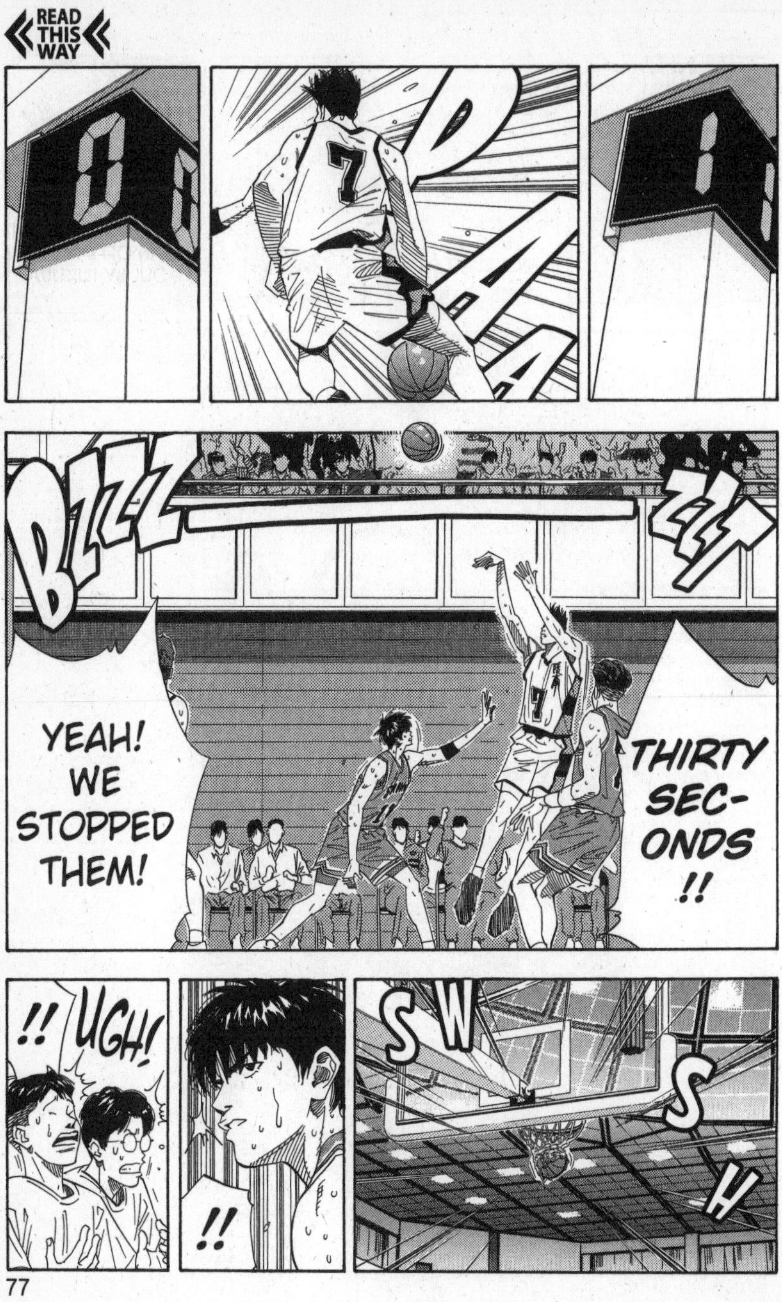
PAA
BZZZZ—ZZT
THIRTY SEC-ONDS!!
YEAH! WE STOPPED THEM!
SWSSH
!!
!!
UGH!

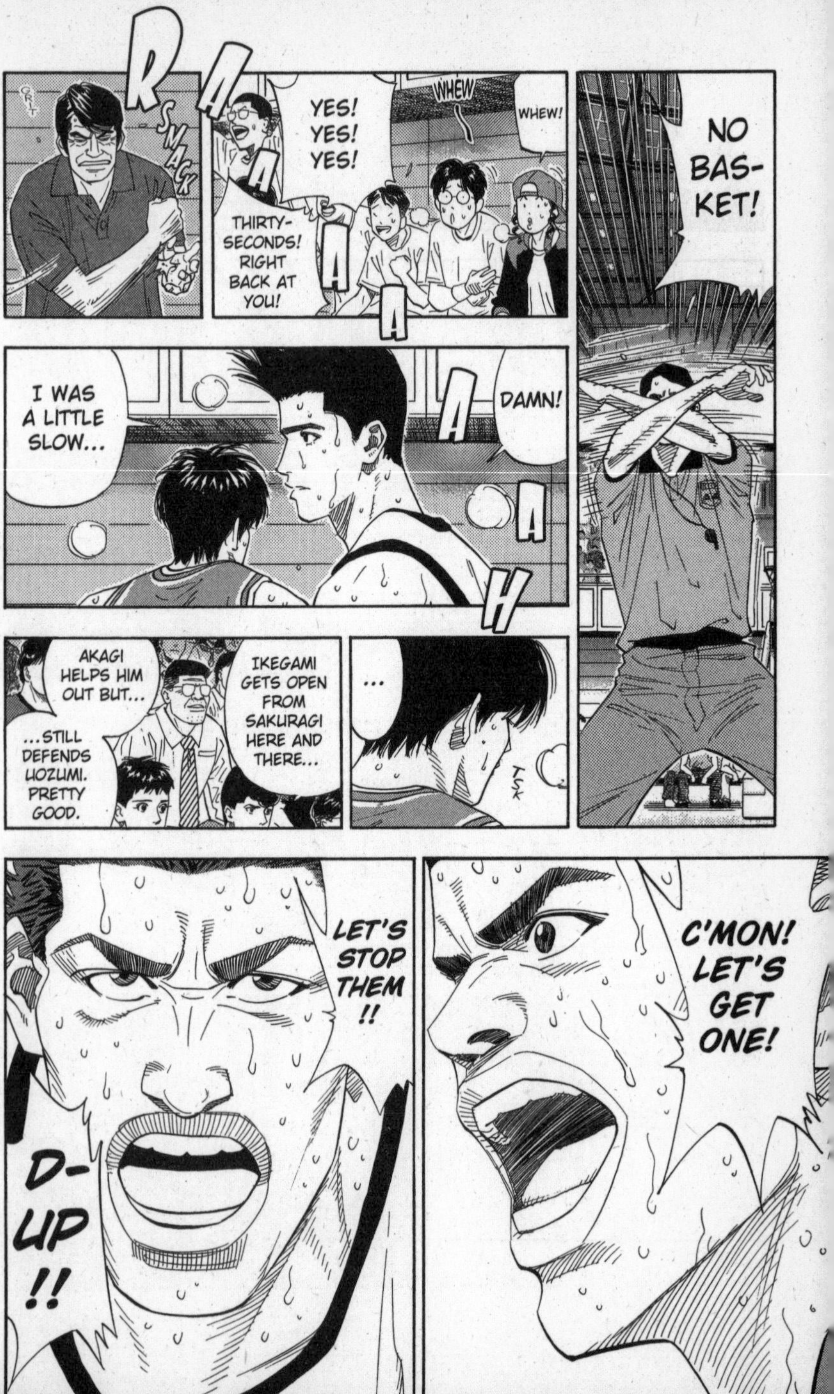
NO BASKET!
WHEW
WHEW!
YES! YES! YES!
THIRTY-SECONDS! RIGHT BACK AT YOU!
RAAAAAAH
GRIT
SNACK
DAMN!
I WAS A LITTLE SLOW...
...
TSK
IKEGAMI GETS OPEN FROM SAKURAGI HERE AND THERE...
AKAGI HELPS HIM OUT BUT...
...STILL DEFENDS UOZUMI. PRETTY GOOD.
C'MON! LET'S GET ONE!
LET'S STOP THEM!!
D-UP!!

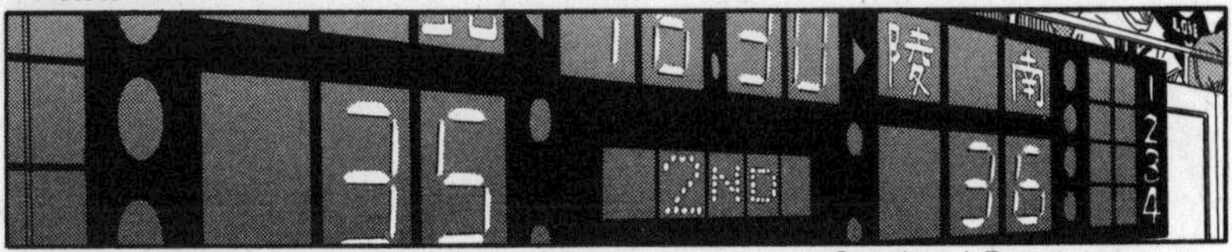
陵
南
35
2ND
36
Scoreboard: Ryonan

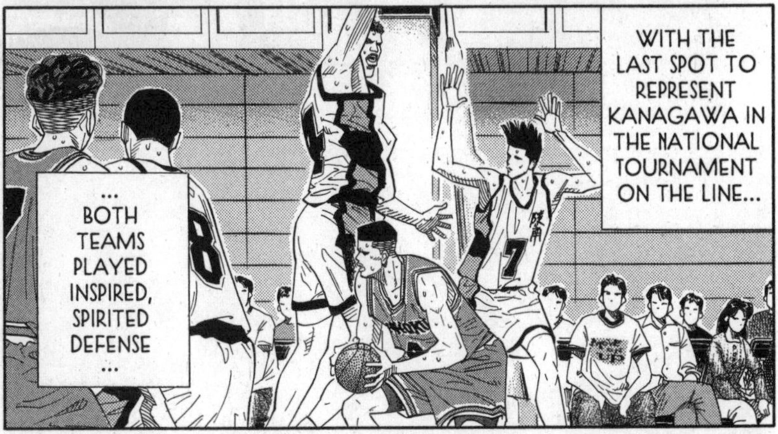
WITH THE LAST SPOT TO REPRESENT KANAGAWA IN THE NATIONAL TOURNAMENT ON THE LINE...
...BOTH TEAMS PLAYED INSPIRED, SPIRITED DEFENSE...

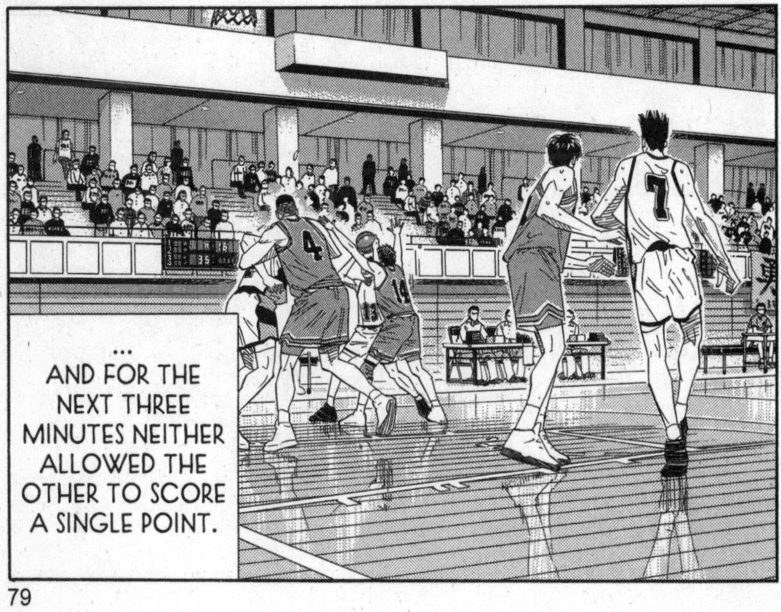
...AND FOR THE NEXT THREE MINUTES NEITHER ALLOWED THE OTHER TO SCORE A SINGLE POINT.

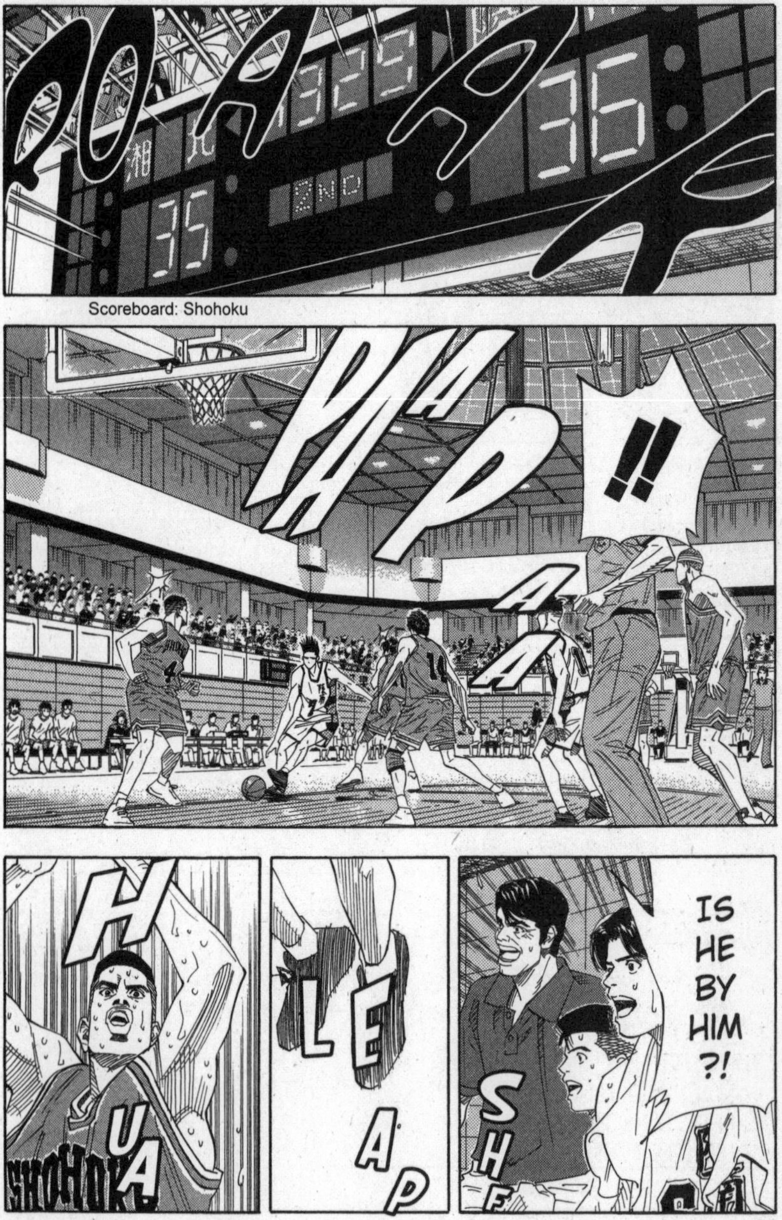

Scoreboard: Shohoku

!!
IS HE BY HIM ?!
SHF
LEAP
HUA
SHOHOKU

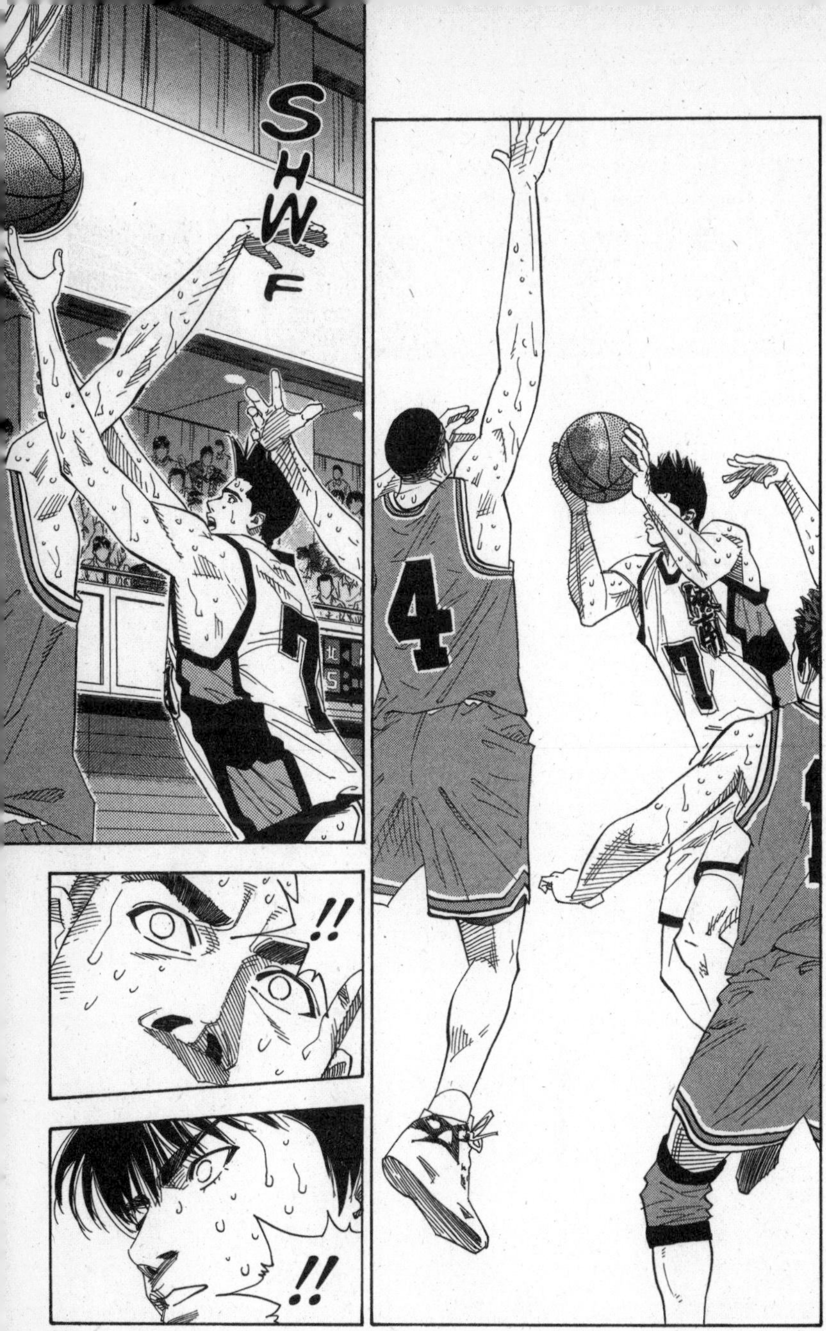
SHWF
!!
!!

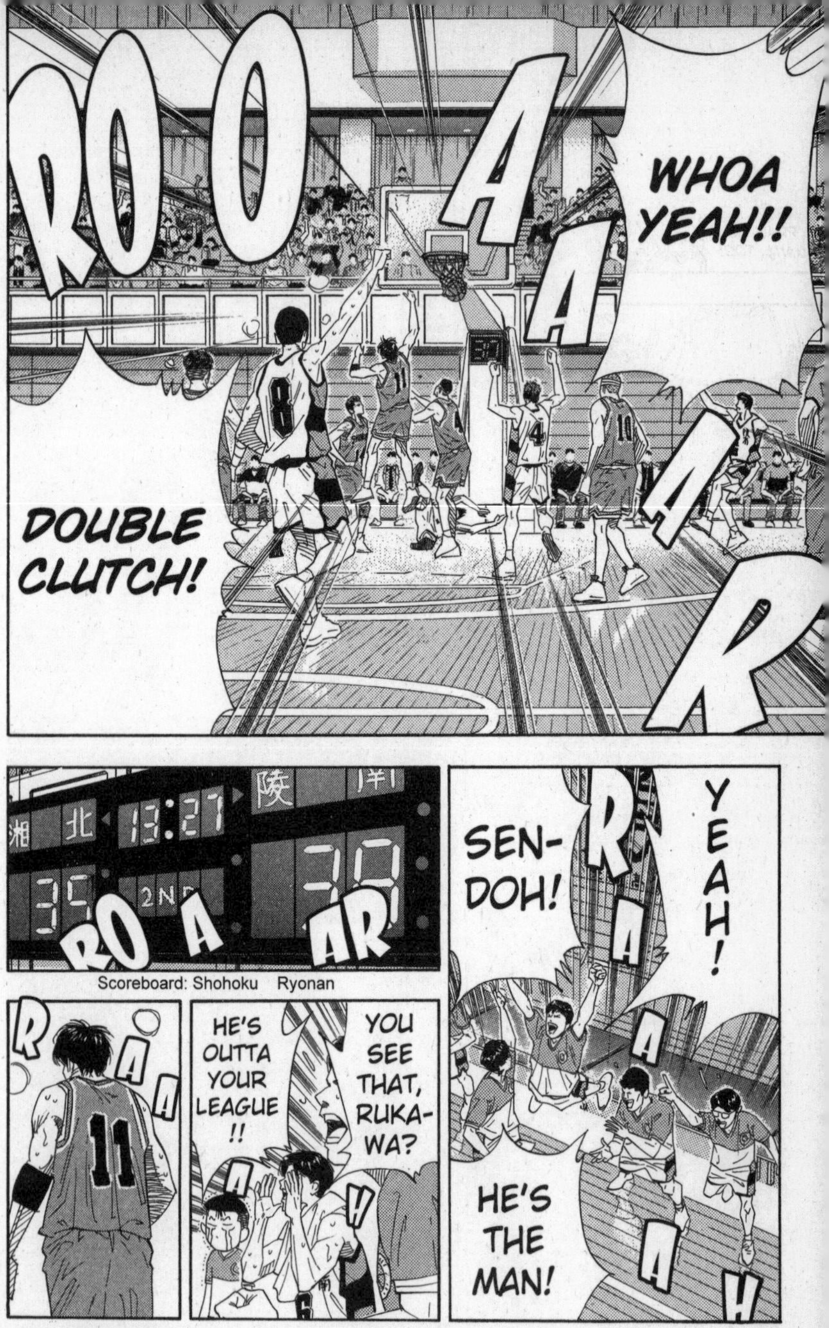
ROOOAAAAR
WHOA YEAH!!
DOUBLE CLUTCH!
YEAH!
SEN-DOH!
RAAAAH
HE'S THE MAN!
湘北 13:27 陵南
2ND
ROAAR
Scoreboard: Shohoku Ryonan
YOU SEE THAT, RUKAWA?
HE'S OUTTA YOUR LEAGUE!!
AAH
RAAA

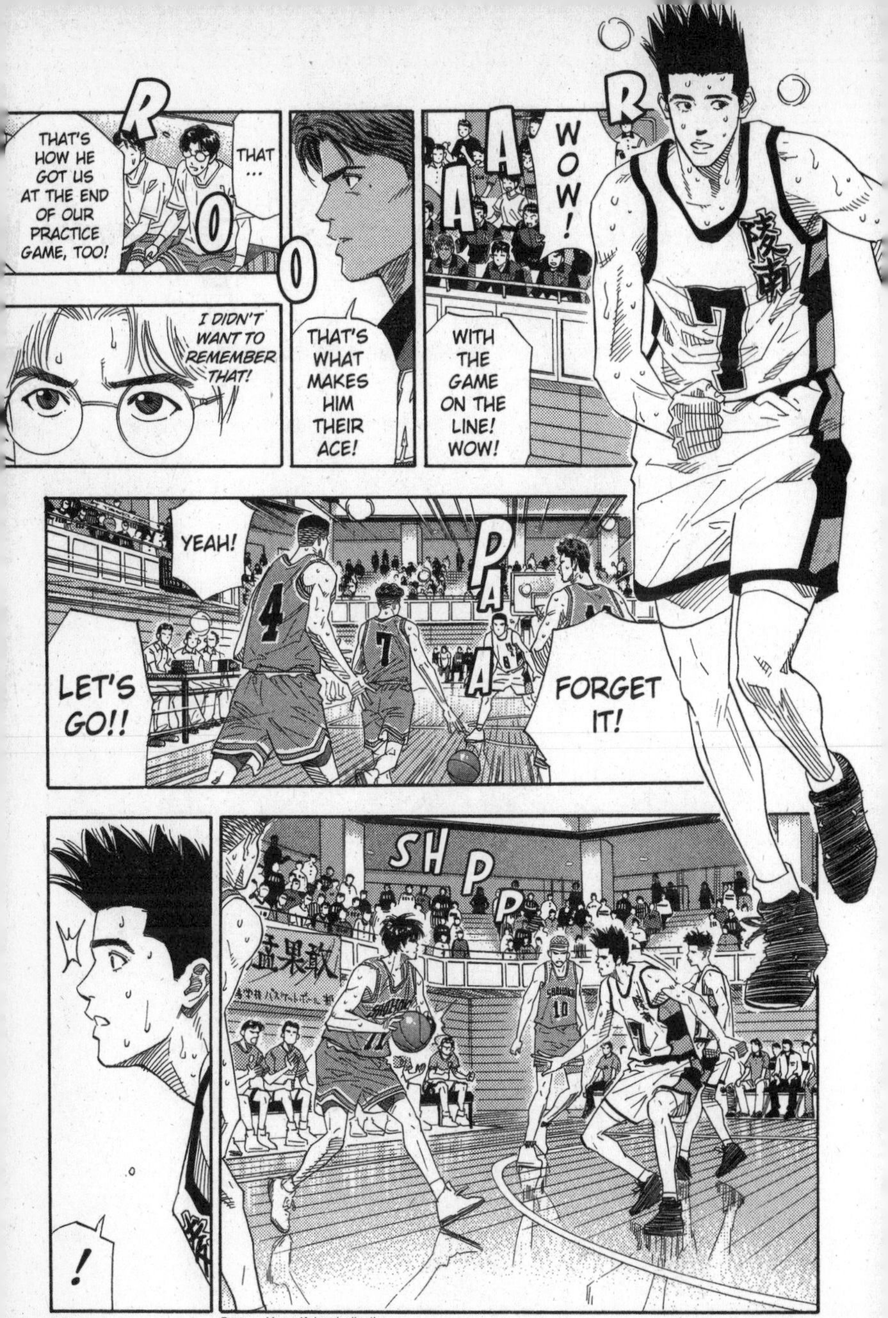
ROOAAR
WOW!
WITH THE GAME ON THE LINE! WOW!
THAT'S WHAT MAKES HIM THEIR ACE!
THAT ...
THAT'S HOW HE GOT US AT THE END OF OUR PRACTICE GAME, TOO!
I DIDN'T WANT TO REMEMBER THAT!
PAA
YEAH!
FORGET IT!
LET'S GO!!
SHPP
!

Banner: *Yumo Kakan* (valiant)
Ryonan High School Basketball Team

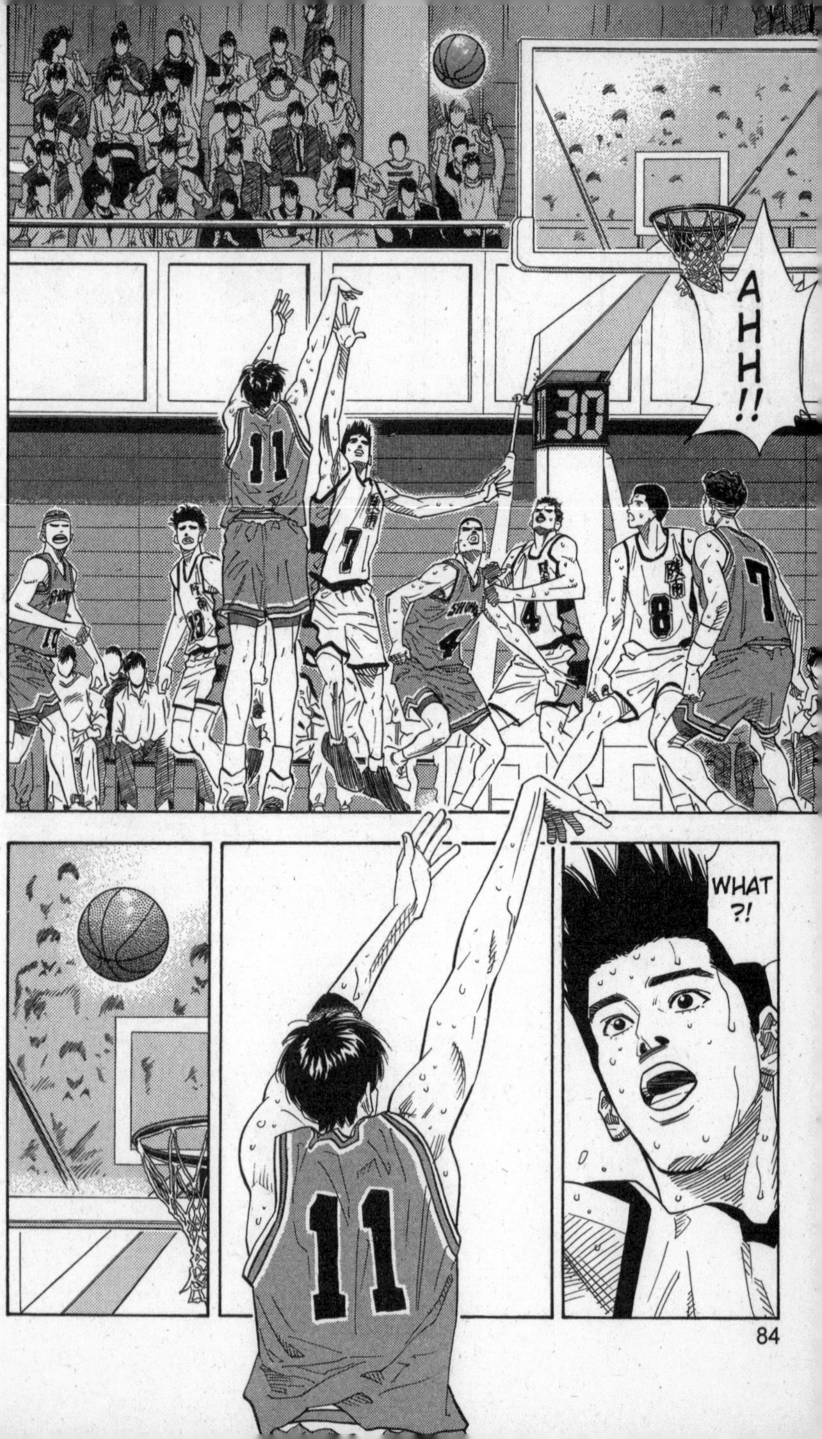
AHH!!
WHAT ?!

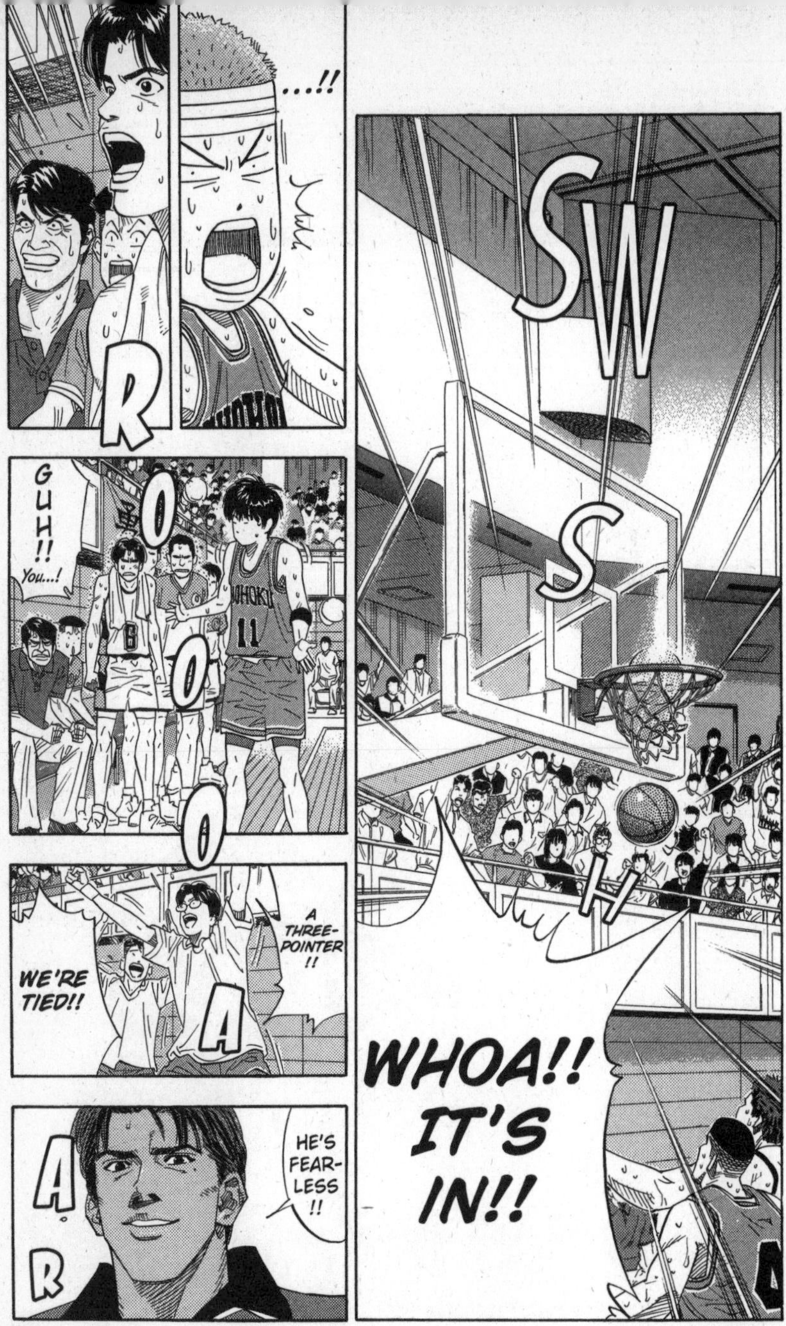
SW
S
SH
WHOA!! IT'S IN!!
...!!
R
GUH!! You...!
O
O
O
A THREE-POINTER!!
WE'RE TIED!!
A
HE'S FEARLESS!!
A
R

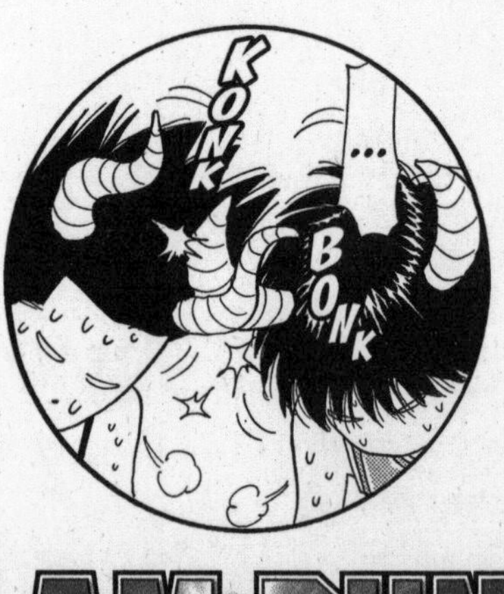
...
KONK
BONK

SLAM DUNK

THE PERSISTENT MAN

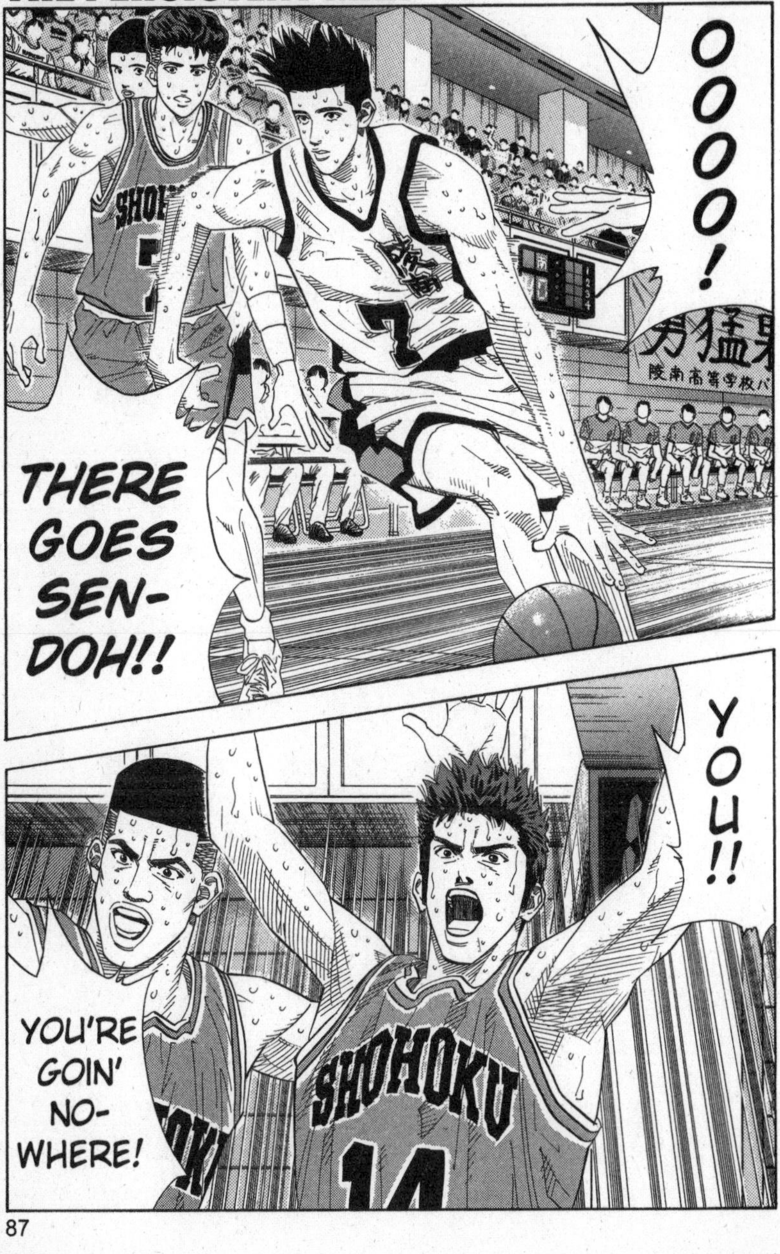

OOOO!
THERE GOES SEN-DOH!!
YOU!!
YOU'RE GOIN' NO-WHERE!

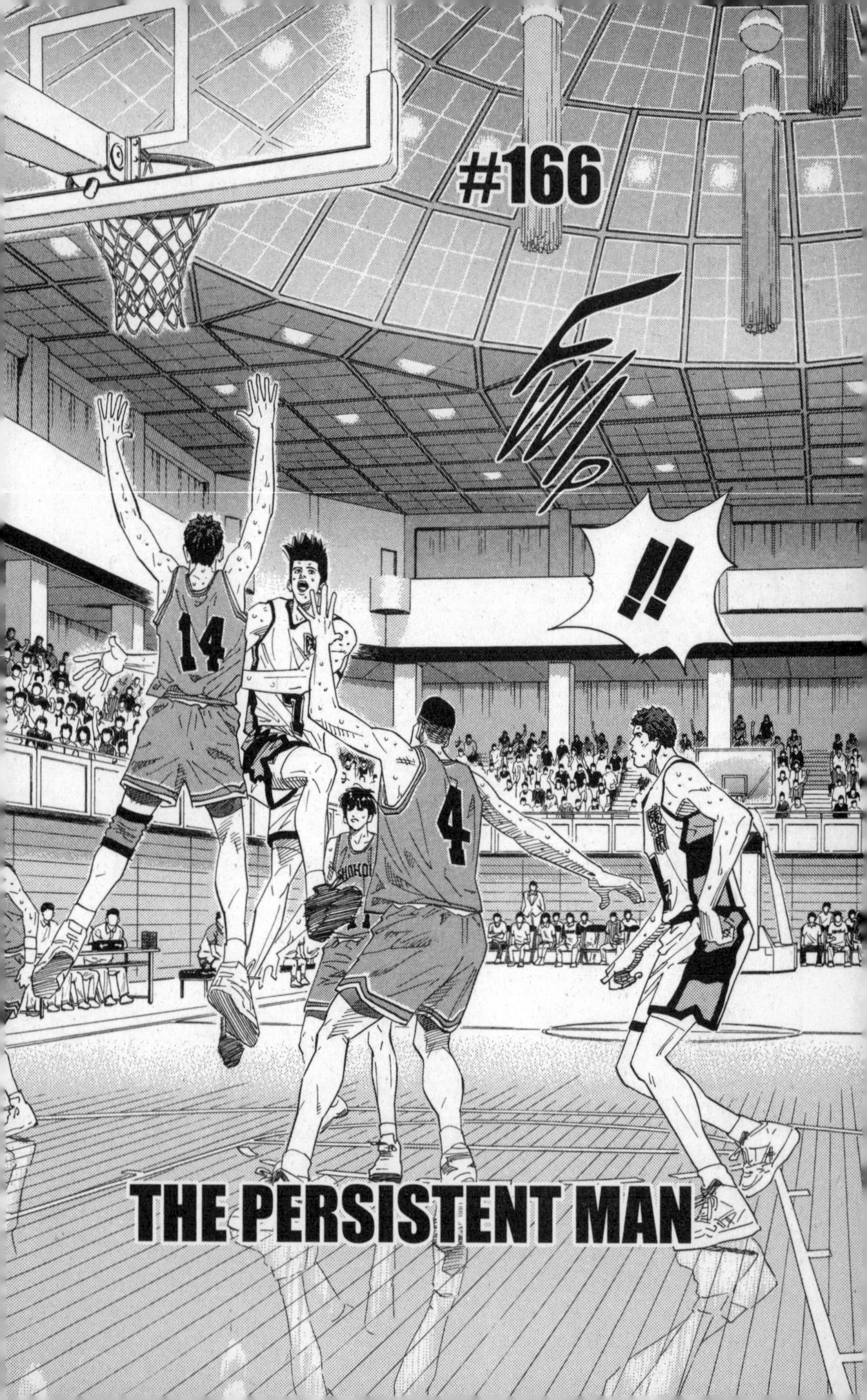
#166
FWIP
!!
SHOHOKU
THE PERSISTENT MAN

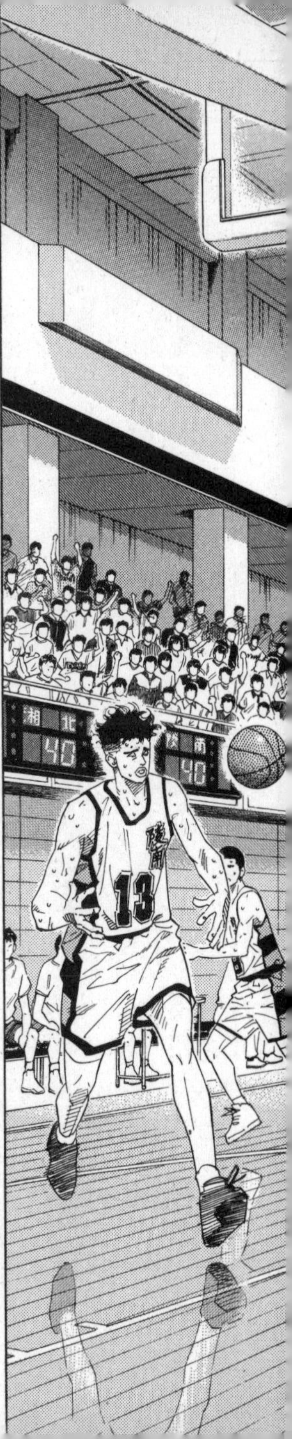

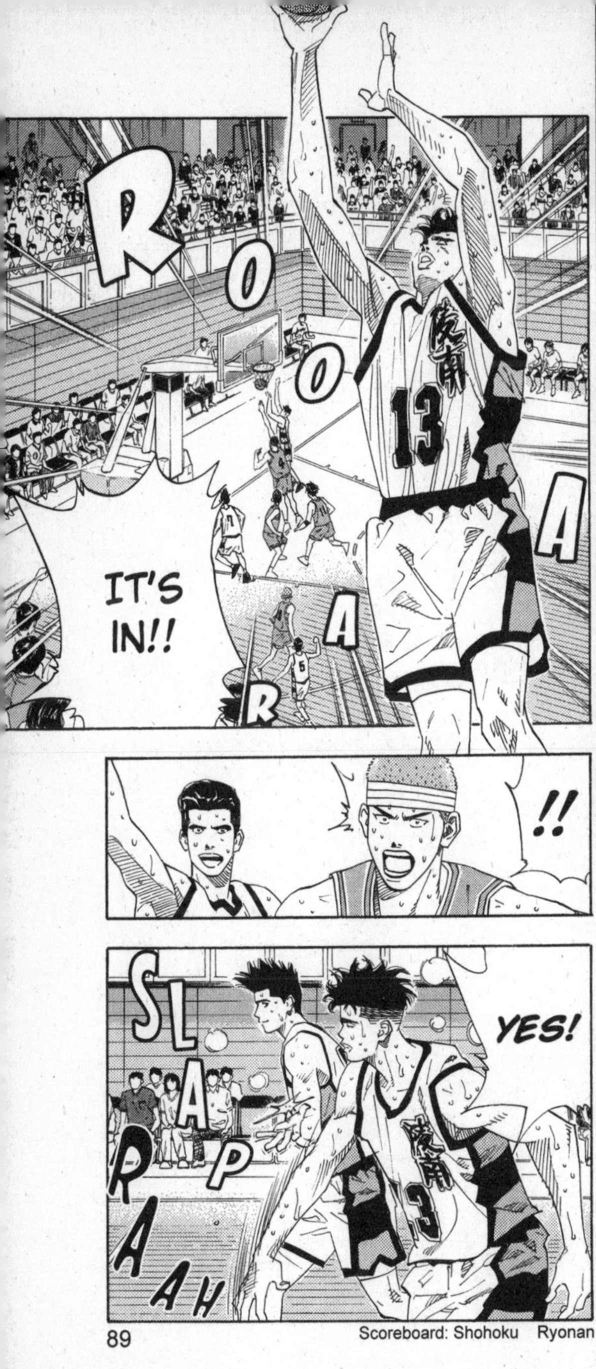
ROOAAR
IT'S IN!!
!!
YES!
SLAP
RAAH

Scoreboard: Shohoku Ryonan

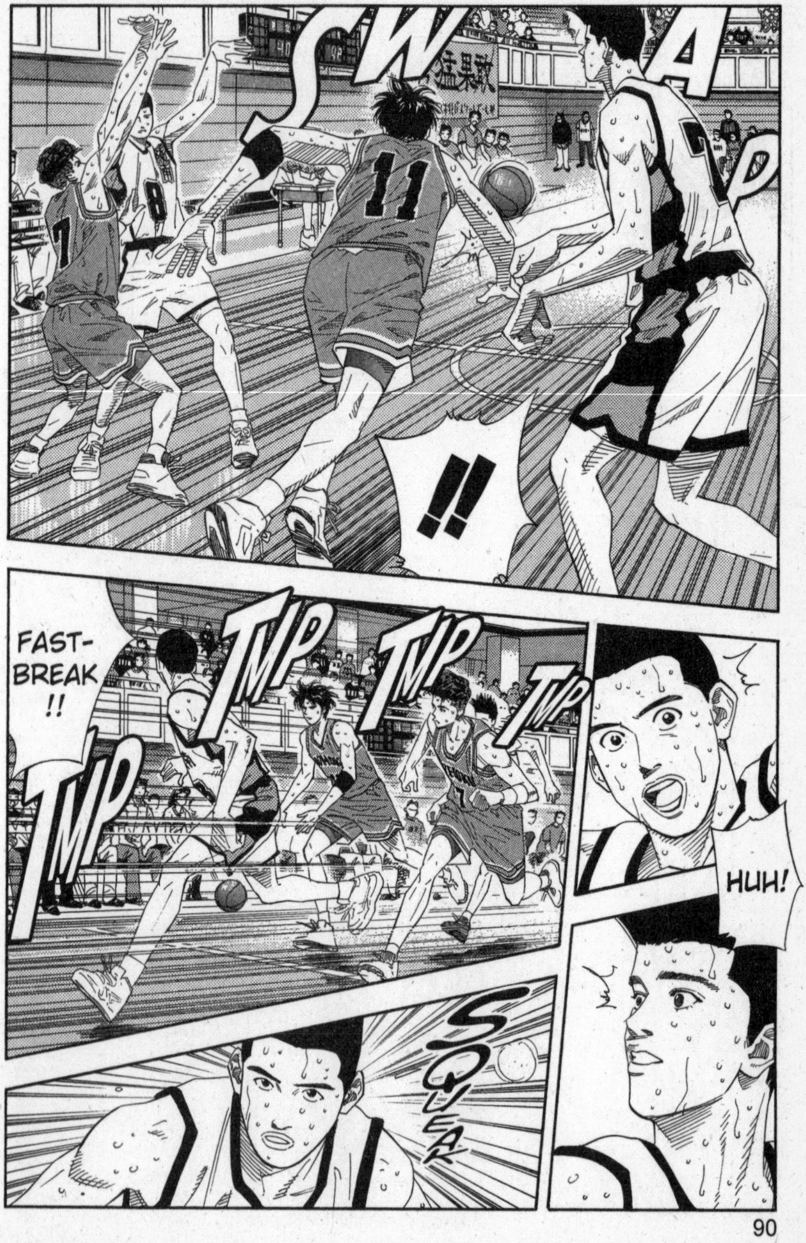
SWAP
!!
HUH!
FAST-BREAK !!
TMP
TMP
TMP
TMP
SQUEAK

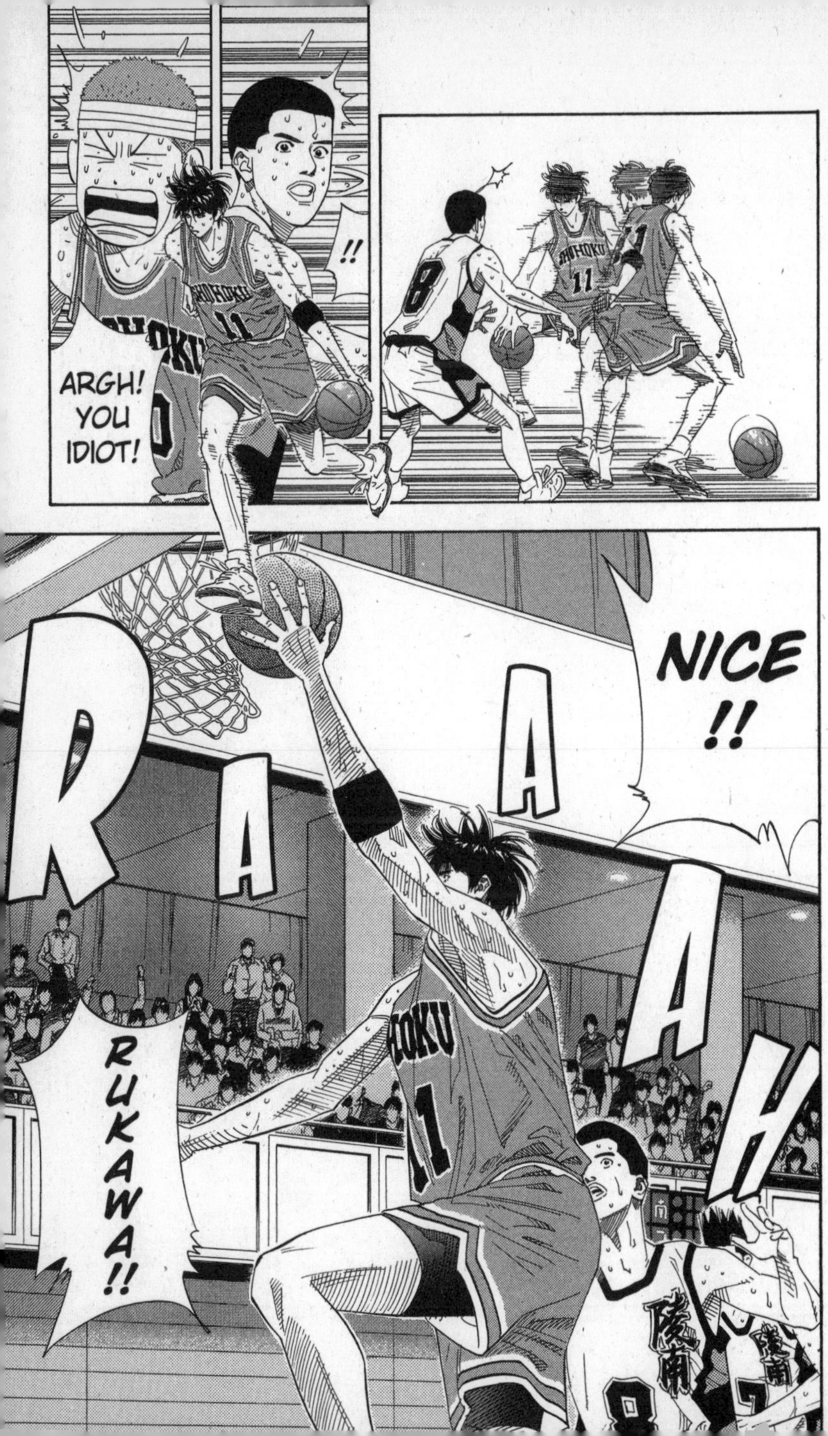
!!
ARGH! YOU IDIOT!
NICE !!
RAAAH
RUKAWA!!

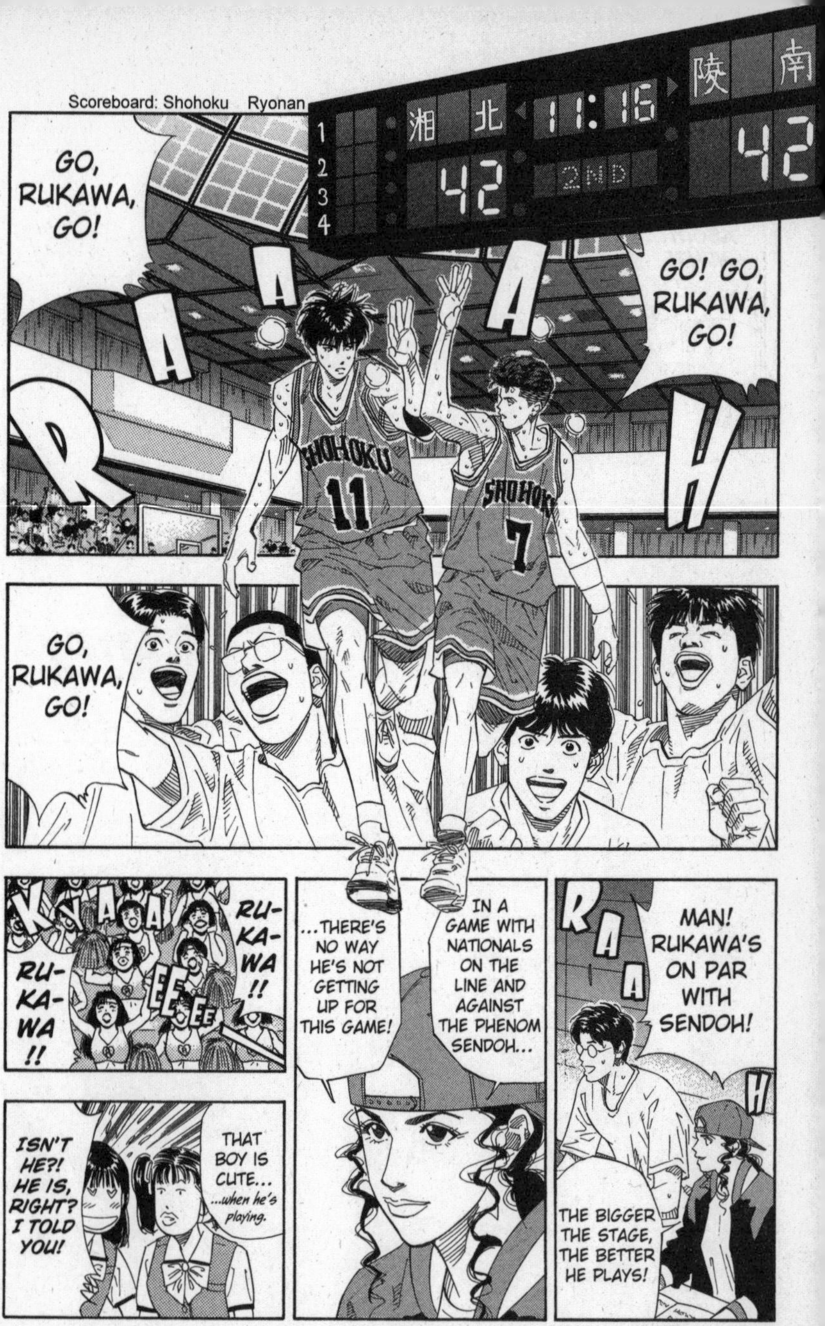
Scoreboard: Shohoku Ryonan
湘北 11:16 陵南
1 2 3 4
42 2ND 42
GO! GO, RUKAWA, GO!
GO, RUKAWA, GO!
RAAAH
GO, RUKAWA, GO!
RAAH
MAN! RUKAWA'S ON PAR WITH SENDOH!
THE BIGGER THE STAGE, THE BETTER HE PLAYS!
IN A GAME WITH NATIONALS ON THE LINE AND AGAINST THE PHENOM SENDOH...
...THERE'S NO WAY HE'S NOT GETTING UP FOR THIS GAME!
RU-KAWA!!
RU-KA-WA!!
KYAAA
EEEE
THAT BOY IS CUTE... ...when he's playing.
ISN'T HE?! HE IS, RIGHT? I TOLD YOU!

READ THIS WAY

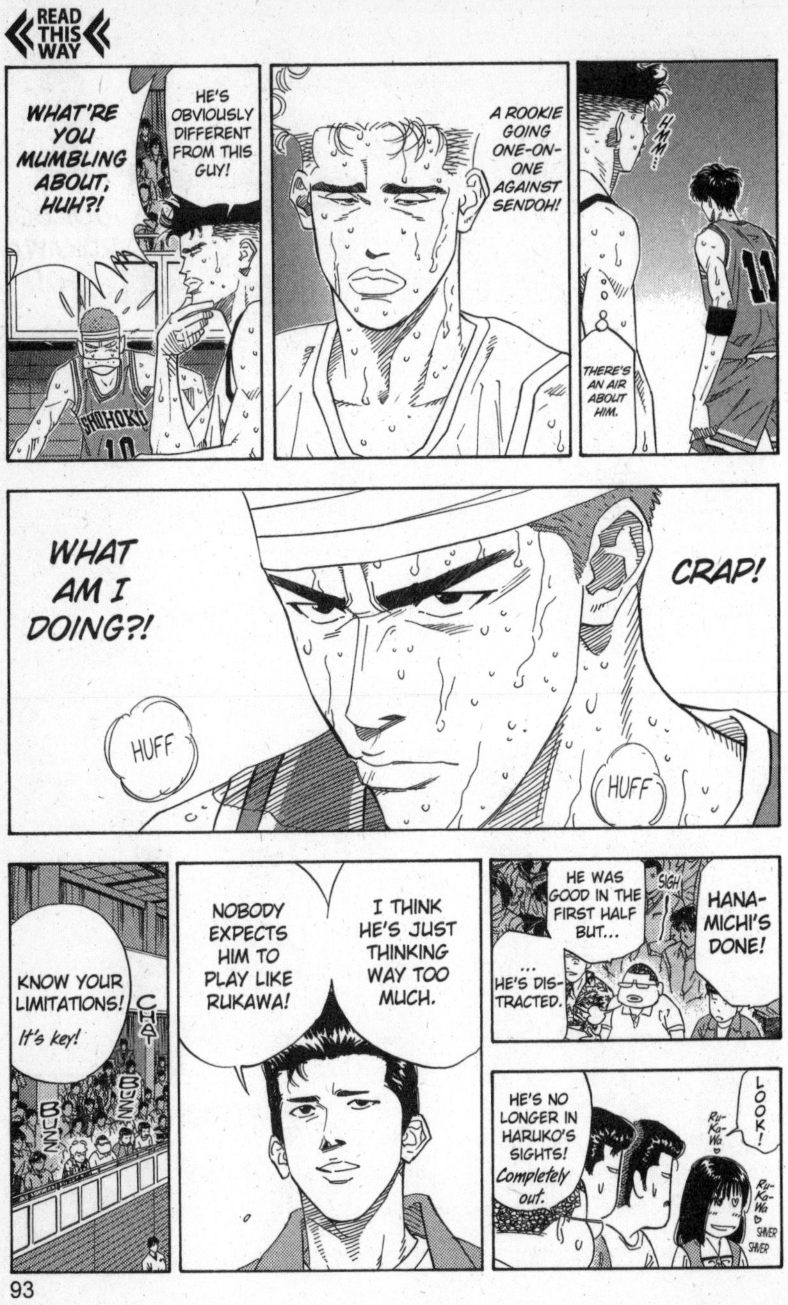
HMM...
THERE'S AN AIR ABOUT HIM.
A ROOKIE GOING ONE-ON-ONE AGAINST SENDOH!
HE'S OBVIOUSLY DIFFERENT FROM THIS GUY!
WHAT'RE YOU MUMBLING ABOUT, HUH?!
CRAP!
WHAT AM I DOING?!
HUFF
HUFF
HANA-MICHI'S DONE!
SIGH
HE WAS GOOD IN THE FIRST HALF BUT...
... HE'S DIS-TRACTED.
LOOK!
Ru-Ka-Wa
Ru-Ka-Wa
SHIVER SHIVER
HE'S NO LONGER IN HARUKO'S SIGHTS! Completely out.
I THINK HE'S JUST THINKING WAY TOO MUCH.
NOBODY EXPECTS HIM TO PLAY LIKE RUKAWA!
KNOW YOUR LIMITATIONS! It's key!
CHAT
BUZZ
BUZZ

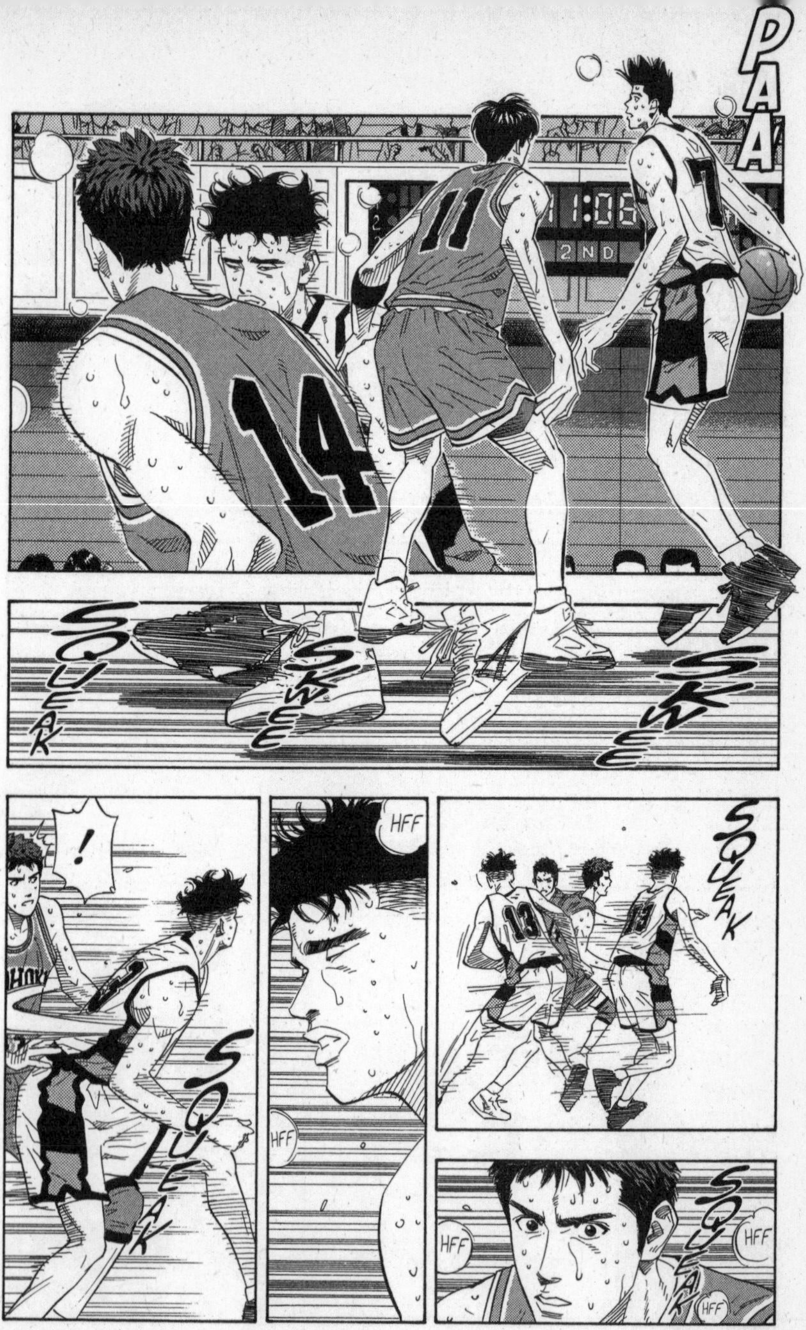
PAA
11:06
2ND
SKWEE
SKWEE
SQUEAK
SQUEAK
HFF
SQUEAK
HFF
HFF
HFF
HFF
!
SQUEAK

READ THIS WAY

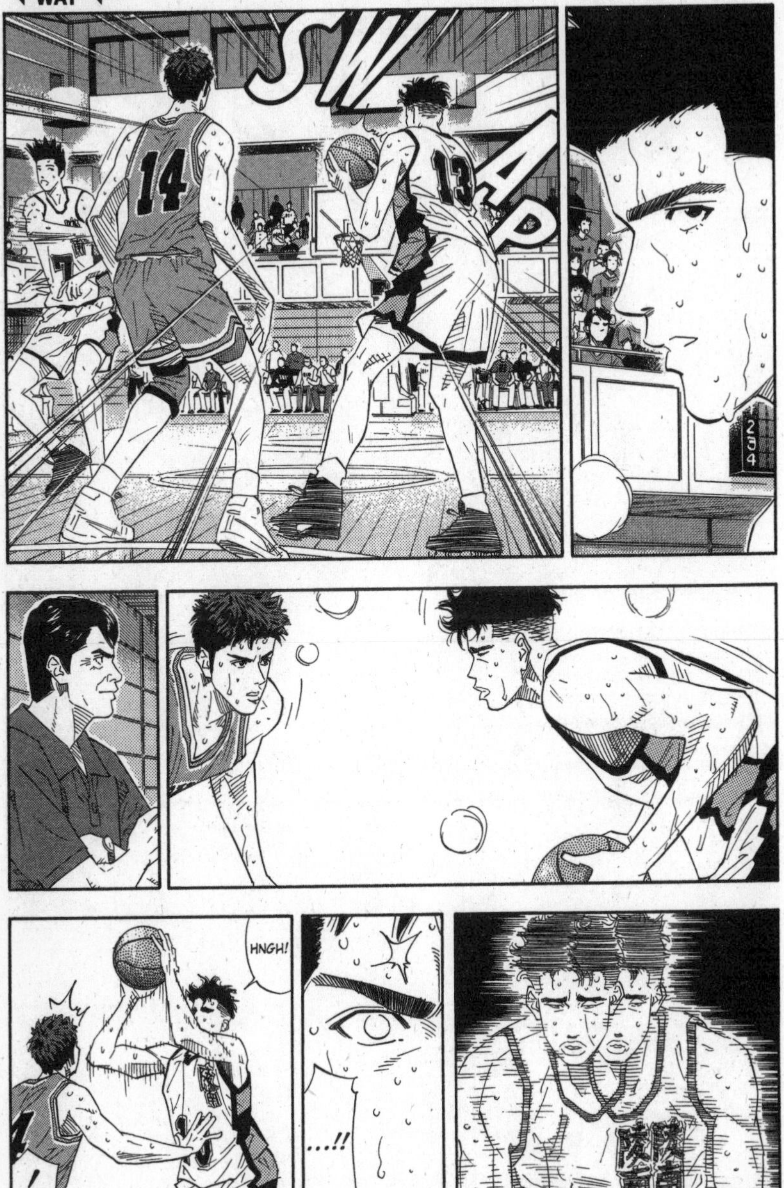
SWAP
...!!
HNGH!
!

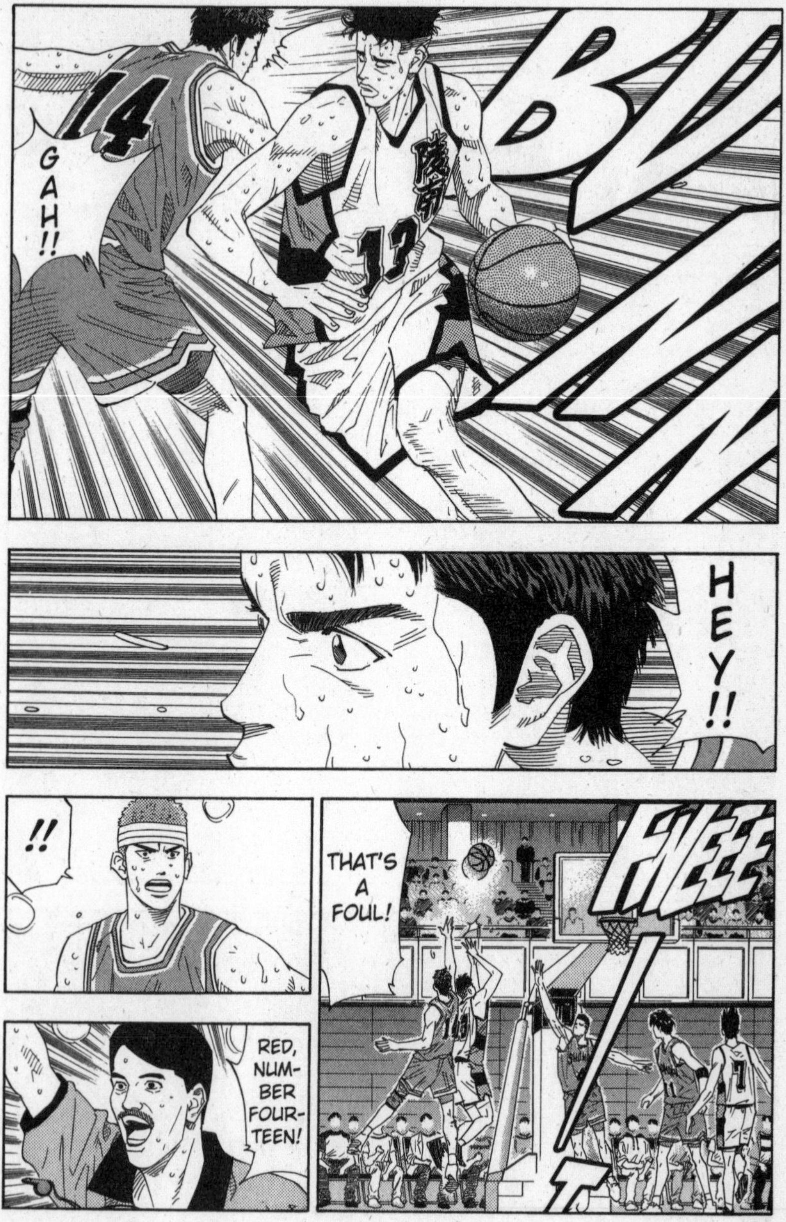
GAH!!
HEY!!
THAT'S A FOUL!
!!
RED, NUMBER FOURTEEN!

READ THIS WAY

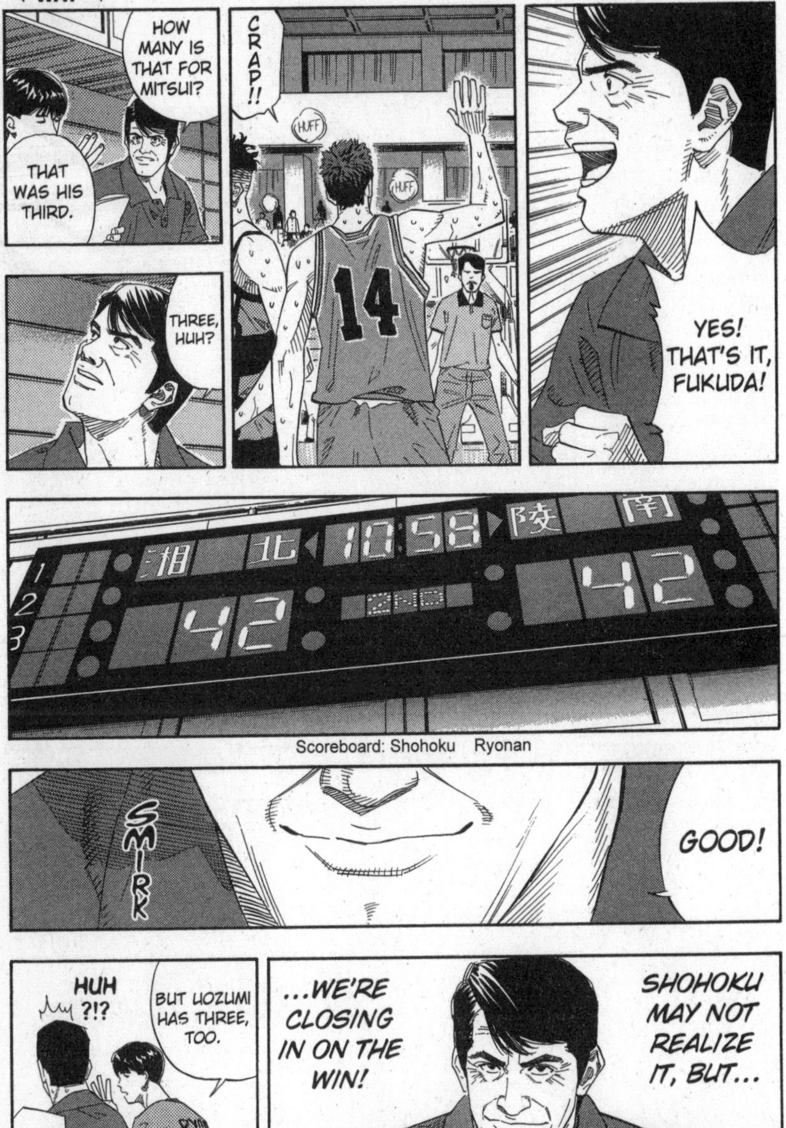
YES! THAT'S IT, FUKUDA!
CRAP!!
HUFF
HUFF
HOW MANY IS THAT FOR MITSUI?
THAT WAS HIS THIRD.
THREE, HUH?
陵南
湘北
10:58
42
42
2ND
Scoreboard: Shohoku Ryonan
GOOD!
SMIRK
SHOHOKU MAY NOT REALIZE IT, BUT...
...WE'RE CLOSING IN ON THE WIN!
BUT UOZUMI HAS THREE, TOO.
HUH ?!?
WHAT ...?!

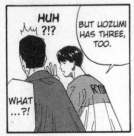

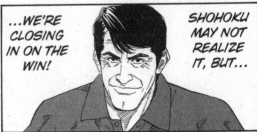

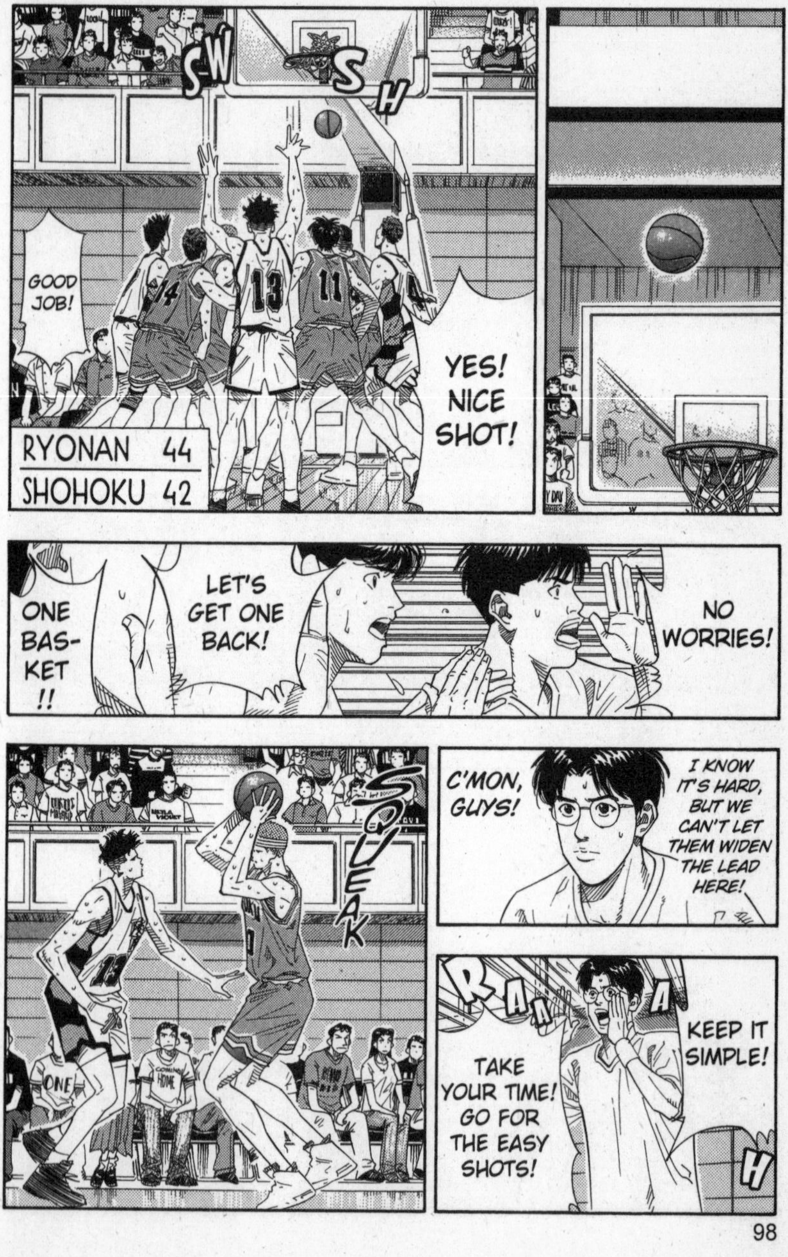
S-WSH
YES! NICE SHOT!
GOOD JOB!
RYONAN 44
SHOHOKU 42
NO WORRIES!
LET'S GET ONE BACK!
ONE BAS-KET!!
I KNOW IT'S HARD, BUT WE CAN'T LET THEM WIDEN THE LEAD HERE!
C'MON, GUYS!
RAAAH
KEEP IT SIMPLE!
TAKE YOUR TIME! GO FOR THE EASY SHOTS!
SQUEEAK

READ THIS WAY

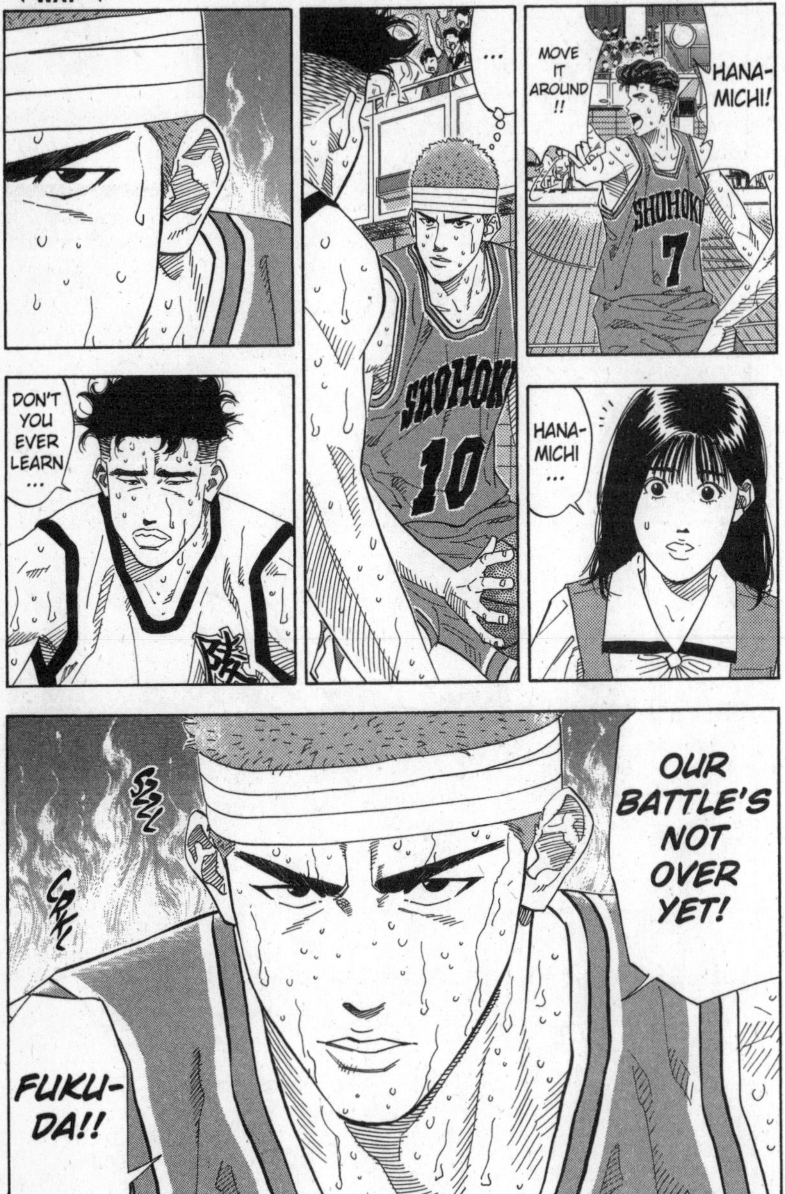

HANA-MICHI!
MOVE IT AROUND!!
HANA-MICHI ...
...
DON'T YOU EVER LEARN ...
OUR BATTLE'S NOT OVER YET!
SZZL
CRKL
FUKU-DA!!

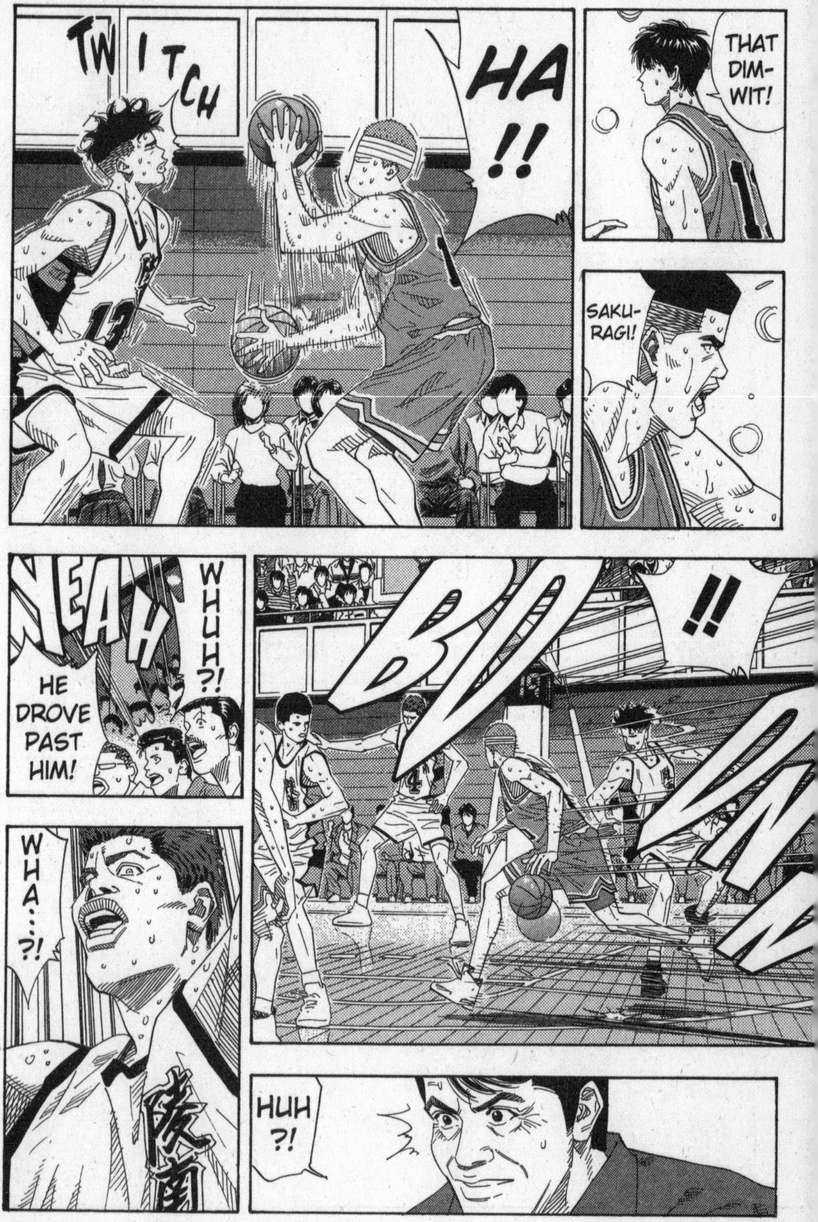
THAT DIM-WIT!
SAKURAGI!
HA!!
TWITCH
BUNN !!
WHUH?!
HE DROVE PAST HIM!
WHA...?!
HUH?!

READ THIS WAY

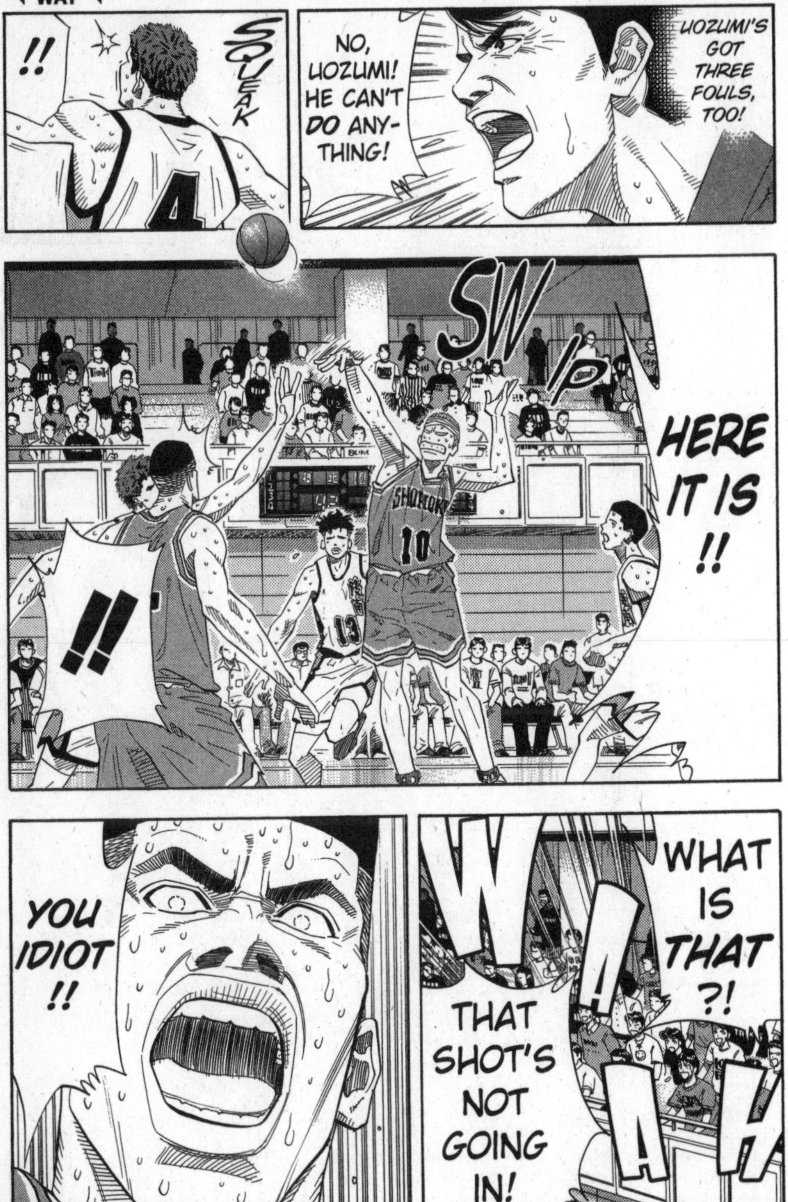

UOZUMI'S GOT THREE FOULS, TOO!
NO, UOZUMI! HE CAN'T DO ANYTHING!
!!
SQUEAK
SWIP
HERE IT IS !!
!!
WHAT IS THAT ?!
WA!
THAT SHOT'S NOT GOING IN!
AH
YOU IDIOT !!

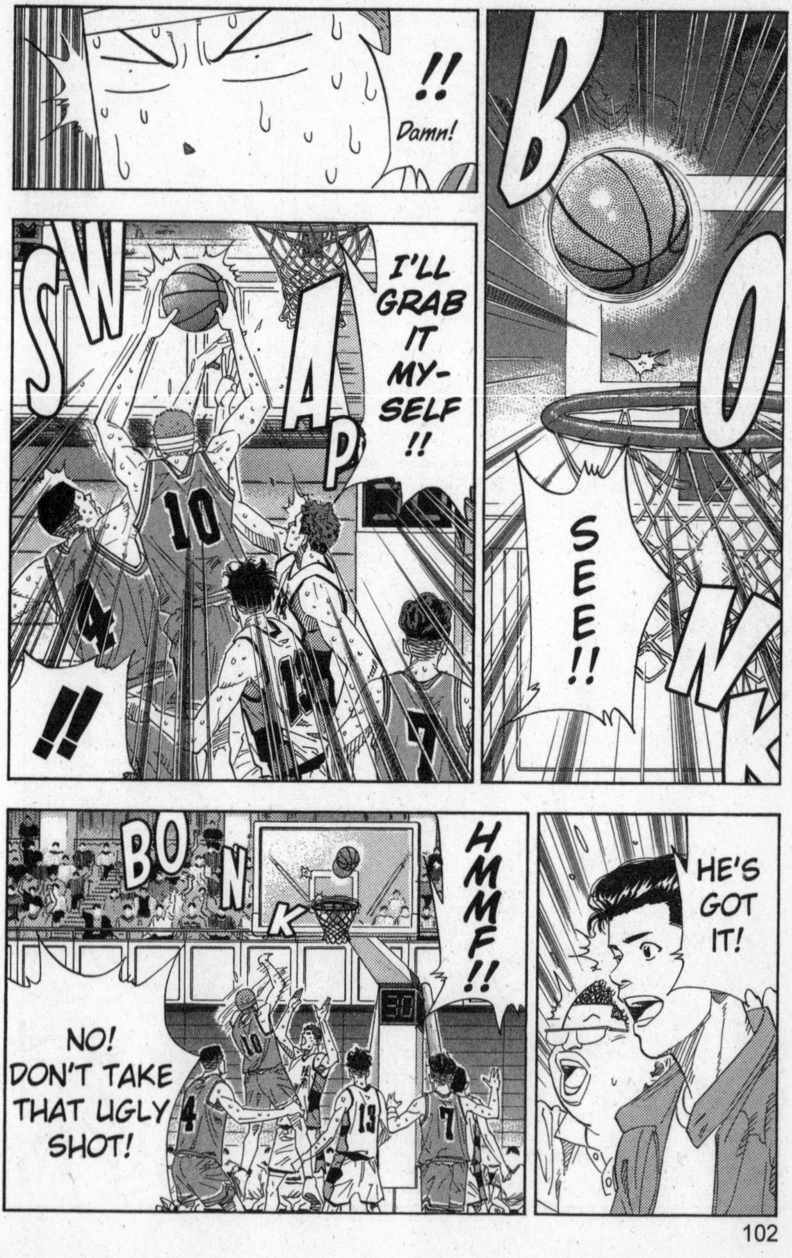
BOONK
SEE!!
!!
Damn!
SWAP
I'LL GRAB IT MY-SELF!!
!!
HE'S GOT IT!
HMMF!!
BONK
NO! DON'T TAKE THAT UGLY SHOT!

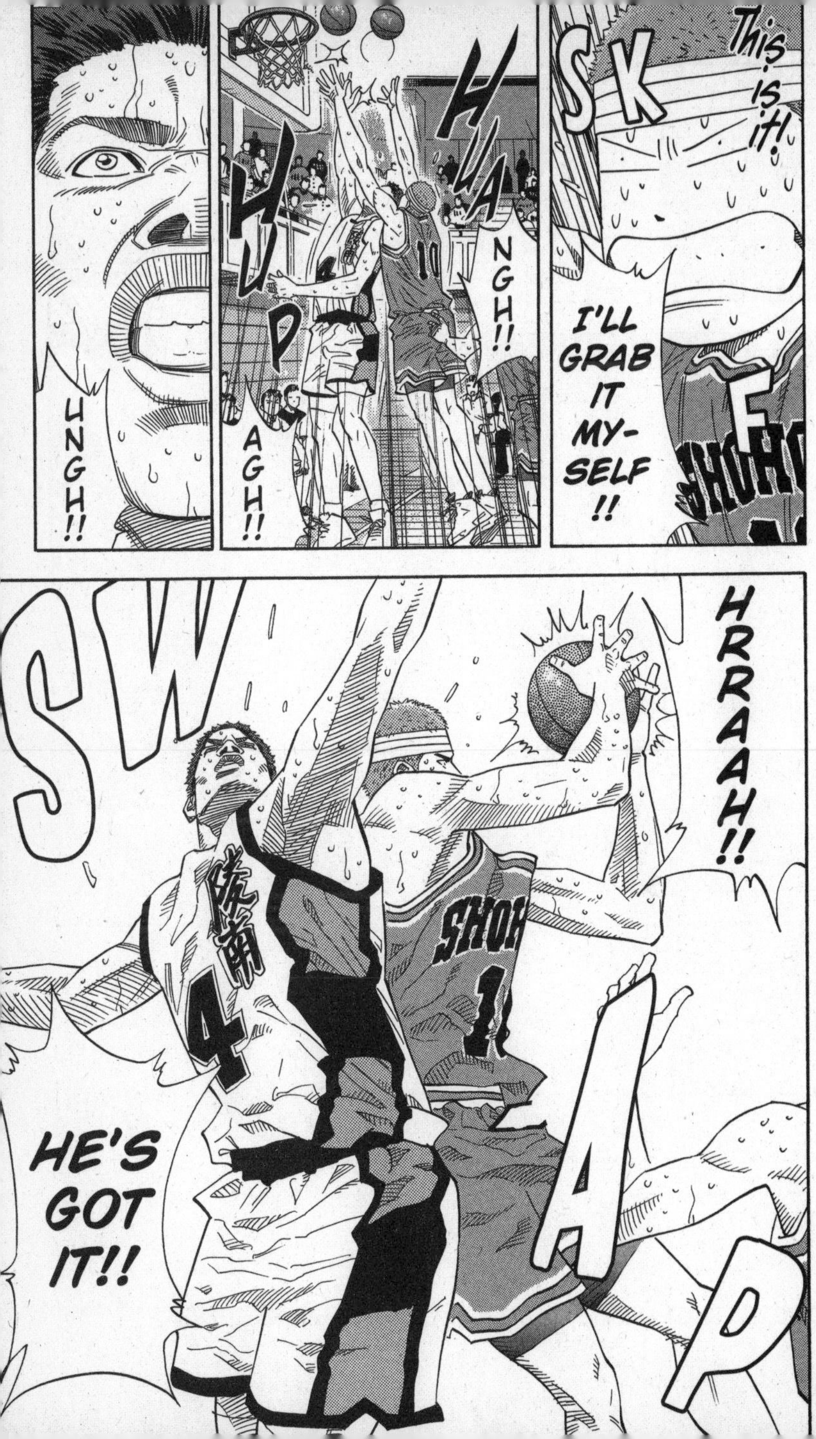
This is it!
SK
I'LL GRAB IT MYSELF!!
HUA
NGH!!
HUP
AGH!!
UNGH!!
HRRAAAH!!
SW
AP
HE'S GOT IT!!

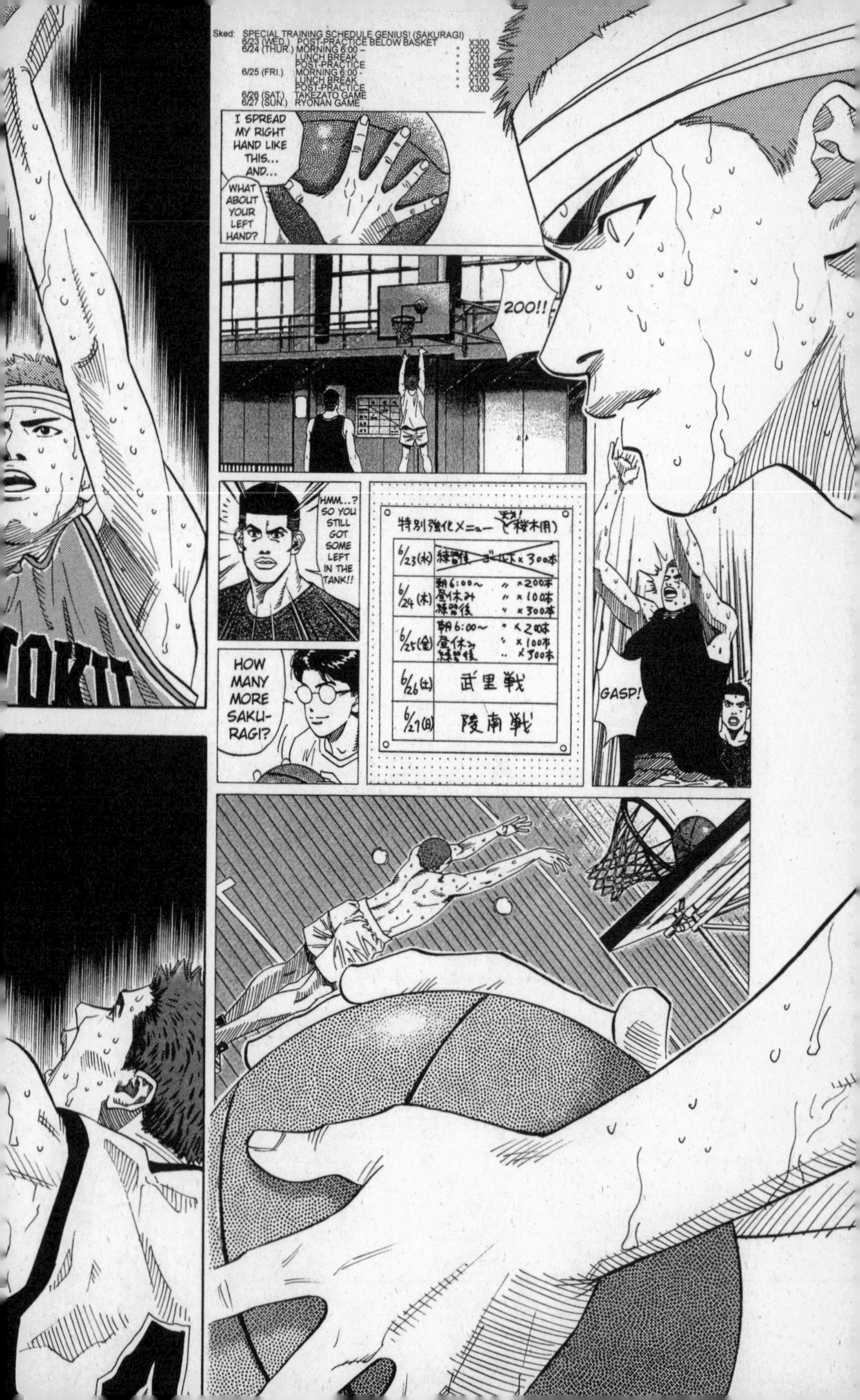
Sked: SPECIAL TRAINING SCHEDULE GENIUS! (SAKURAGI)
6/23 (WED.) POST-PRACTICE BELOW BASKET X300
6/24 (THUR.) MORNING 6:00 – X200
LUNCH BREAK X100
POST-PRACTICE X300
6/25 (FRI.) MORNING 6:00 - X200
LUNCH BREAK X100
POST-PRACTICE X300
6/26 (SAT.) TAKEZATO GAME
6/27 (SUN.) RYONAN GAME
I SPREAD MY RIGHT HAND LIKE THIS... AND...
WHAT ABOUT YOUR LEFT HAND?
200!!
GASP!
特別強化メニュー 天才! 桜木用
6/23(水) 練習後 ゴール下×300本
6/24(木) 朝6:00～ 〃×200本 昼休み 〃×100本 練習後 〃×300本
6/25(金) 朝6:00～ 〃×200本 昼休み 〃×100本 練習後 〃×300本
6/26(土) 武里戦
6/27(日) 陵南戦
HMM...? SO YOU STILL GOT SOME LEFT IN THE TANK!!
HOW MANY MORE SAKURAGI?

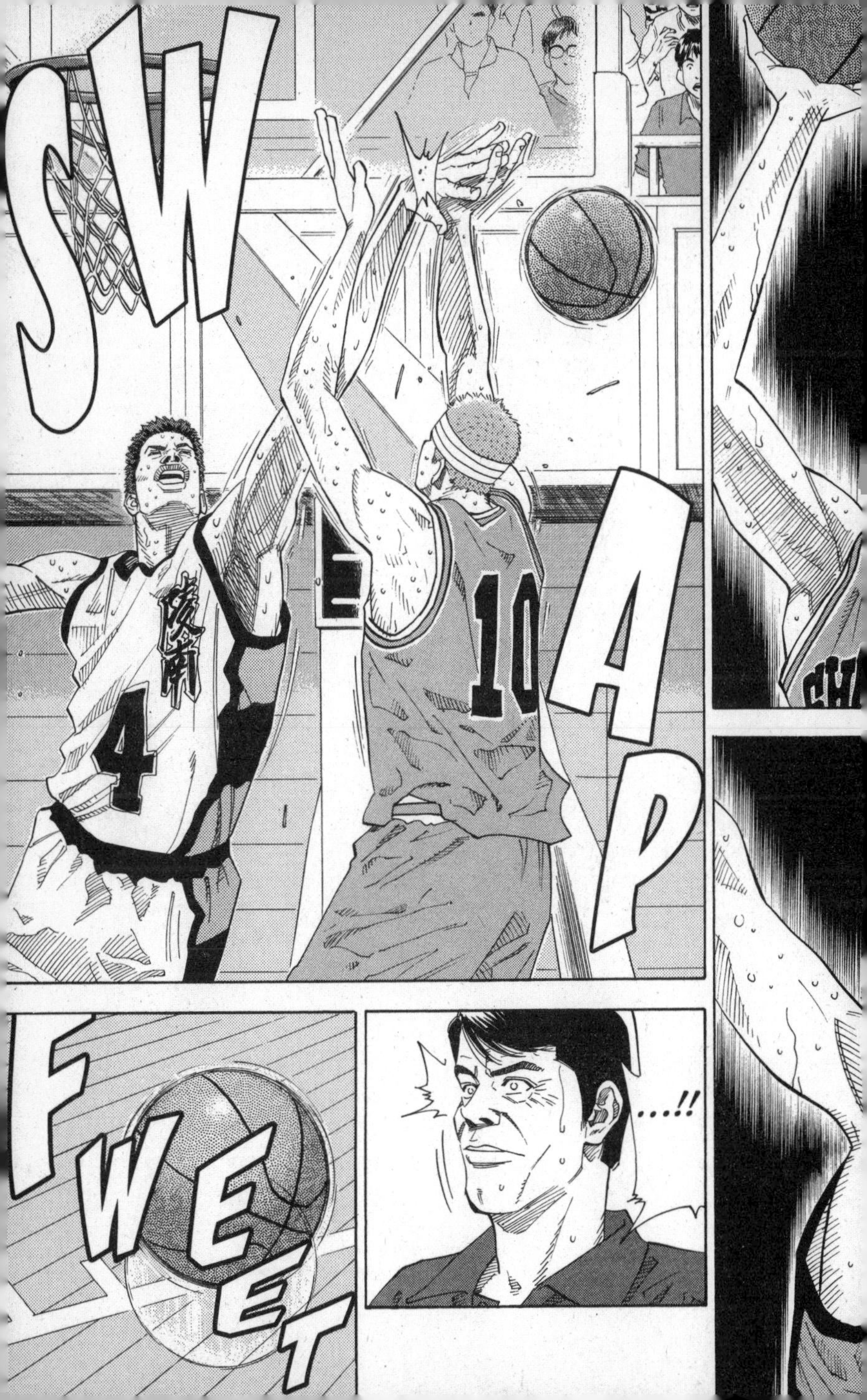
SWAP
...!!
FWEET

FINE PLAY

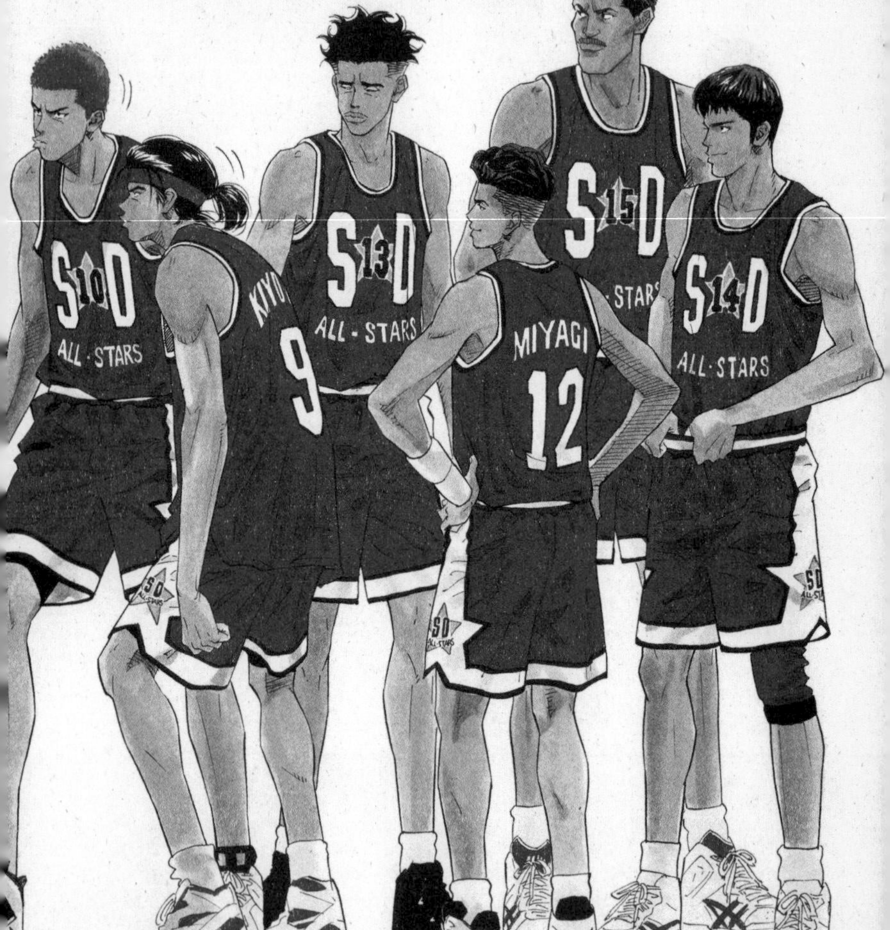
S 10 D
ALL · STARS
KIYO
9
S 13 D
ALL - STARS
MIYAGI
12
S 15 D
STARS
S 14 D
ALL · STARS

#167

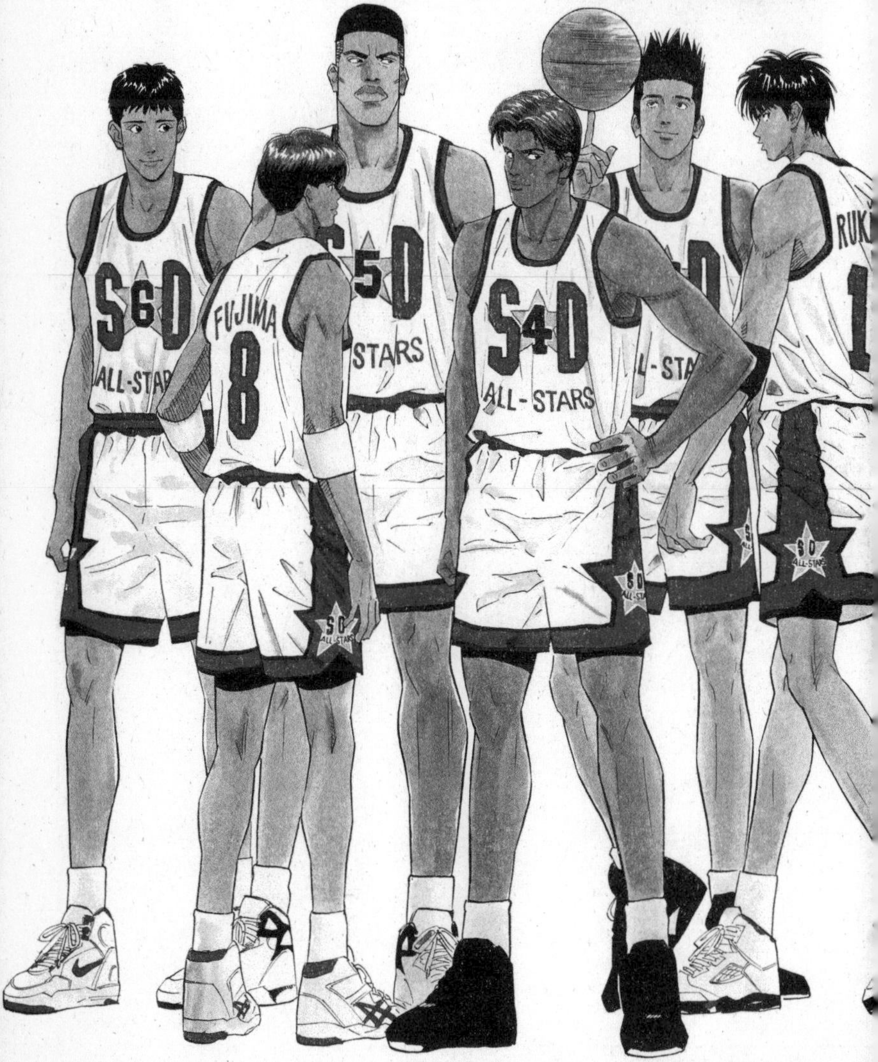
S 6 D ALL-STARS
FUJIMA 8
S 5 D STARS
S 4 D ALL-STARS
ALL-STA
RUK 1

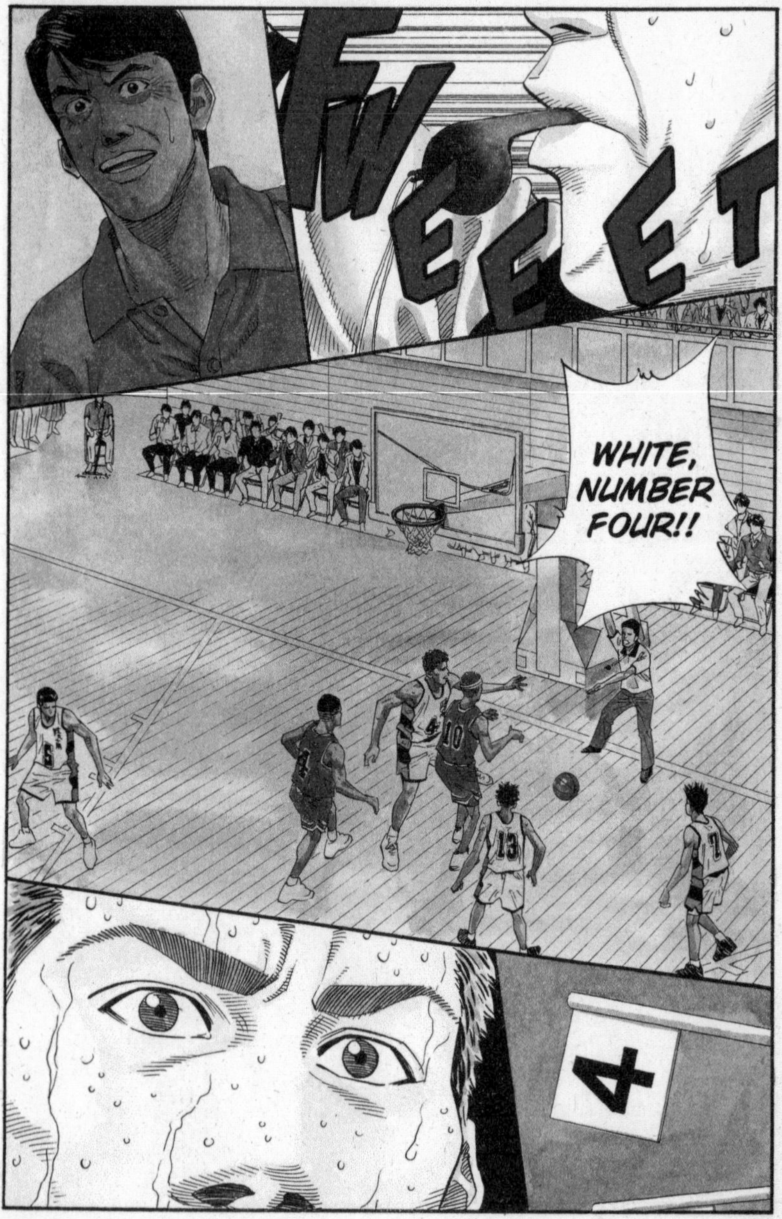
FWEEET
WHITE, NUMBER FOUR!!
4

READ THIS WAY

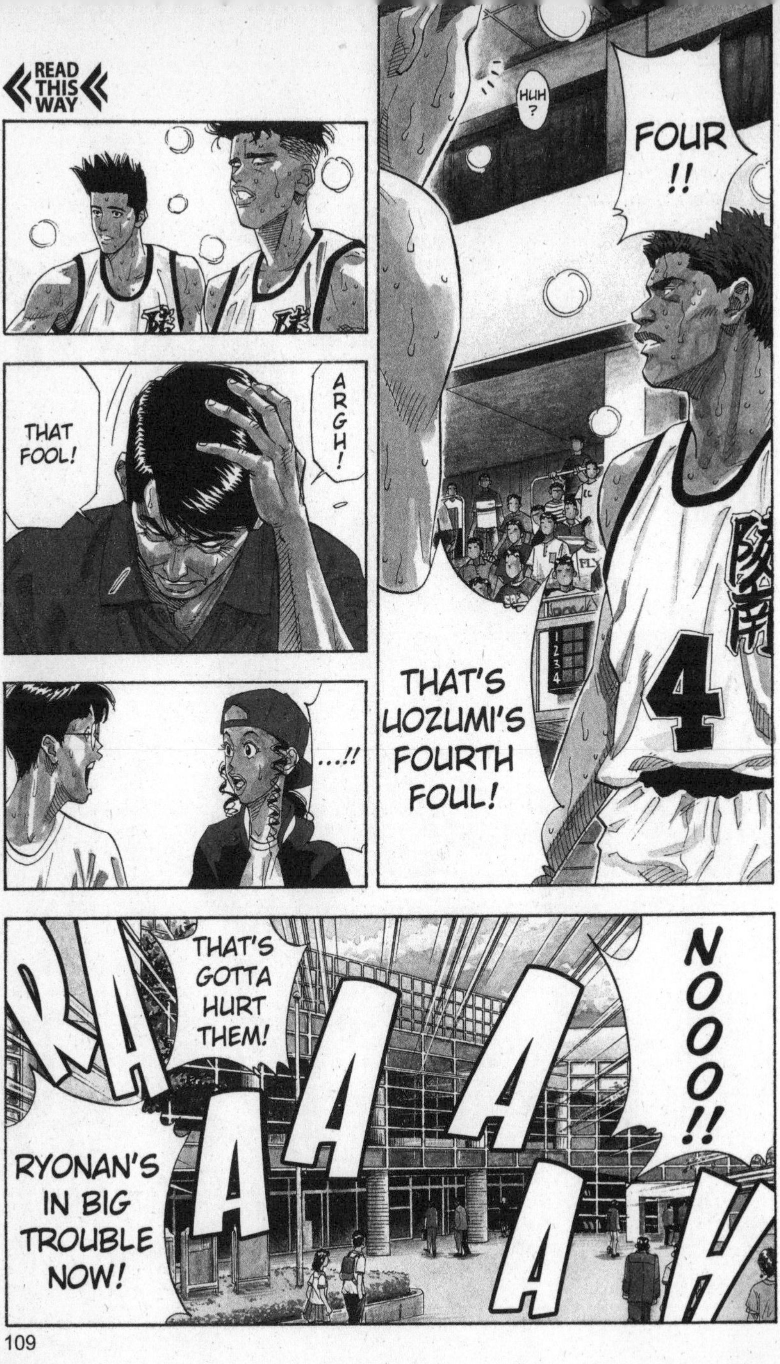
FOUR!!
HUH?
THAT'S UOZUMI'S FOURTH FOUL!
ARGH!
THAT FOOL!
...!!
NOOOO!!
RAAAAAAAH
THAT'S GOTTA HURT THEM!
RYONAN'S IN BIG TROUBLE NOW!

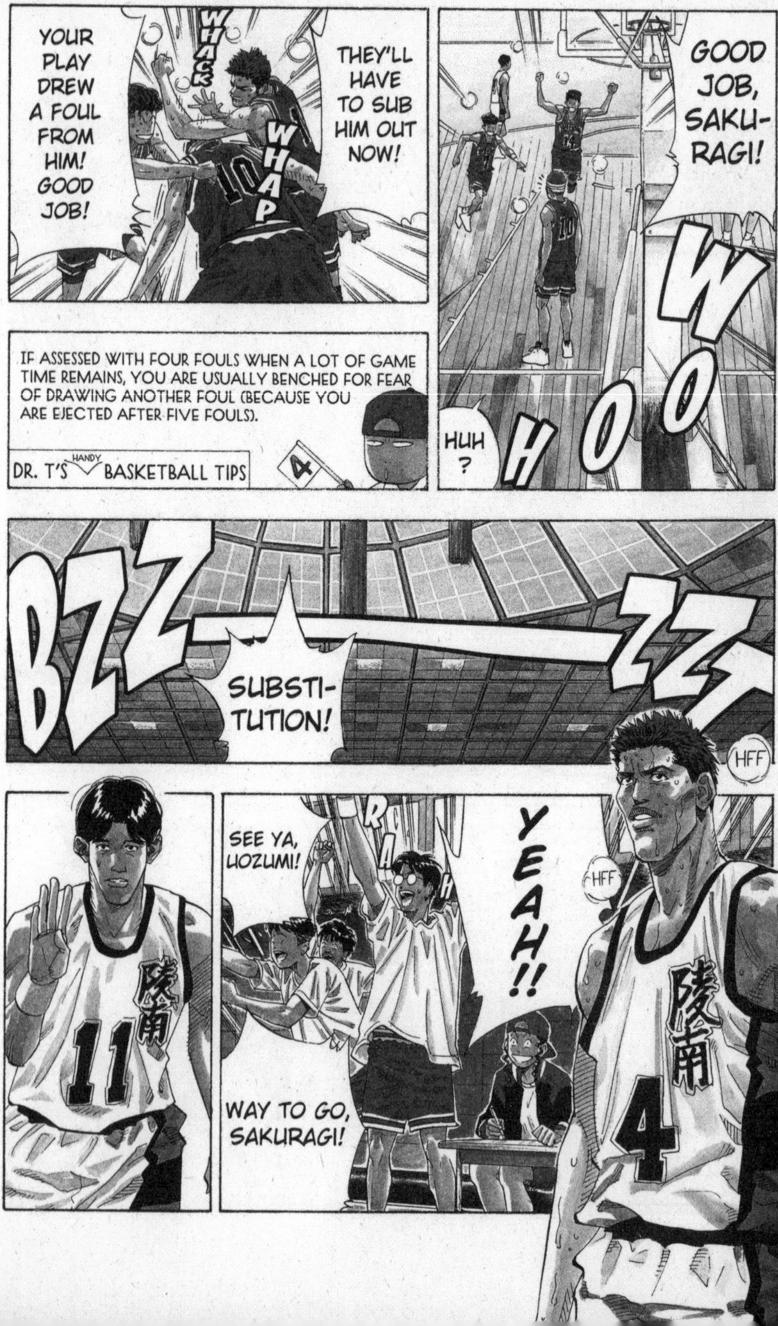
GOOD JOB, SAKURAGI!
WHOOO
HUH?
THEY'LL HAVE TO SUB HIM OUT NOW!
WHACK
WHAP
YOUR PLAY DREW A FOUL FROM HIM! GOOD JOB!
IF ASSESSED WITH FOUR FOULS WHEN A LOT OF GAME TIME REMAINS, YOU ARE USUALLY BENCHED FOR FEAR OF DRAWING ANOTHER FOUL (BECAUSE YOU ARE EJECTED AFTER FIVE FOULS).
DR. T'S HANDY BASKETBALL TIPS
4
BZZ—ZZT
SUBSTITUTION!
HFF
HFF
YEAH!!
RAH
SEE YA, UOZUMI!
WAY TO GO, SAKURAGI!

READ THIS WAY

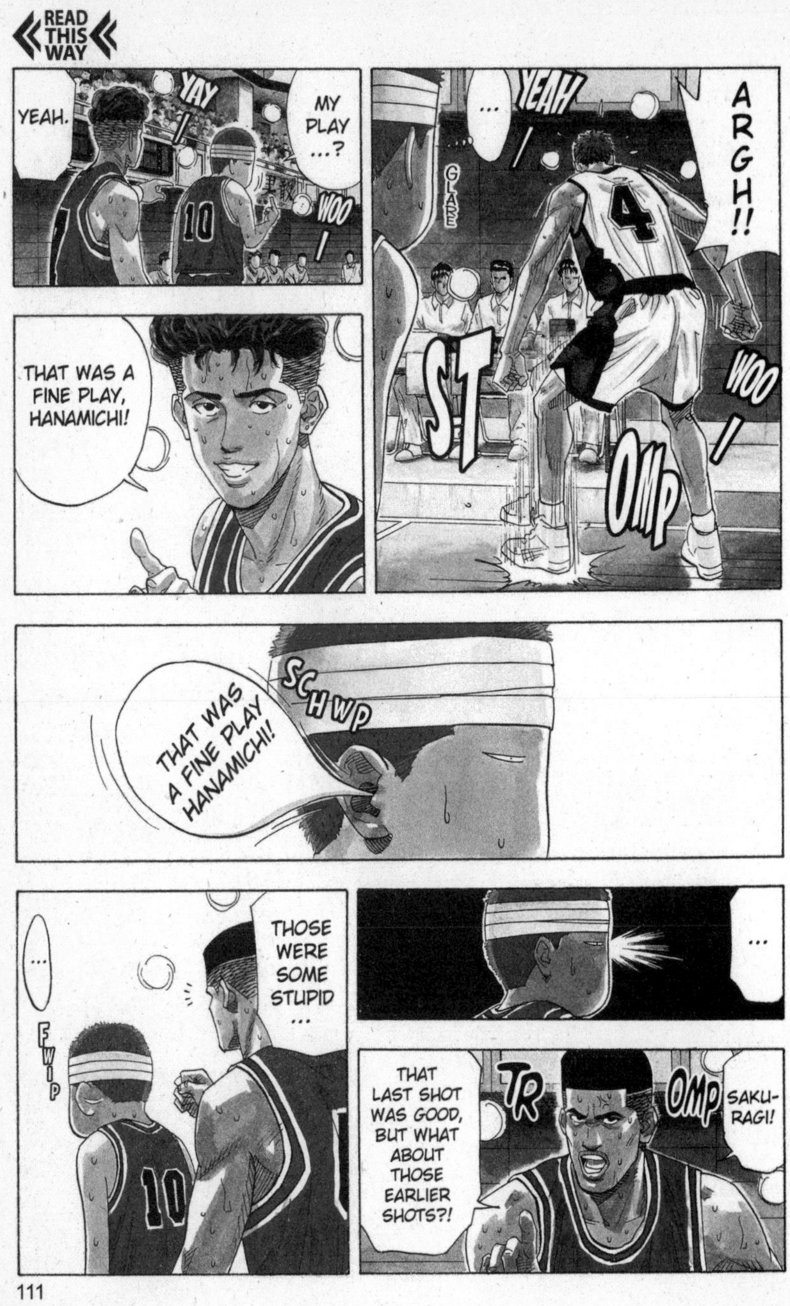
...
YEAH
ARGH!!
GLARE
ST
OMP
WOO
MY PLAY ...?
YAY
WOO
YEAH.
THAT WAS A FINE PLAY, HANAMICHI!
SCHWP
THAT WAS A FINE PLAY HANAMICHI!
...
SAKU-RAGI!
OMP
TR
THAT LAST SHOT WAS GOOD, BUT WHAT ABOUT THOSE EARLIER SHOTS?!
THOSE WERE SOME STUPID ...
...
FWIP

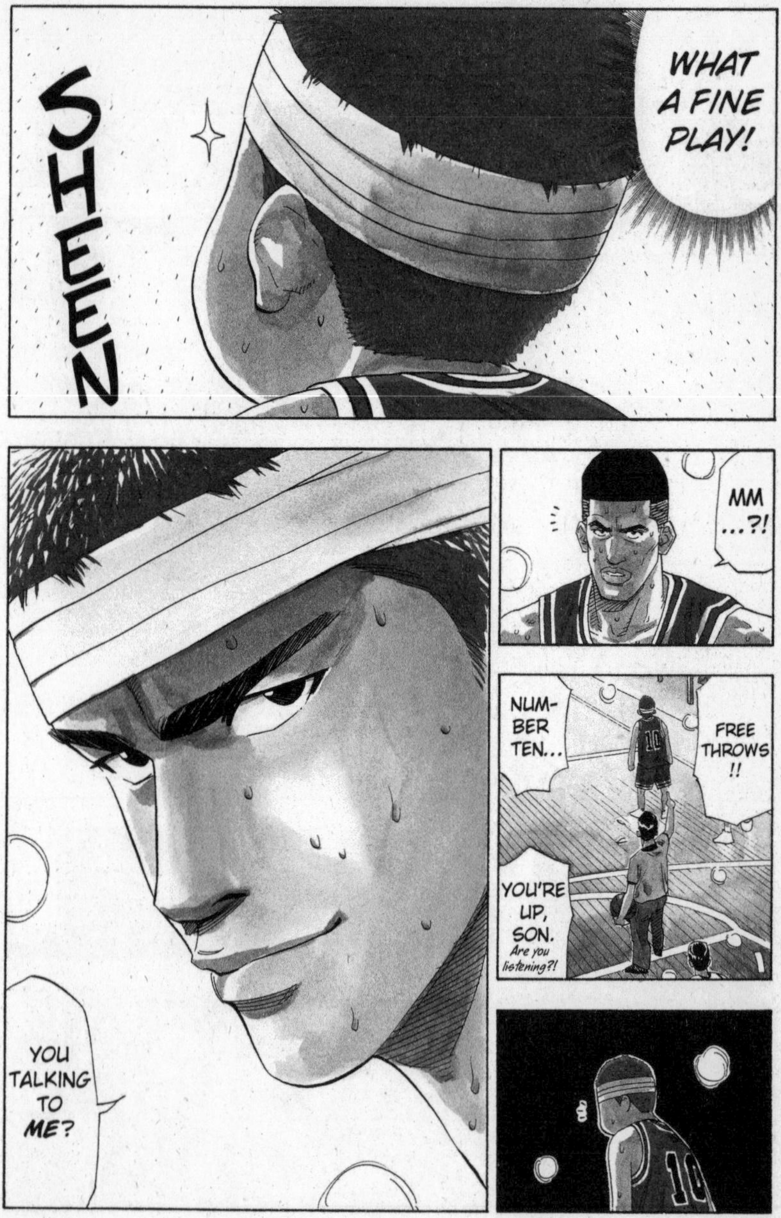
WHAT A FINE PLAY!
SHEEN
MM ...?!
FREE THROWS !!
NUM-BER TEN...
YOU'RE UP, SON.
Are you listening?!
YOU TALKING TO ME?

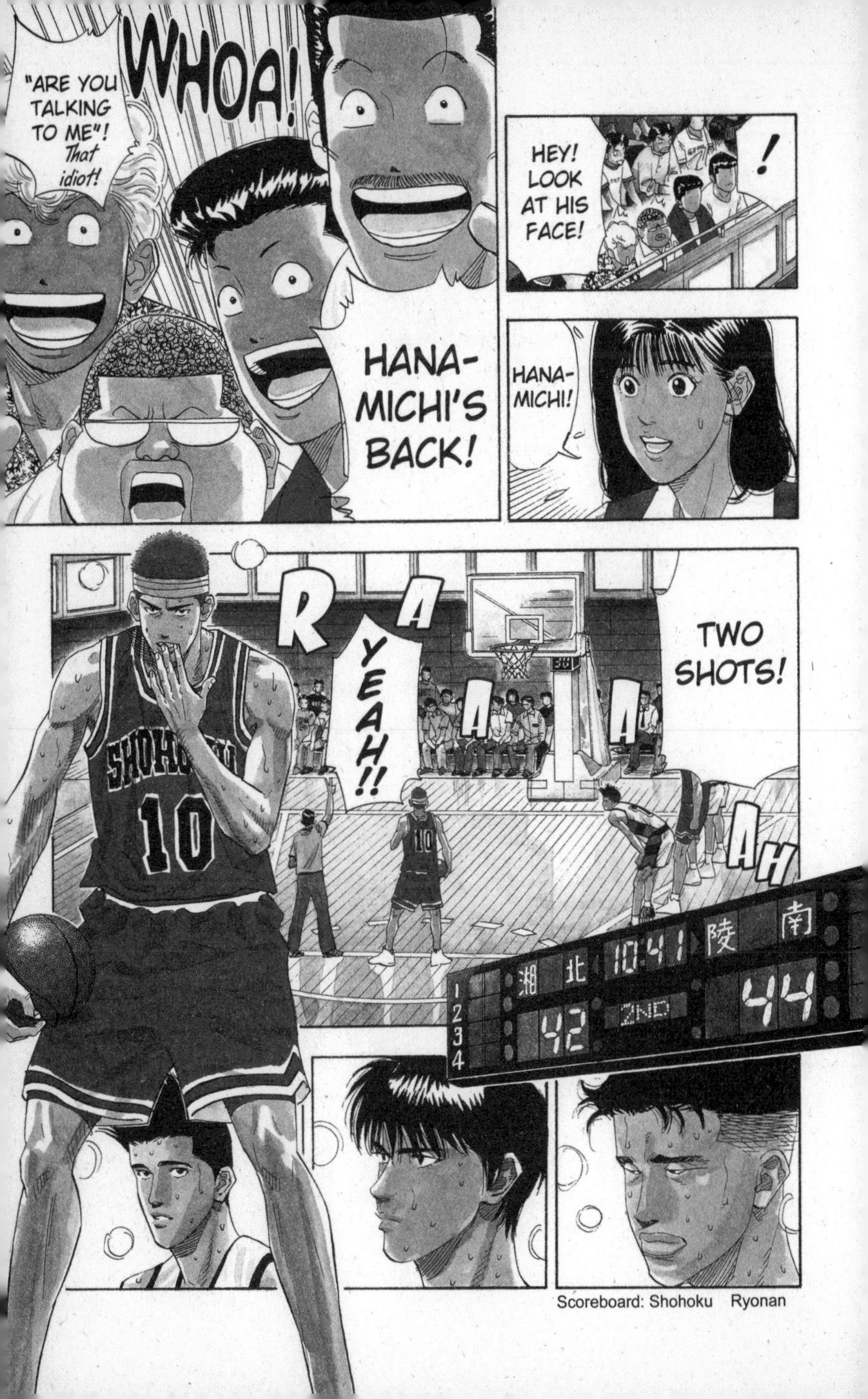

!
HEY! LOOK AT HIS FACE!
HANA-MICHI!
WHOA!
"ARE YOU TALKING TO ME"! That idiot!
HANA-MICHI'S BACK!
TWO SHOTS!
RAAAA
YEAH!!
AH
南 陵
10:41
湘 北
42
2ND
44
1 2 3 4

Scoreboard: Shohoku Ryonan

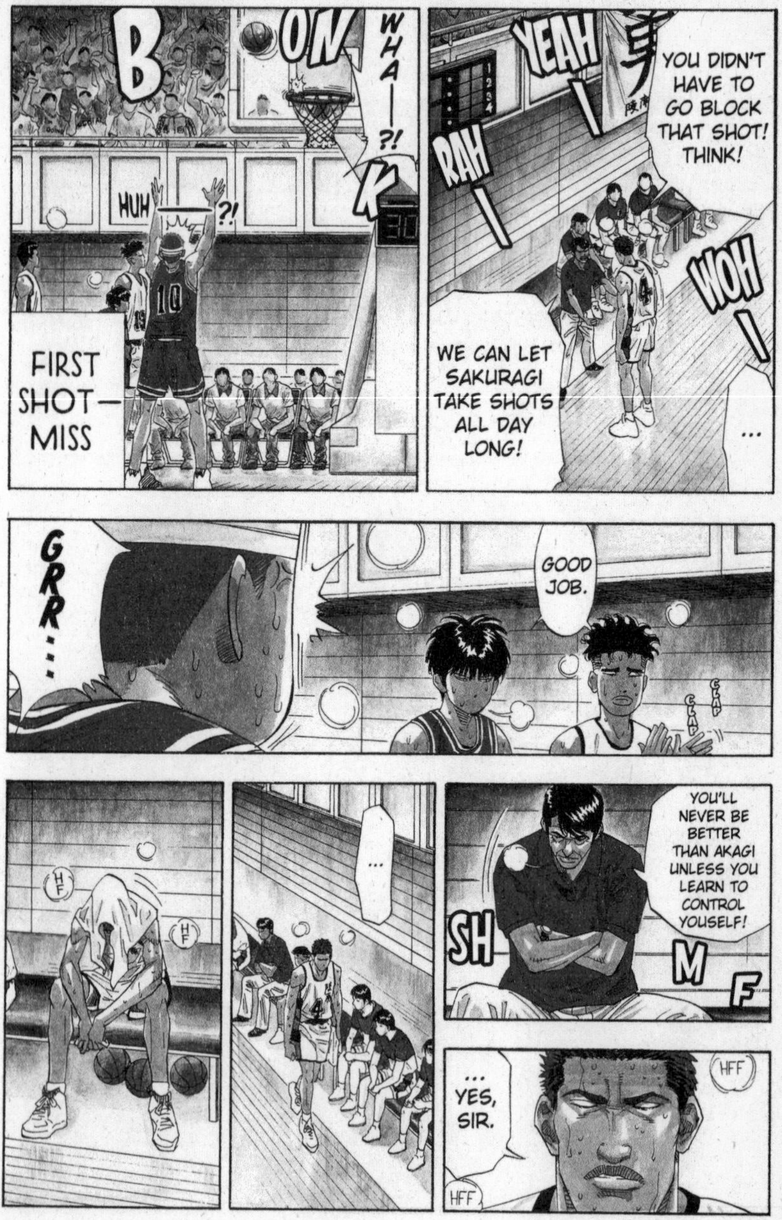
YEAH
YOU DIDN'T HAVE TO GO BLOCK THAT SHOT! THINK!
RAH
WOH
WE CAN LET SAKURAGI TAKE SHOTS ALL DAY LONG!
...
BONK
WHA—?!
HUH
?!
FIRST SHOT—MISS
GOOD JOB.
CLAP CLAP
GRR...
YOU'LL NEVER BE BETTER THAN AKAGI UNLESS YOU LEARN TO CONTROL YOUSELF!
SHMF
HFF
... YES, SIR.
HFF
...
HF
HF

READ THIS WAY

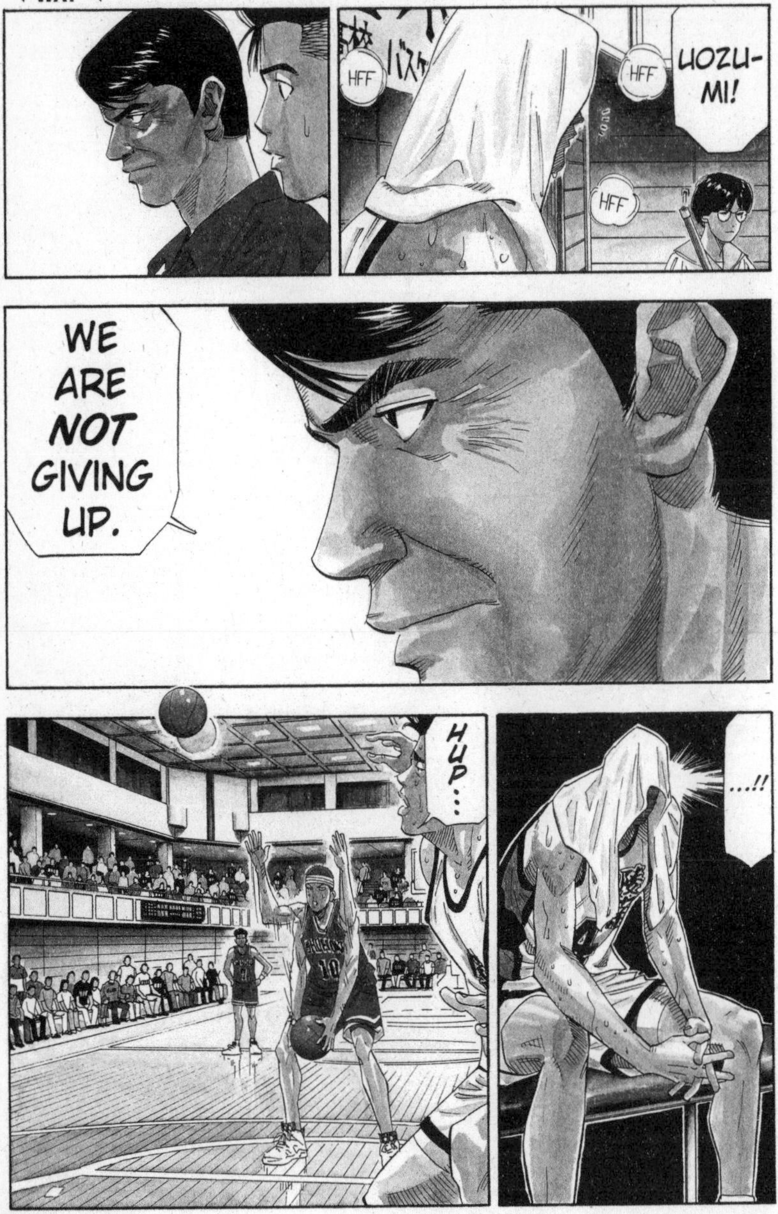
UOZU-MI!
HFF
HFF
HFF
WE ARE *NOT* GIVING UP.
...!!
HUP...

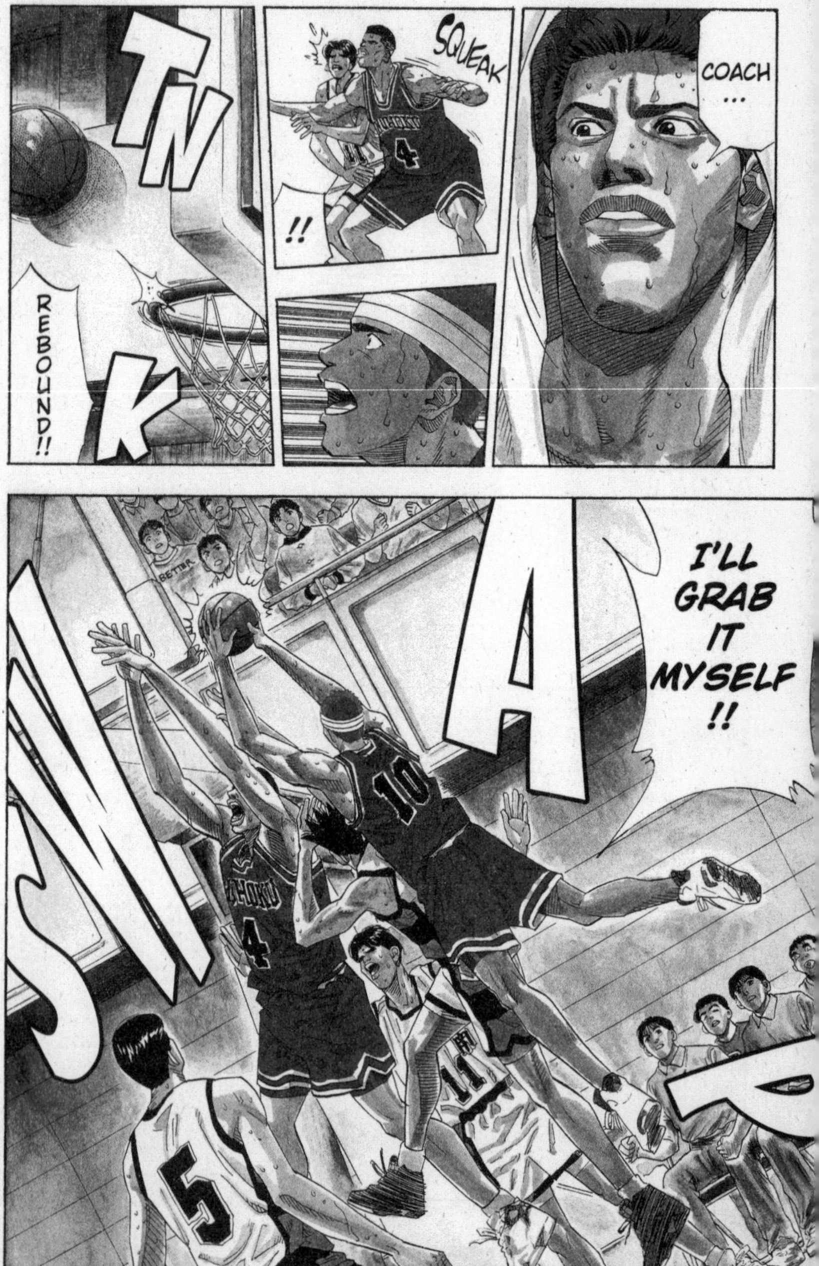
COACH ...
SQUEAK
!!
TNK
REBOUND!!
I'LL GRAB IT MYSELF !!

READ THIS WAY

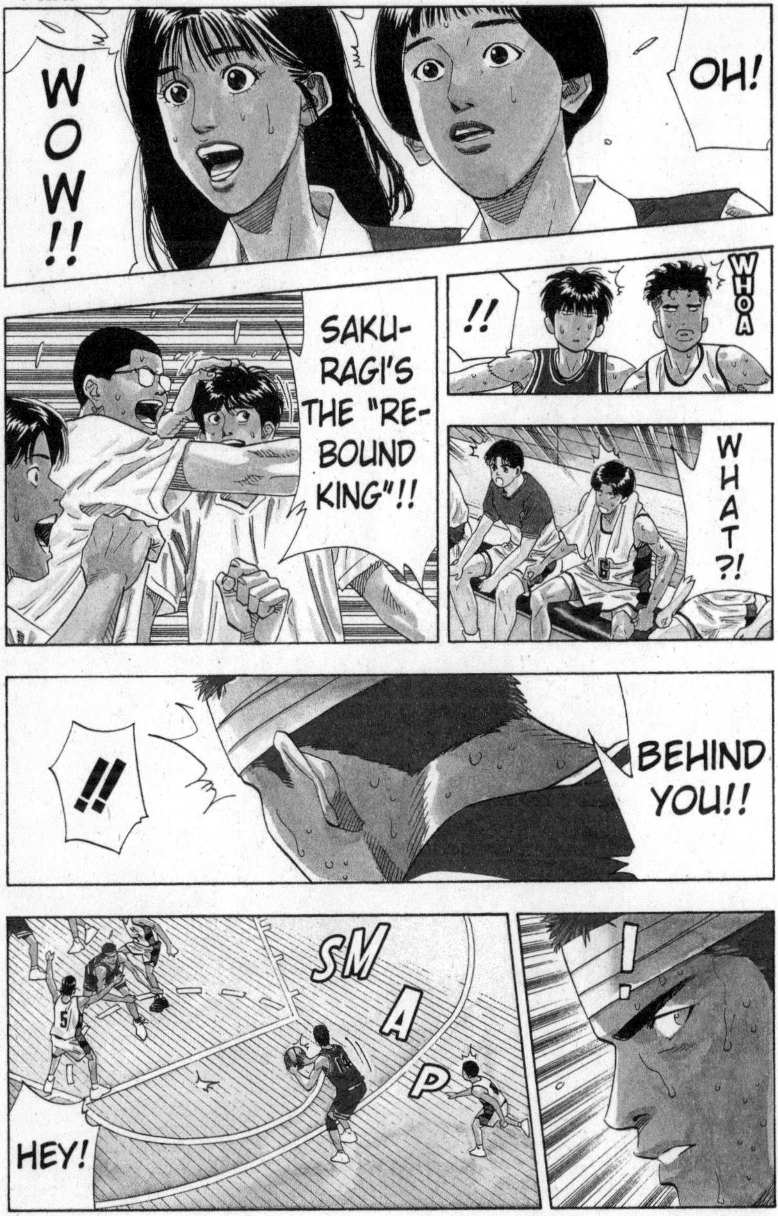

OH!
WOW!!
WHOA
!!
WHAT?!
SAKURAGI'S THE "REBOUND KING"!!
BEHIND YOU!!
!!
!
SMAP
HEY!

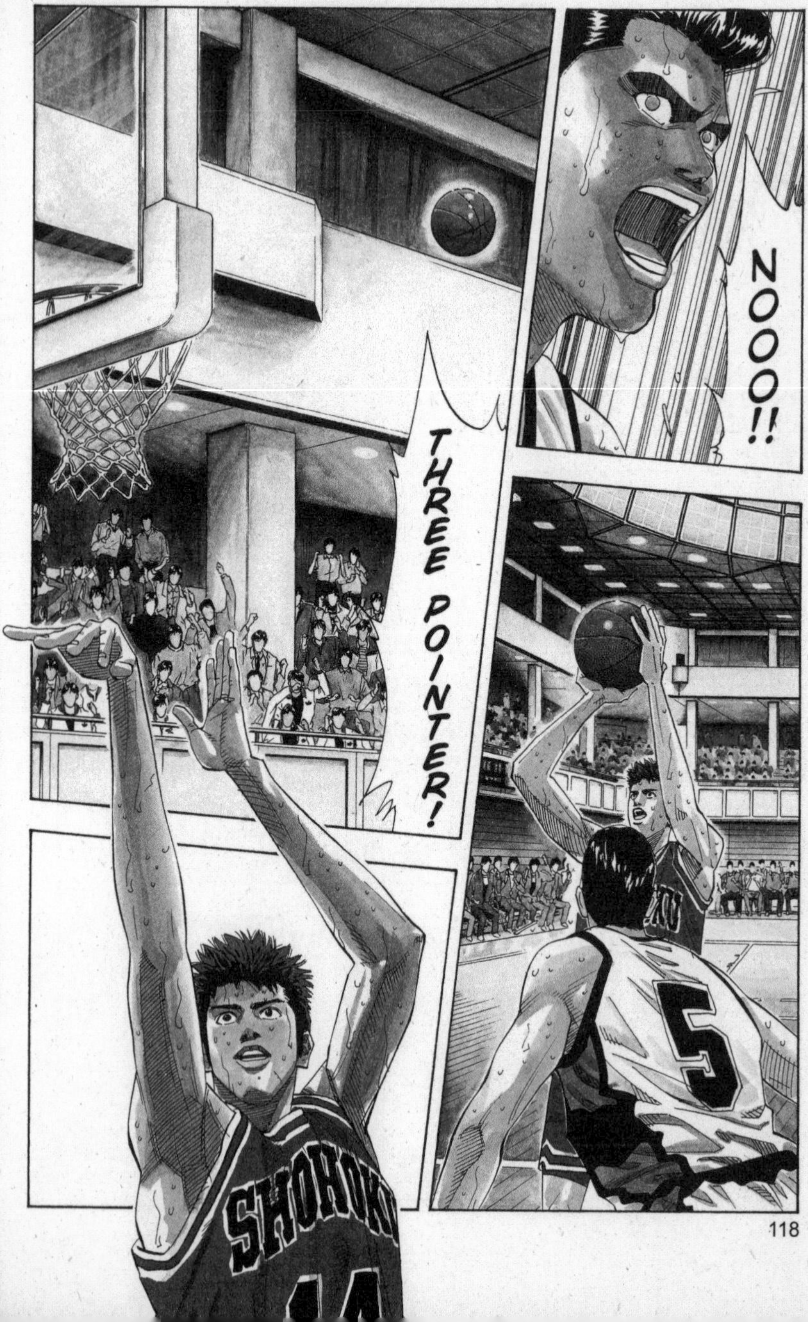
NOOOO!!
THREE POINTER!

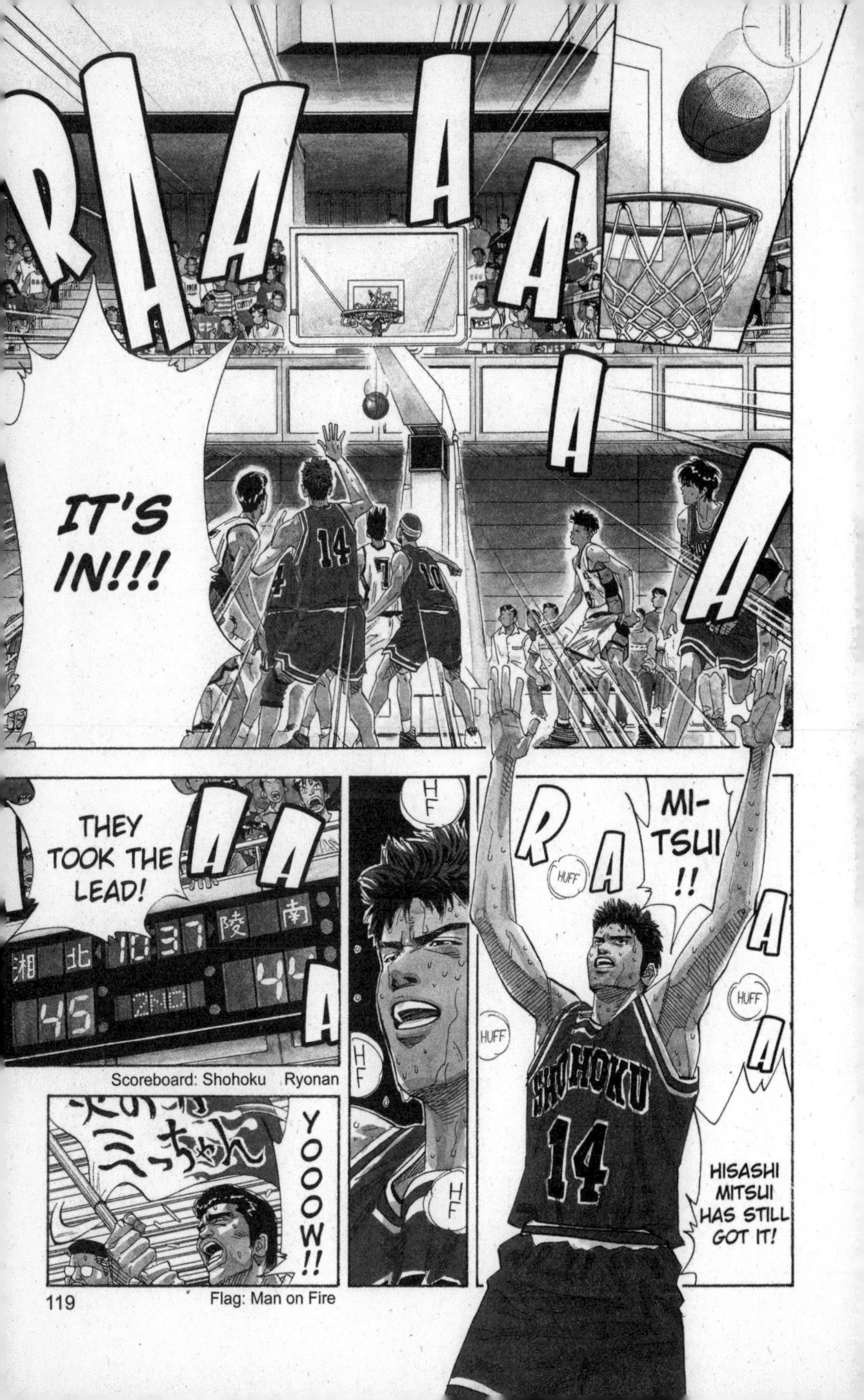
RAAAAAAAAA
IT'S IN!!!
MI-TSUI!!
RAAAA
HUFF
HUFF
HUFF
HISASHI MITSUI HAS STILL GOT IT!
HF
HF
HF
THEY TOOK THE LEAD!
AAA
YOOOOW!!

Scoreboard: Shohoku Ryonan

Flag: Man on Fire

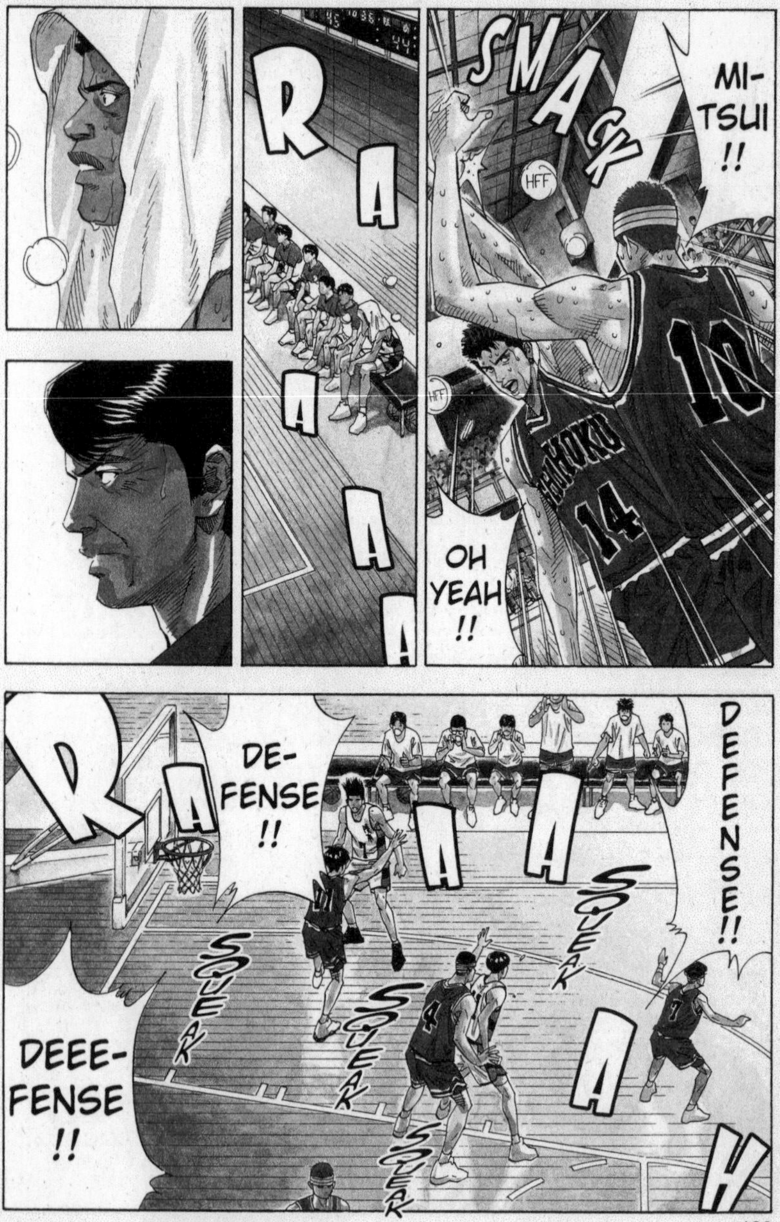
SMACK
MI-
TSUI
!!
HFF
HFF
OH
YEAH
!!
RAAAA
DEFENSE!!
SQUEAK
DE-
FENSE
!!
RAAAAH
SQUEAK
SQUEAK
SQUEAK
DEEE-
FENSE
!!

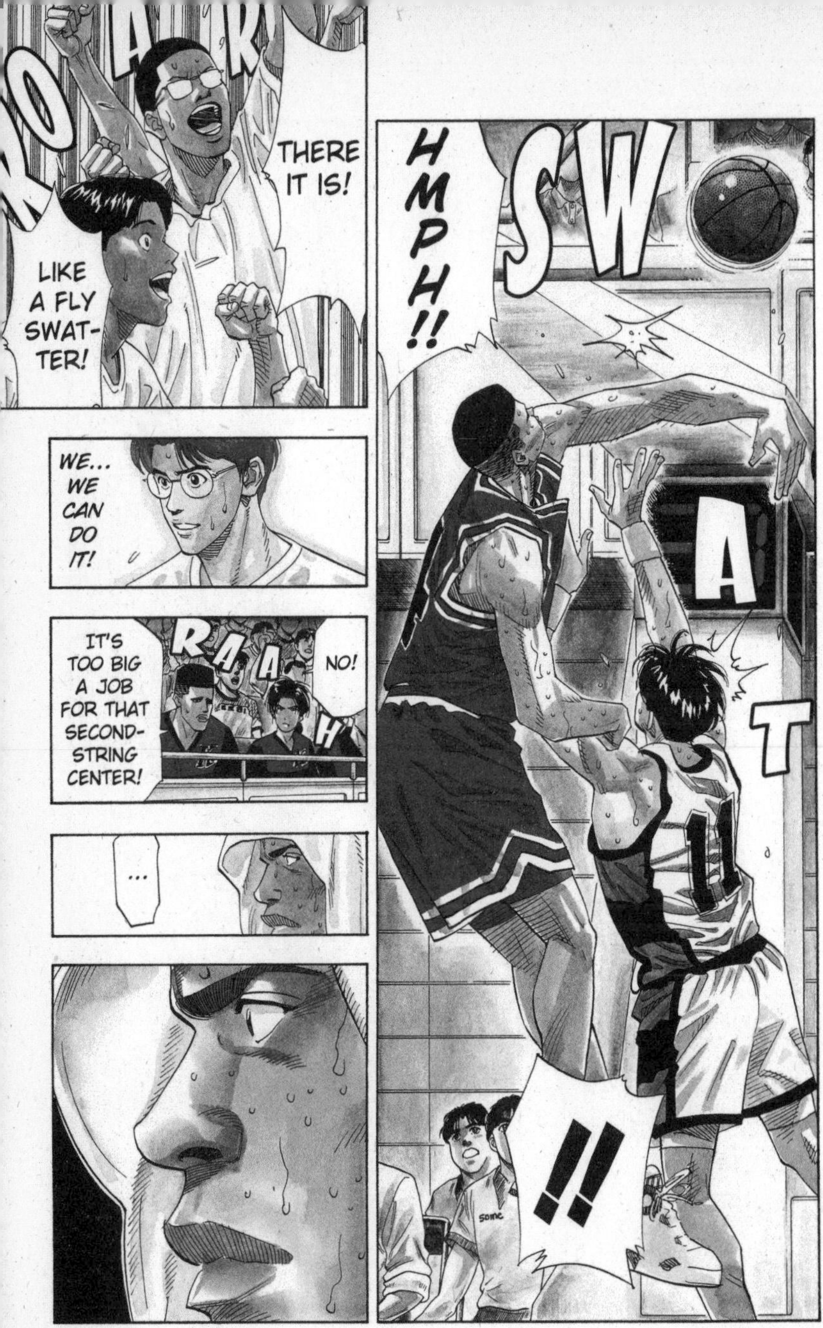

HMPH!!
SWAT
!!
THERE IT IS!
LIKE A FLY SWATTER!
WE... WE CAN DO IT!
NO!
RAAAH
IT'S TOO BIG A JOB FOR THAT SECOND-STRING CENTER!
...

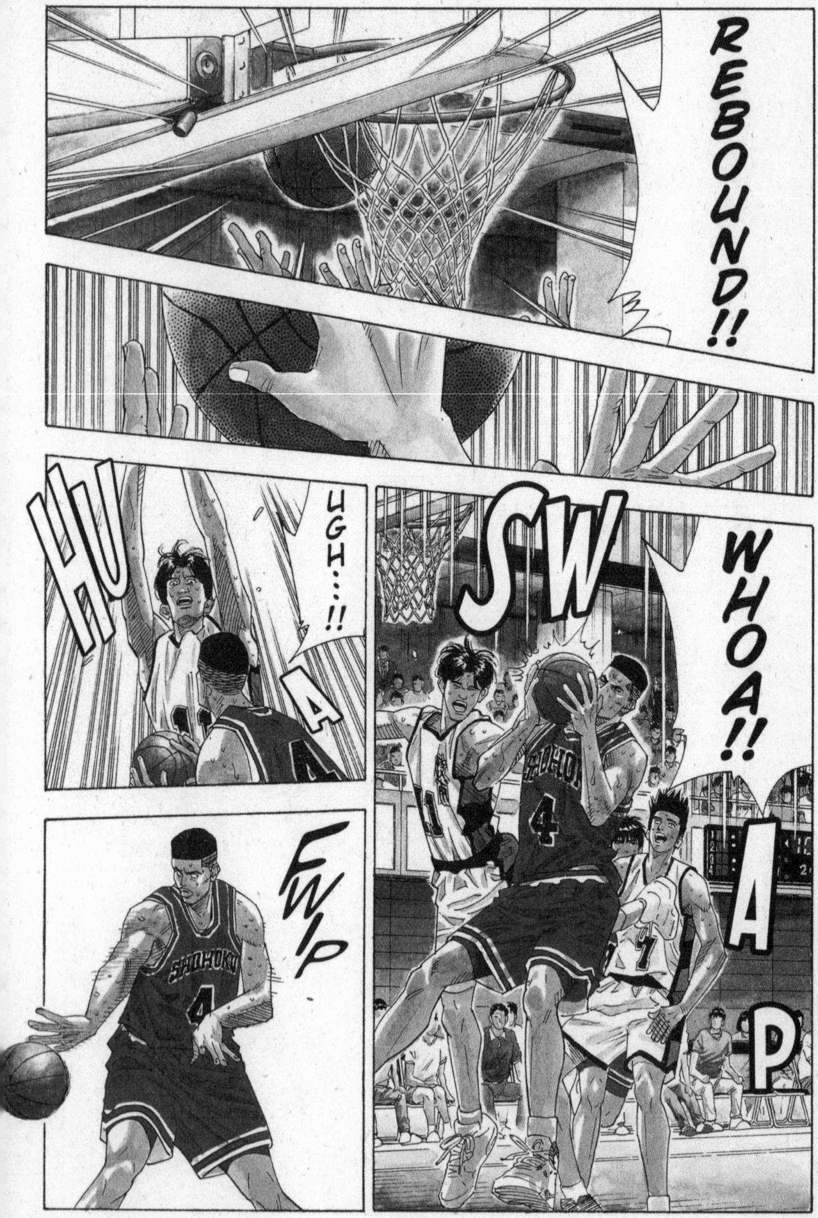
REBOUND!!
WHOA!!
SW
A
P
HU
UGH...!!
A
FWIP

READ THIS WAY

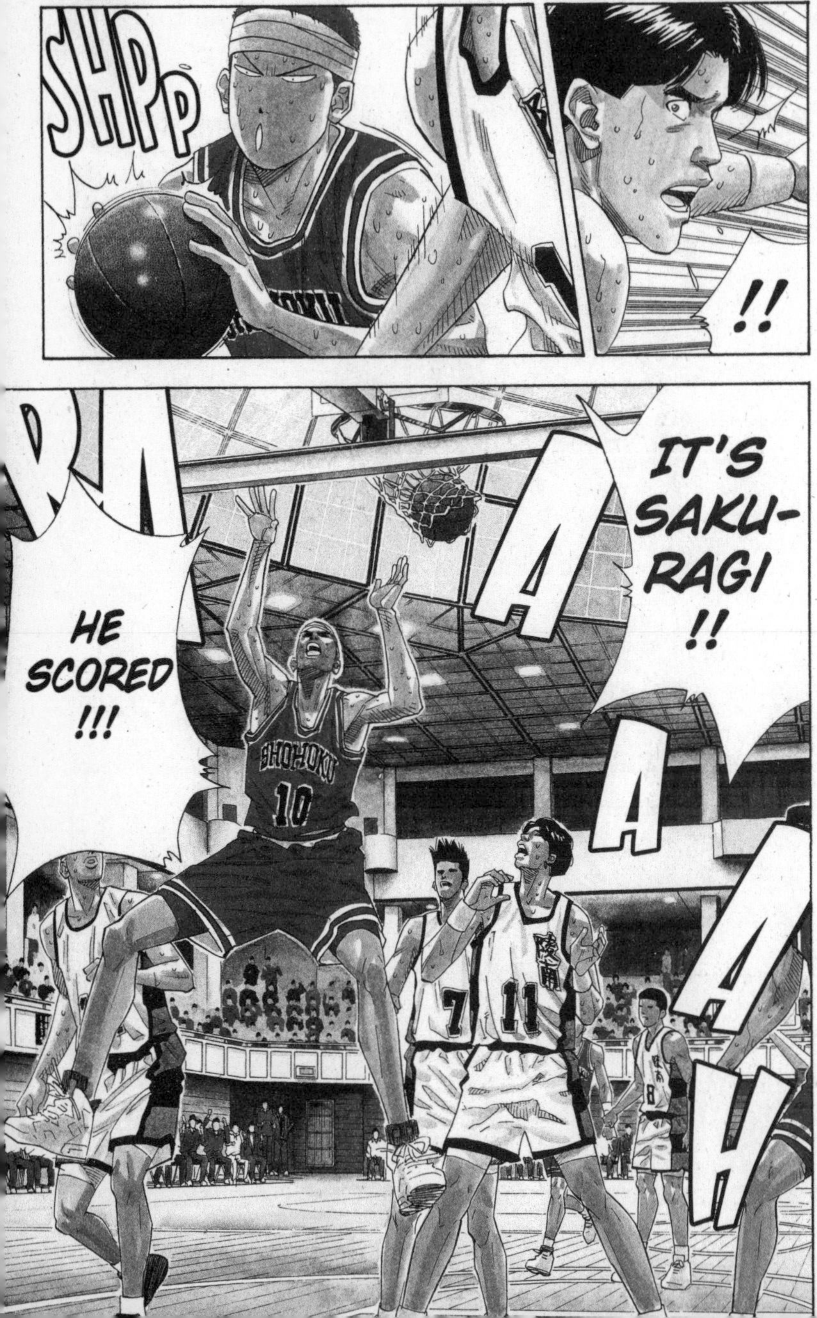
!!
SHPP
IT'S SAKU-RAGI!!
HE SCORED!!!

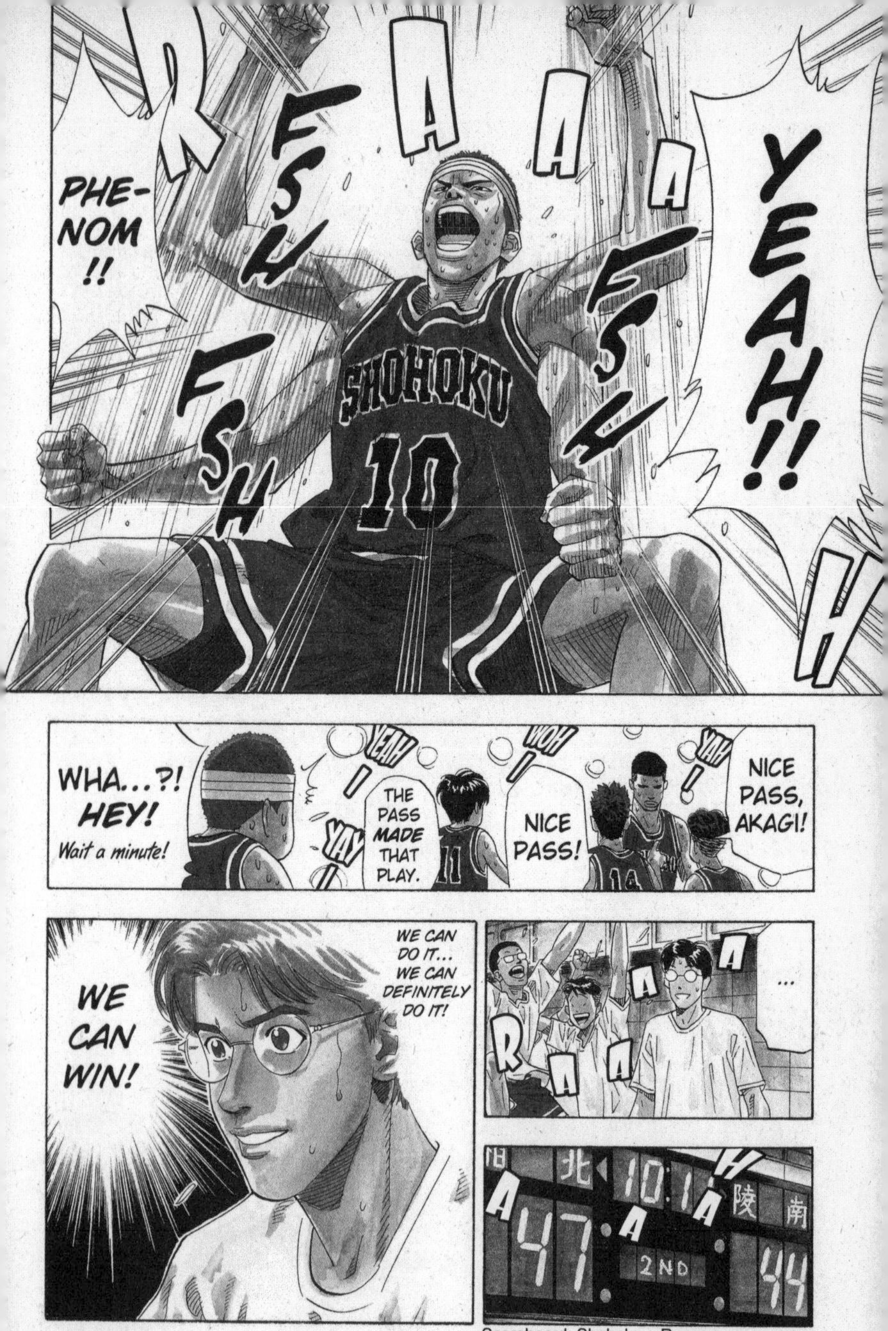
YEAH!!
H
A
A
A
A
FSH
FSH
FSH
FSH
PHE-NOM!!
NICE PASS, AKAGI!
YAH!
NICE PASS!
WOH!
THE PASS MADE THAT PLAY.
YEAH!
YAY
WHA...?! HEY! Wait a minute!
...
RAAAA
47
2ND
44
AAAAH
WE CAN DO IT... WE CAN DEFINITELY DO IT!
WE CAN WIN!
Scoreboard: Shohoku Ryonan

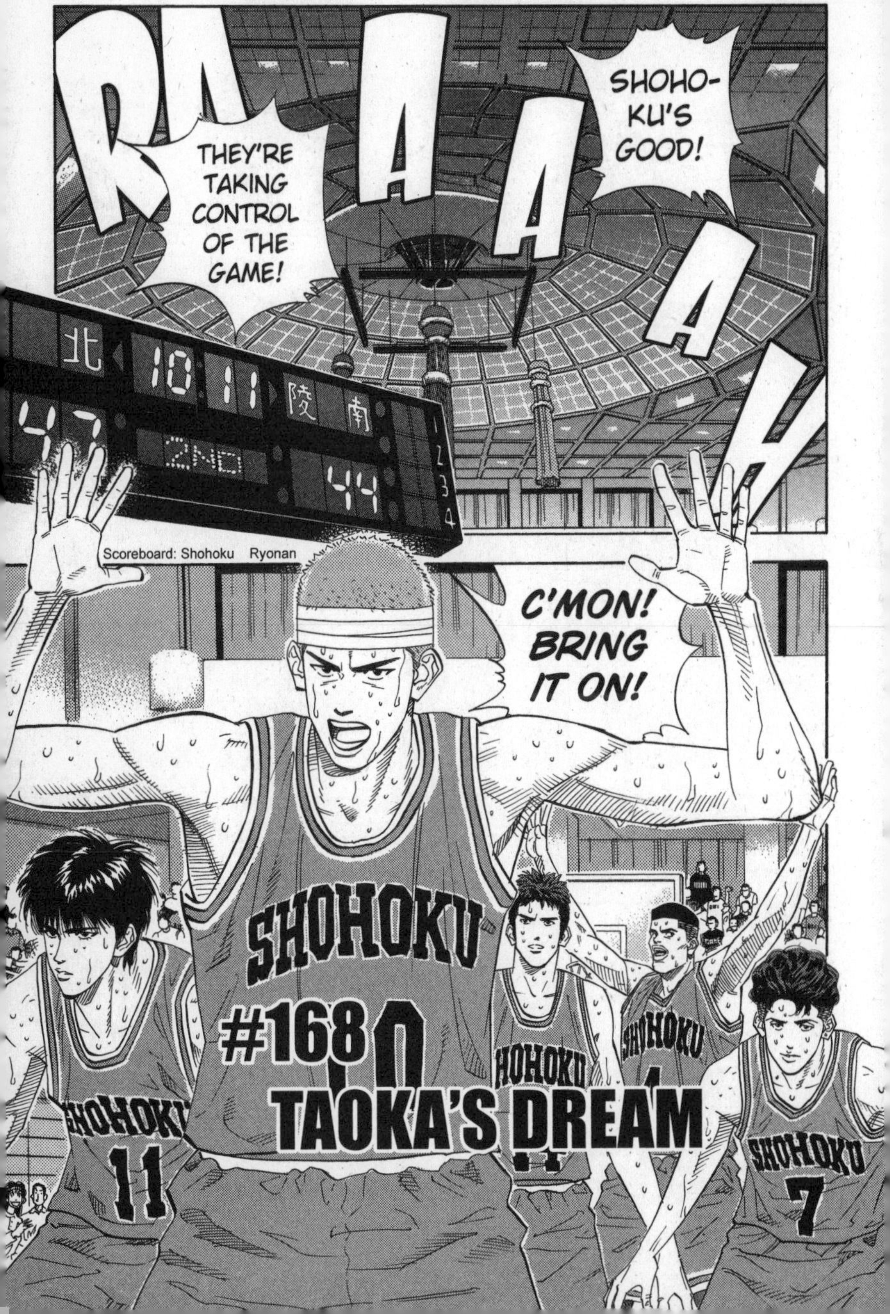
RAAAAH
SHOHO-KU'S GOOD!
THEY'RE TAKING CONTROL OF THE GAME!
北 10:11 陵南
47 2ND 44
1 2 3 4
Scoreboard: Shohoku Ryonan
C'MON! BRING IT ON!
SHOHOKU
11
7

#168 TAOKA'S DREAM

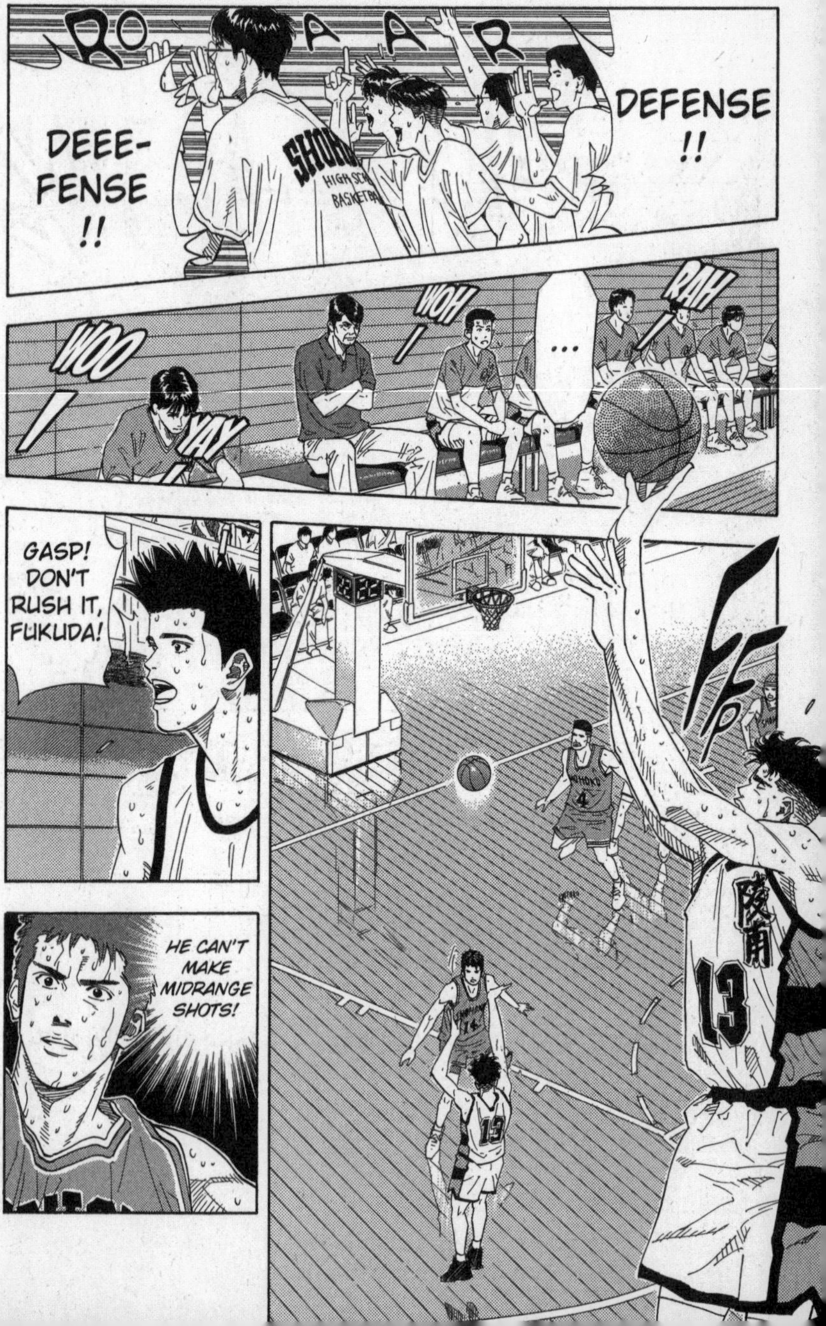
ROAAR
DEFENSE !!
DEEE-FENSE !!
RAH
WOH
...
WOO
YAY
FFP
GASP! DON'T RUSH IT, FUKUDA!
HE CAN'T MAKE MIDRANGE SHOTS!

READ THIS WAY

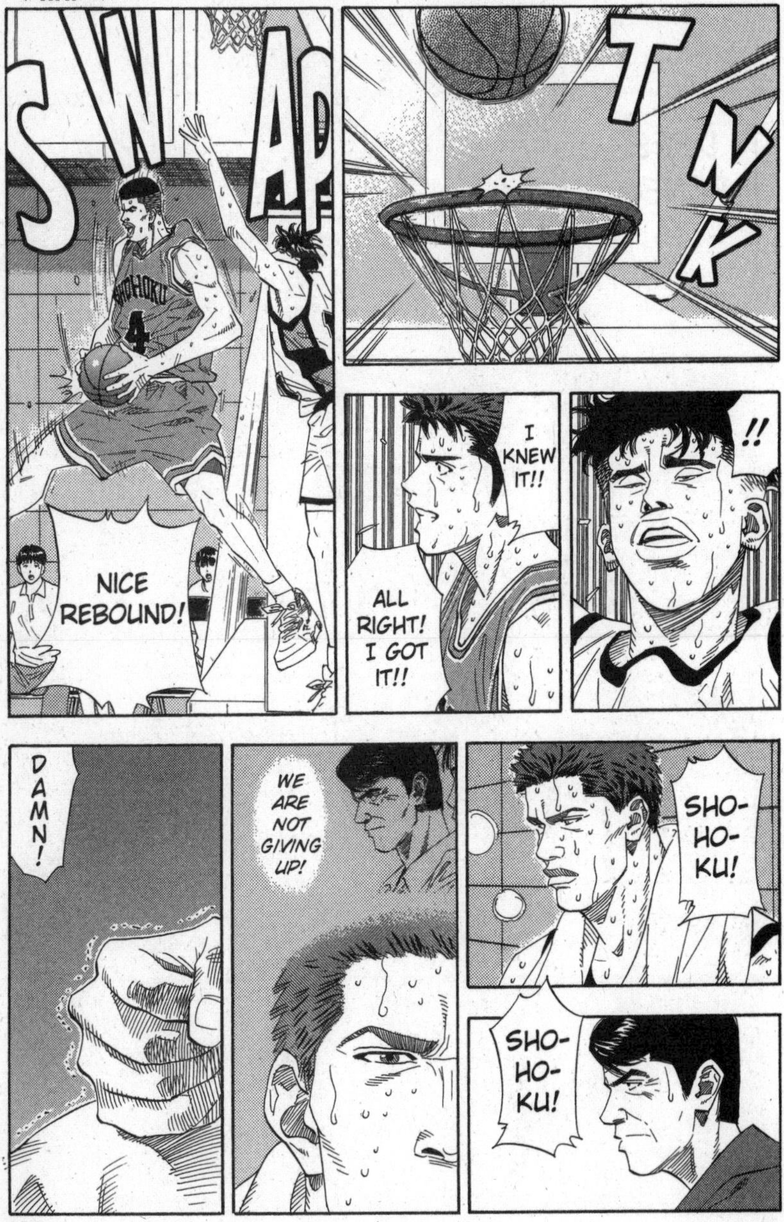
TNK
!!
I KNEW IT!!
ALL RIGHT! I GOT IT!!
SWAP
NICE REBOUND!
SHO-HO-KU!
SHO-HO-KU!
WE ARE NOT GIVING UP!
DAMN!

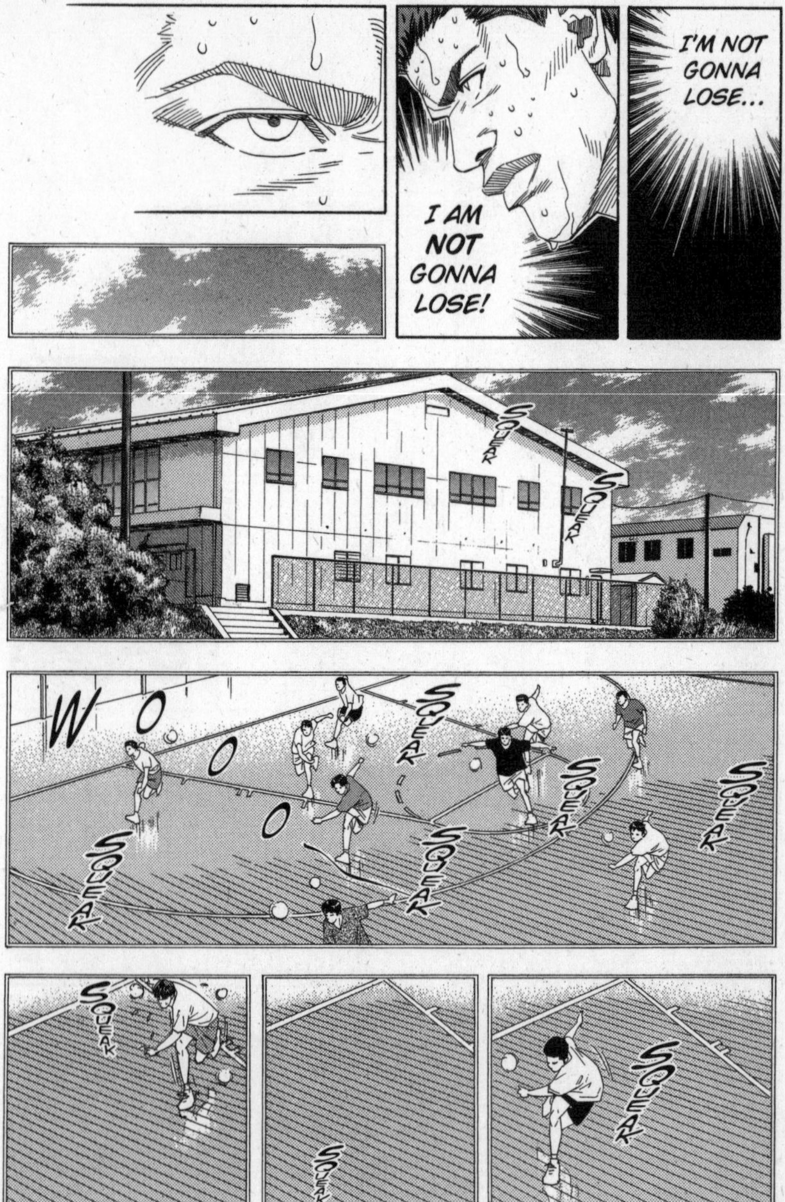
I'M NOT GONNA LOSE...
I AM NOT GONNA LOSE!
SQUEAK
SQUEAK
WOOO
SQUEAK
SQUEAK
SQUEAK
SQUEAK
SQUEAK
SQUEAK
SQUEAK
SQUEAK

READ THIS WAY

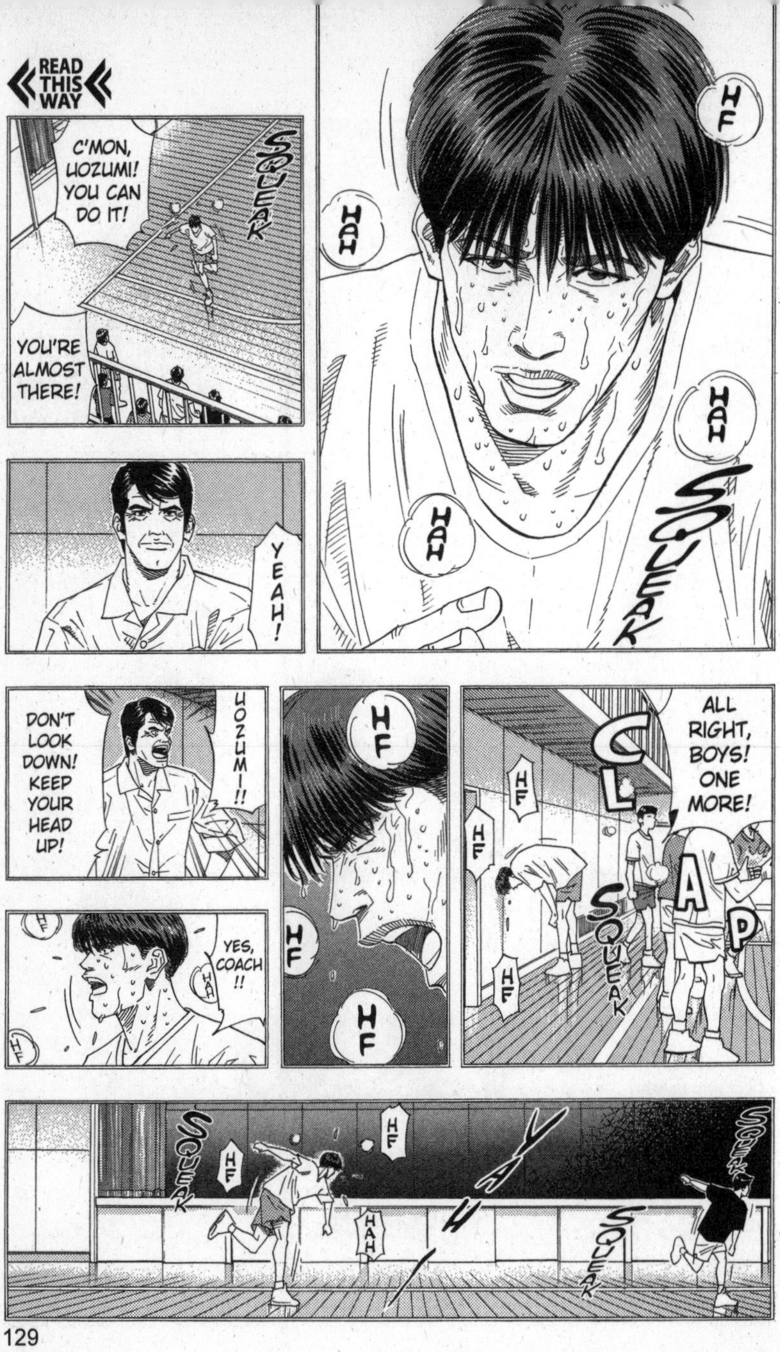
HF
HAH
HAH
SQUEAK
HAH
SQUEAK
C'MON, UOZUMI! YOU CAN DO IT!
YOU'RE ALMOST THERE!
YEAH!
ALL RIGHT, BOYS! ONE MORE!
CLAP
HF
HF
SQUEAK
HF
HF
HF
HF
HF
UOZUMI!!
DON'T LOOK DOWN! KEEP YOUR HEAD UP!
YES, COACH!!
HF
HAH
HF
SQUEAK
SQUEAK
YAH!
HF
HF
HAH
SQUEAK

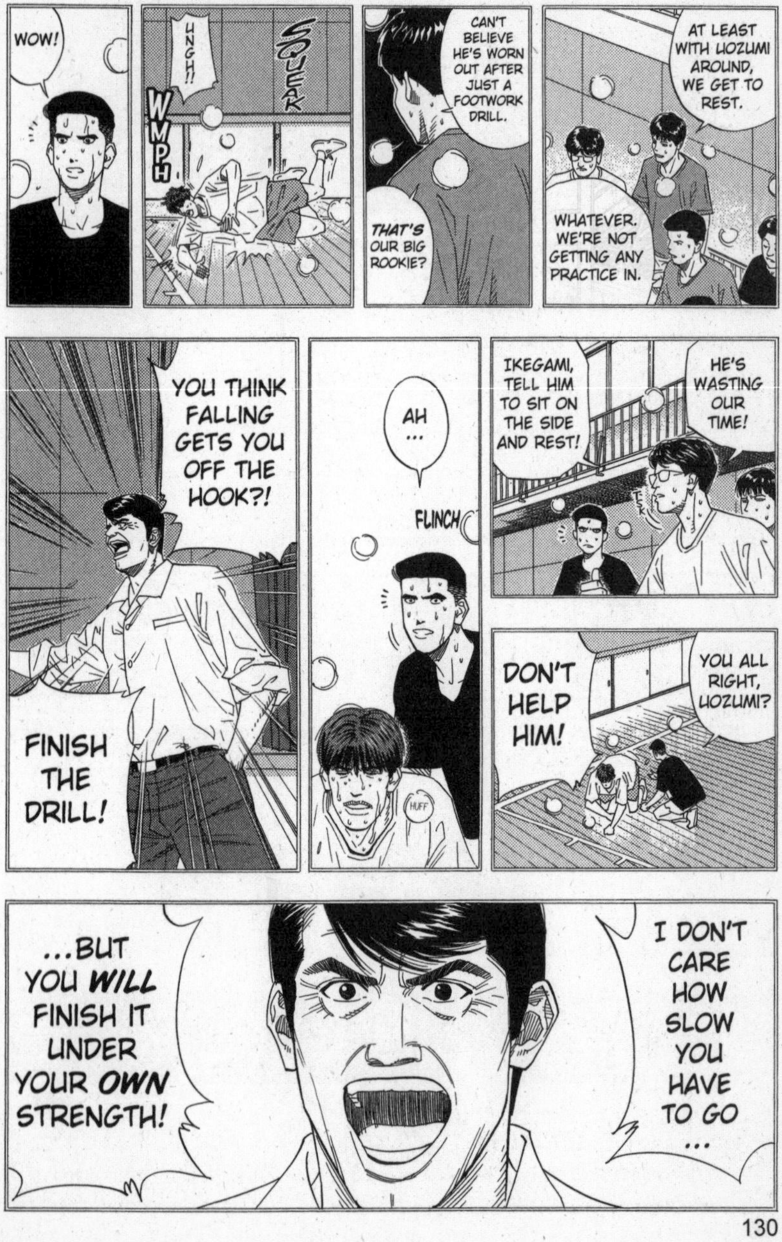
AT LEAST WITH UOZUMI AROUND, WE GET TO REST.
WHATEVER. WE'RE NOT GETTING ANY PRACTICE IN.
CAN'T BELIEVE HE'S WORN OUT AFTER JUST A FOOTWORK DRILL.
THAT'S OUR BIG ROOKIE?
SQUEAK
UNGH!!
WMPH
WOW!
HE'S WASTING OUR TIME!
IKEGAMI, TELL HIM TO SIT ON THE SIDE AND REST!
TSK
YOU ALL RIGHT, UOZUMI?
DON'T HELP HIM!
AH ...
FLINCH
HUFF
YOU THINK FALLING GETS YOU OFF THE HOOK?!
FINISH THE DRILL!
I DON'T CARE HOW SLOW YOU HAVE TO GO ...
...BUT YOU WILL FINISH IT UNDER YOUR OWN STRENGTH!

READ THIS WAY

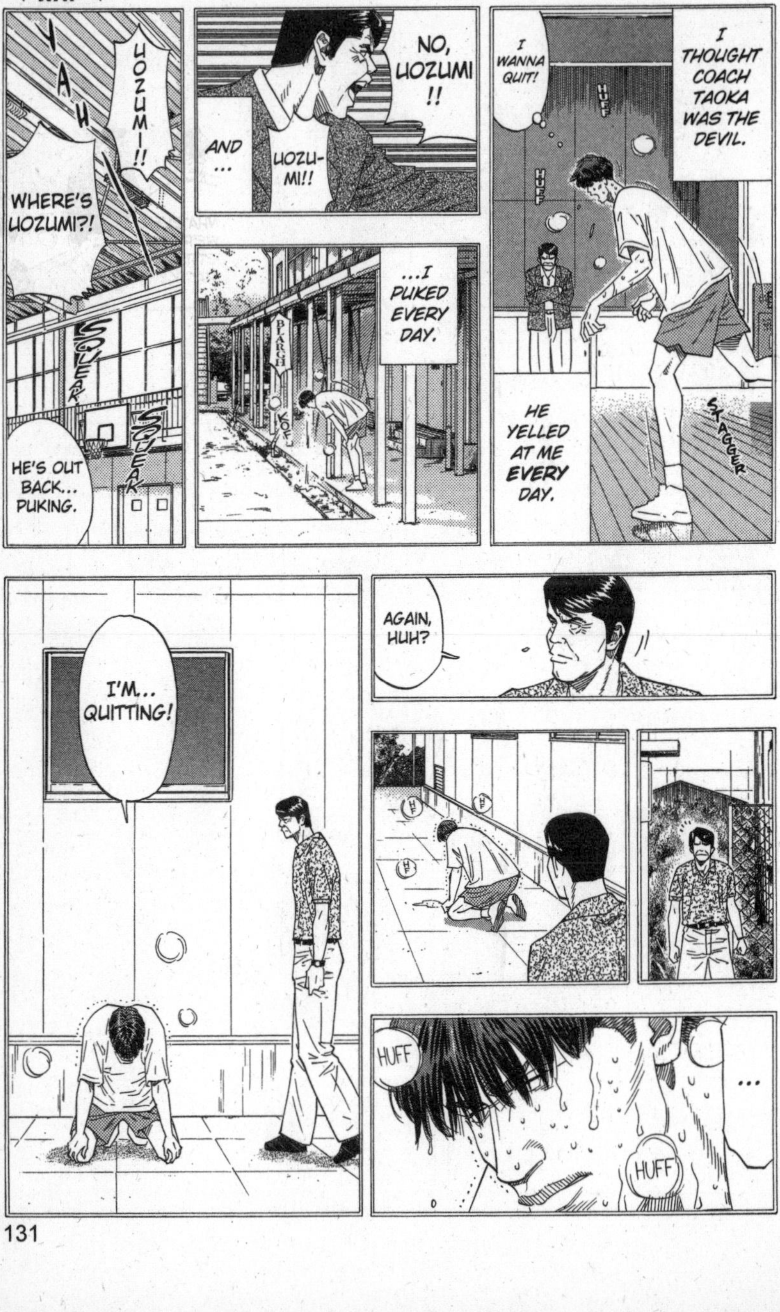
I THOUGHT COACH TAOKA WAS THE DEVIL.
I WANNA QUIT!
HUFF
HUFF
HE YELLED AT ME EVERY DAY.
STAGGER
NO, UOZUMI!!
AND...
UOZU-MI!!
...I PUKED EVERY DAY.
BLARGH
KOF
YAH
UOZUMI!!
WHERE'S UOZUMI?!
SQUEAK
SQUEAK
HE'S OUT BACK... PUKING.
AGAIN, HUH?
HF
HF
HF
HUFF
...
HUFF
I'M... QUITTING!

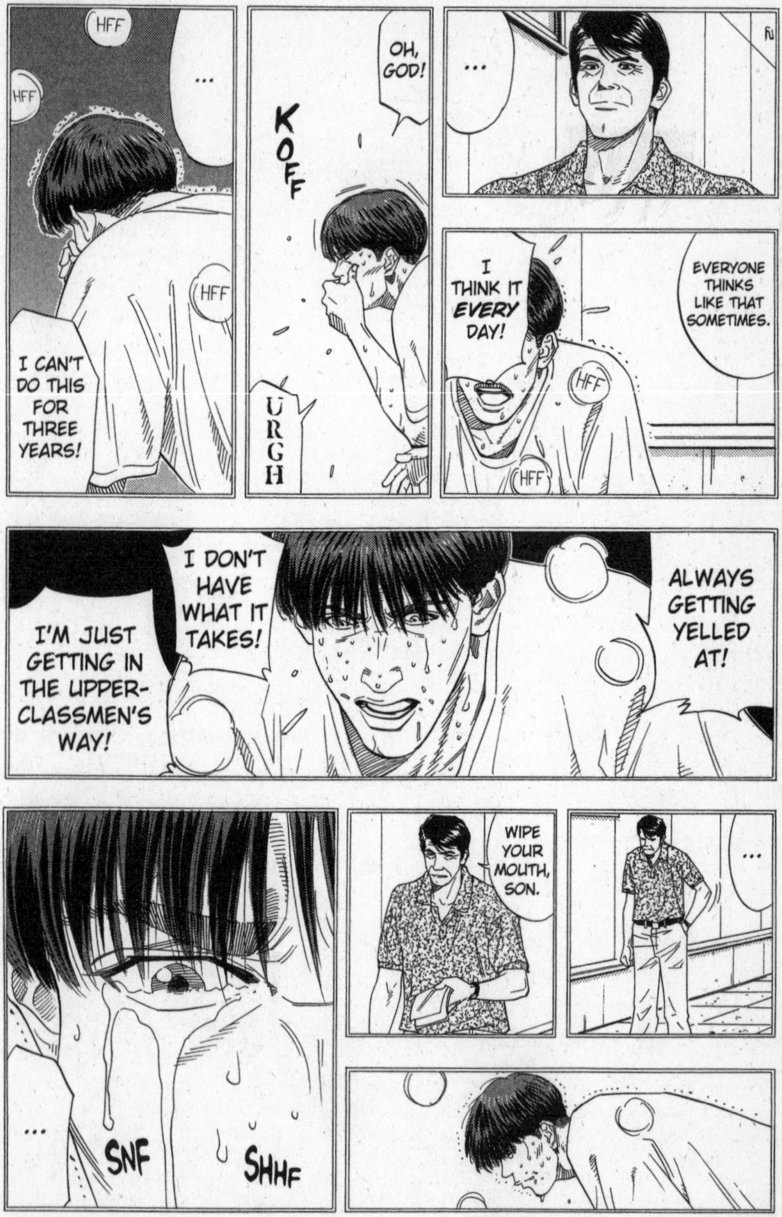

FU
...
EVERYONE THINKS LIKE THAT SOMETIMES.
I THINK IT *EVERY* DAY!
HFF
HFF
OH, GOD!
KOFF
URGH
HFF
...
HFF
HFF
I CAN'T DO THIS FOR THREE YEARS!
ALWAYS GETTING YELLED AT!
I DON'T HAVE WHAT IT TAKES!
I'M JUST GETTING IN THE UPPER-CLASSMEN'S WAY!
...
WIPE YOUR MOUTH, SON.
SHHF
SNF
...

READ THIS WAY

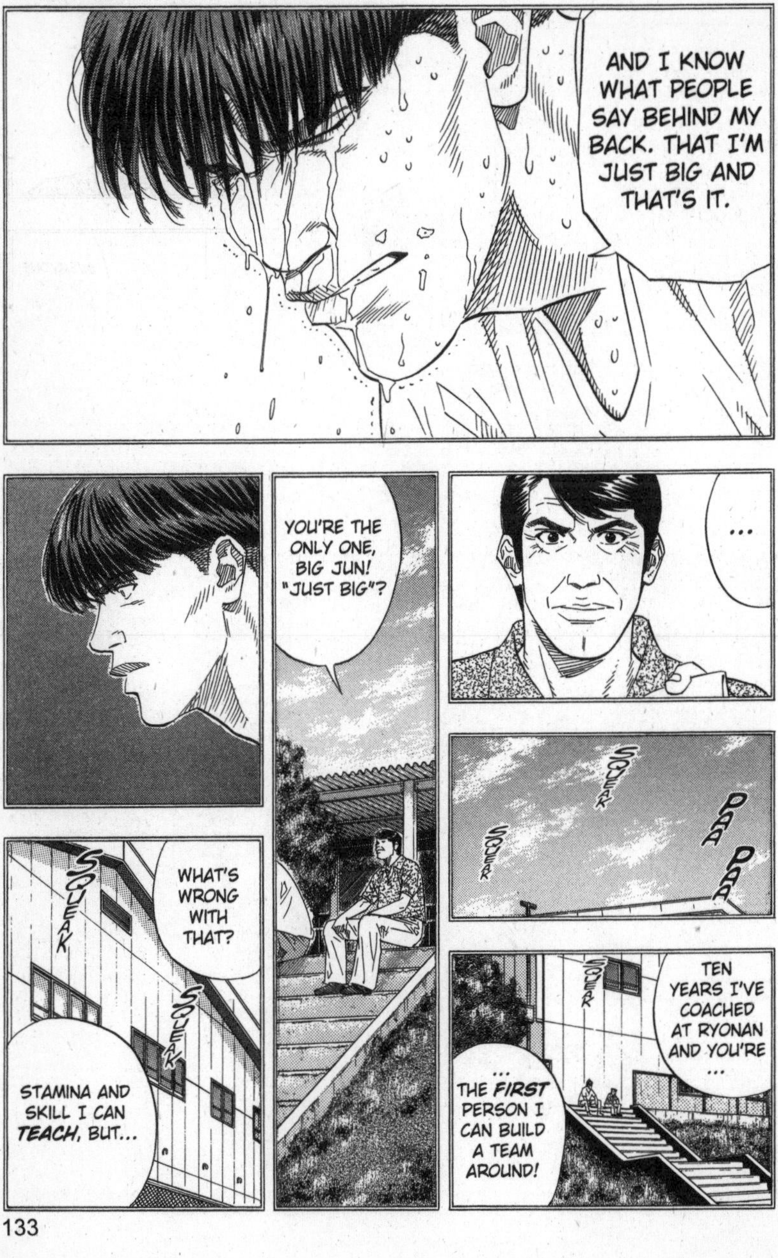
AND I KNOW WHAT PEOPLE SAY BEHIND MY BACK. THAT I'M JUST BIG AND THAT'S IT.
...
YOU'RE THE ONLY ONE, BIG JUN! "JUST BIG"?
WHAT'S WRONG WITH THAT?
SQUEAK
SQUEAK
STAMINA AND SKILL I CAN *TEACH*, BUT...
SQUEEK
PAA PAA
SQUEAK
SQUEAK
TEN YEARS I'VE COACHED AT RYONAN AND YOU'RE ...
... THE *FIRST* PERSON I CAN BUILD A TEAM AROUND!

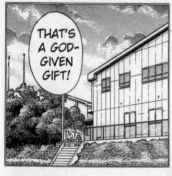

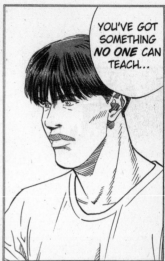

YOU'VE GOT SOMETHING *NO ONE* CAN TEACH...
... NOT ANY COACH IN THE WORLD.
THAT'S A GOD-GIVEN GIFT!
UOZUMI ...
WHEN YOU BECOME A SENIOR...
...RYONAN'S GOING TO THE NATIONALS FOR THE FIRST TIME EVER!
THAT'S MY DREAM!
...!!
HMM ?
THINK IT'S FUNNY FOR AN OLD MAN TO HAVE A DREAM LIKE THAT?

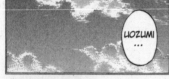

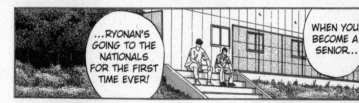

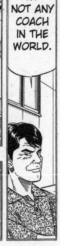

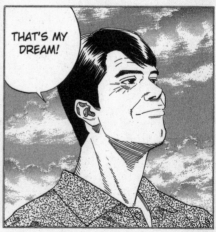

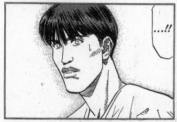

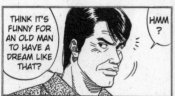

READ THIS WAY

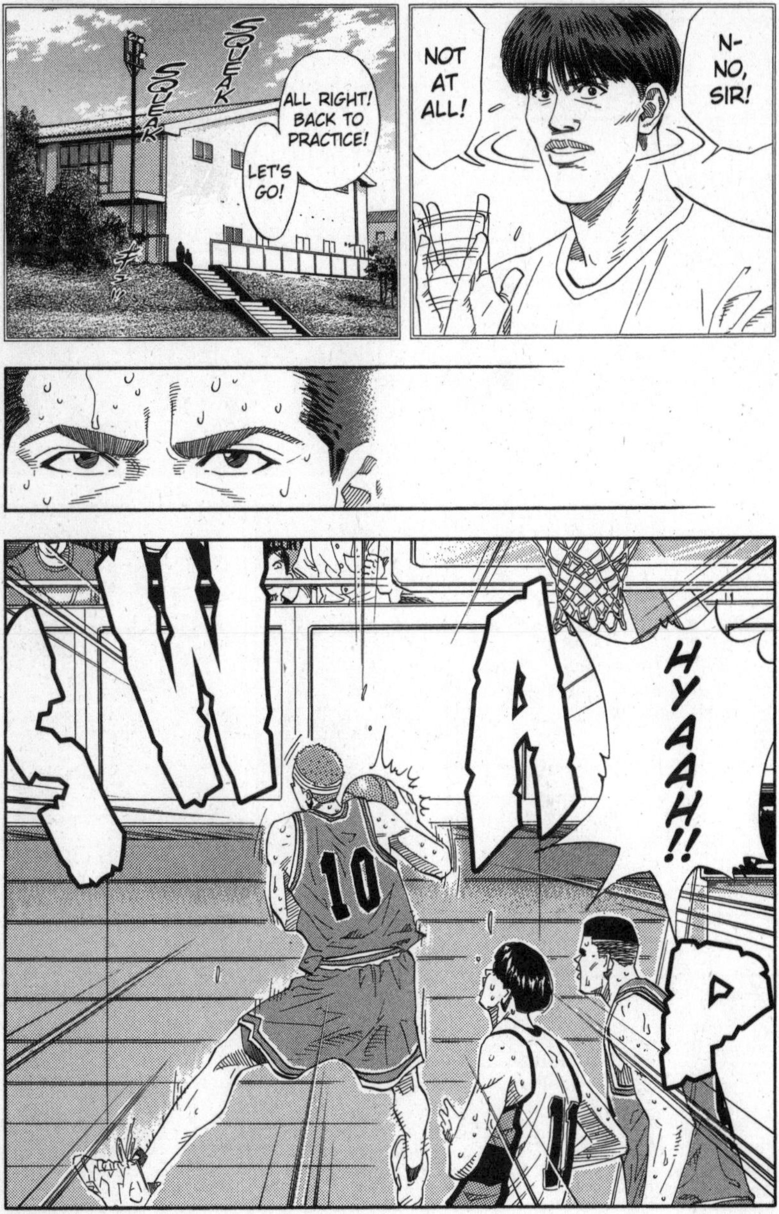
N-NO, SIR!
NOT AT ALL!
SQUEAK
SQUEAK
ALL RIGHT! BACK TO PRACTICE!
LET'S GO!
HYAAAH!!

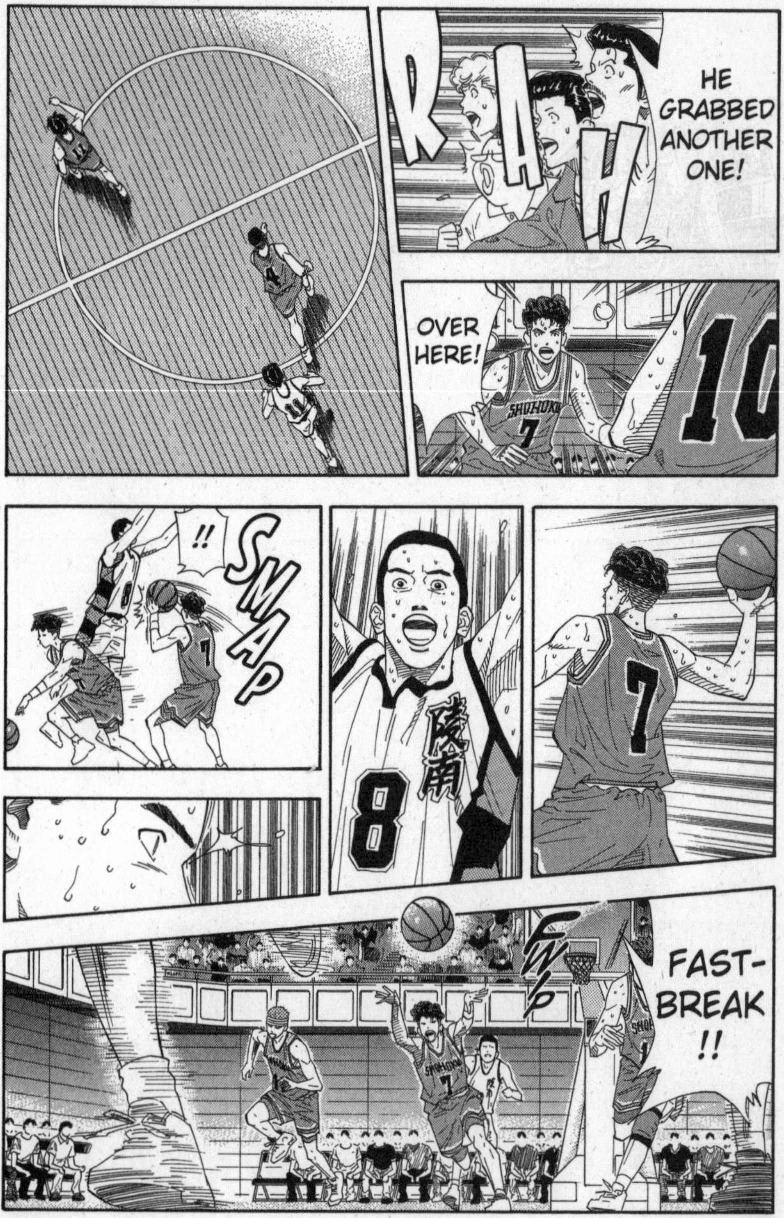
RAH
HE GRABBED ANOTHER ONE!
OVER HERE!
!!
SMAP
FAST-BREAK !!
FWIP

READ THIS WAY

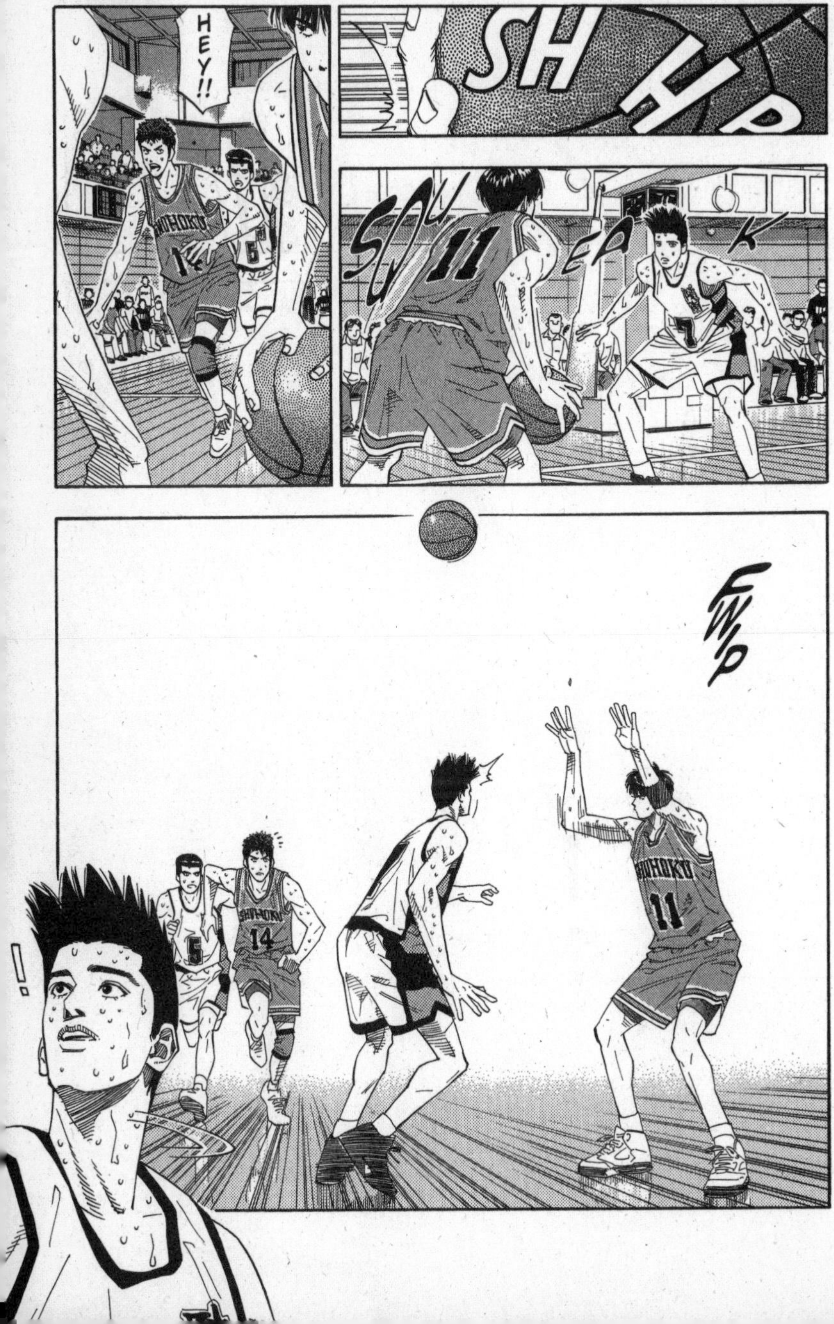

SHHP
SQUEAK
HEY!!
FWIP
!

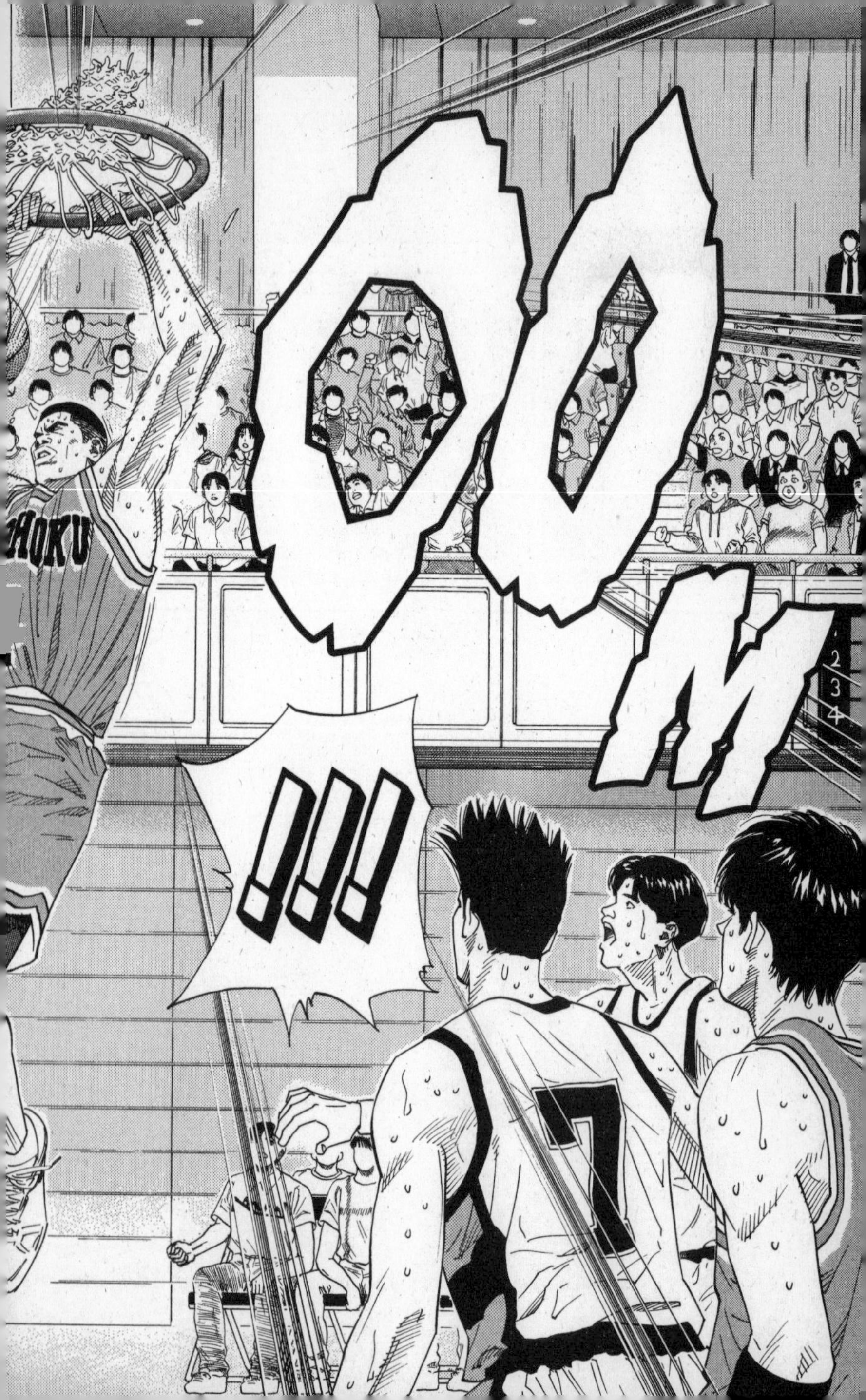
OOM
!!!

READ THIS WAY

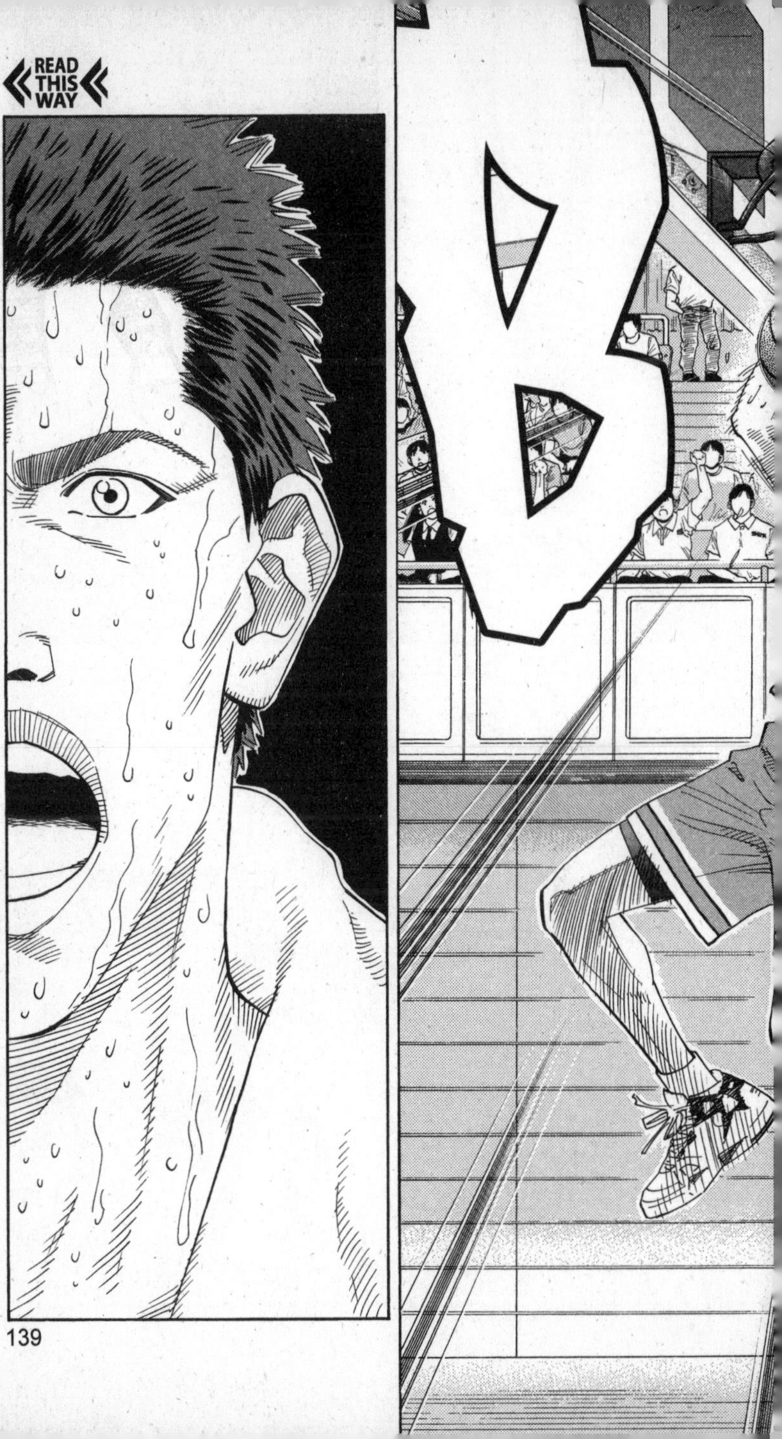

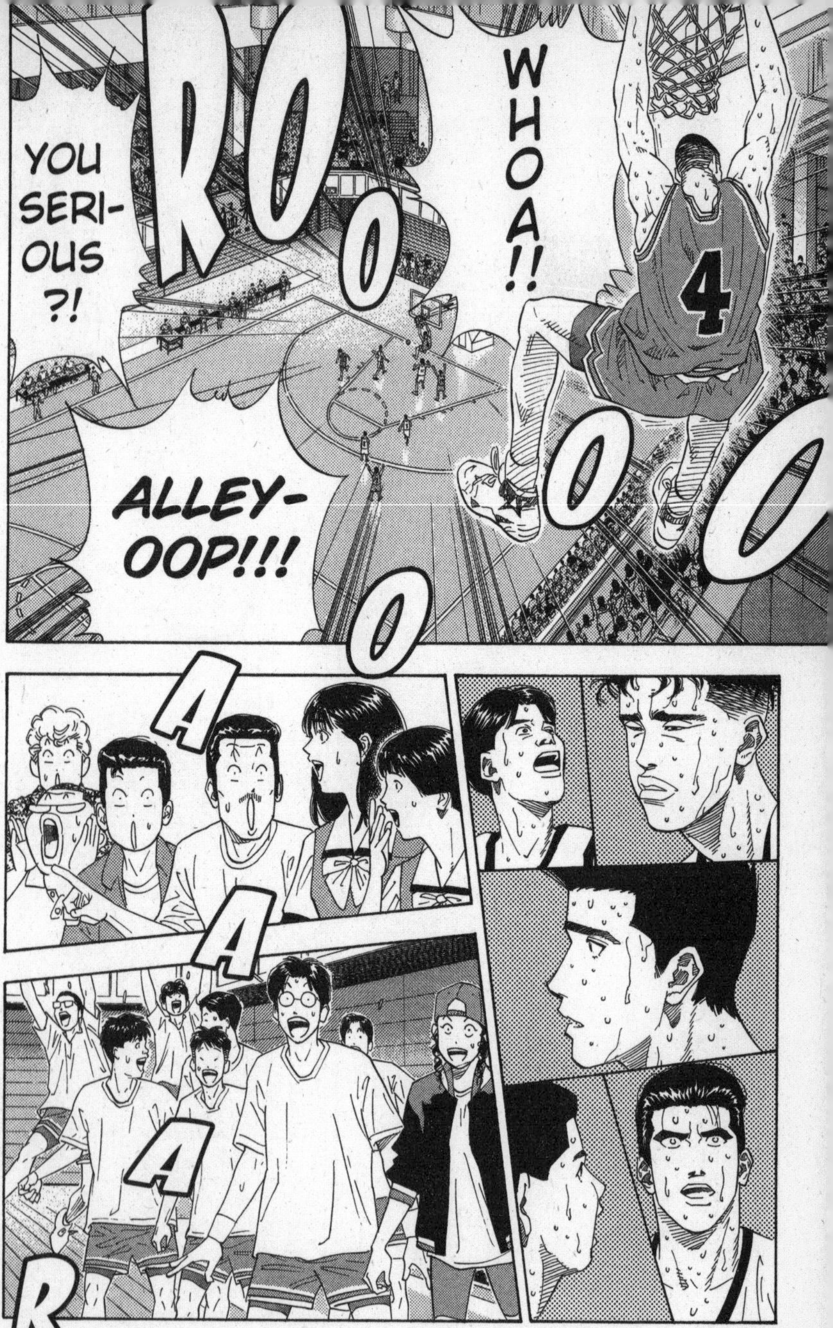
WHOA!!
ROOOOOAAAR
YOU SERIOUS?!
ALLEY-OOP!!!

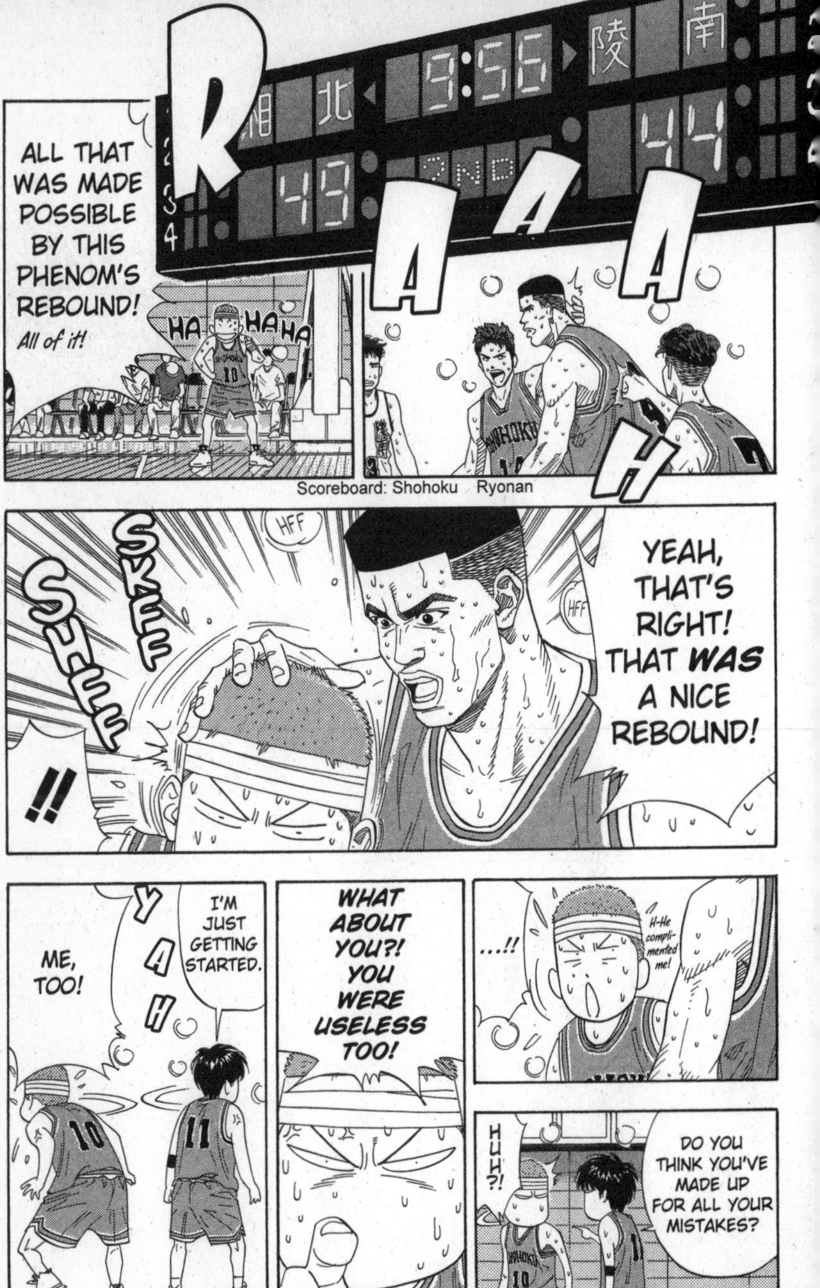

陵南
9:56
北
49
2ND
44
RAAAAH
ALL THAT WAS MADE POSSIBLE BY THIS PHENOM'S REBOUND!
All of it!
HA HAHA
Scoreboard: Shohoku Ryonan
HFF
YEAH, THAT'S RIGHT! THAT WAS A NICE REBOUND!
HFF
SKEFF
SHEFF
!!
...!!
H-He complimented me!
HUH?!
DO YOU THINK YOU'VE MADE UP FOR ALL YOUR MISTAKES?
WHAT ABOUT YOU?! YOU WERE USELESS TOO!
I'M JUST GETTING STARTED.
YAAH
ME, TOO!

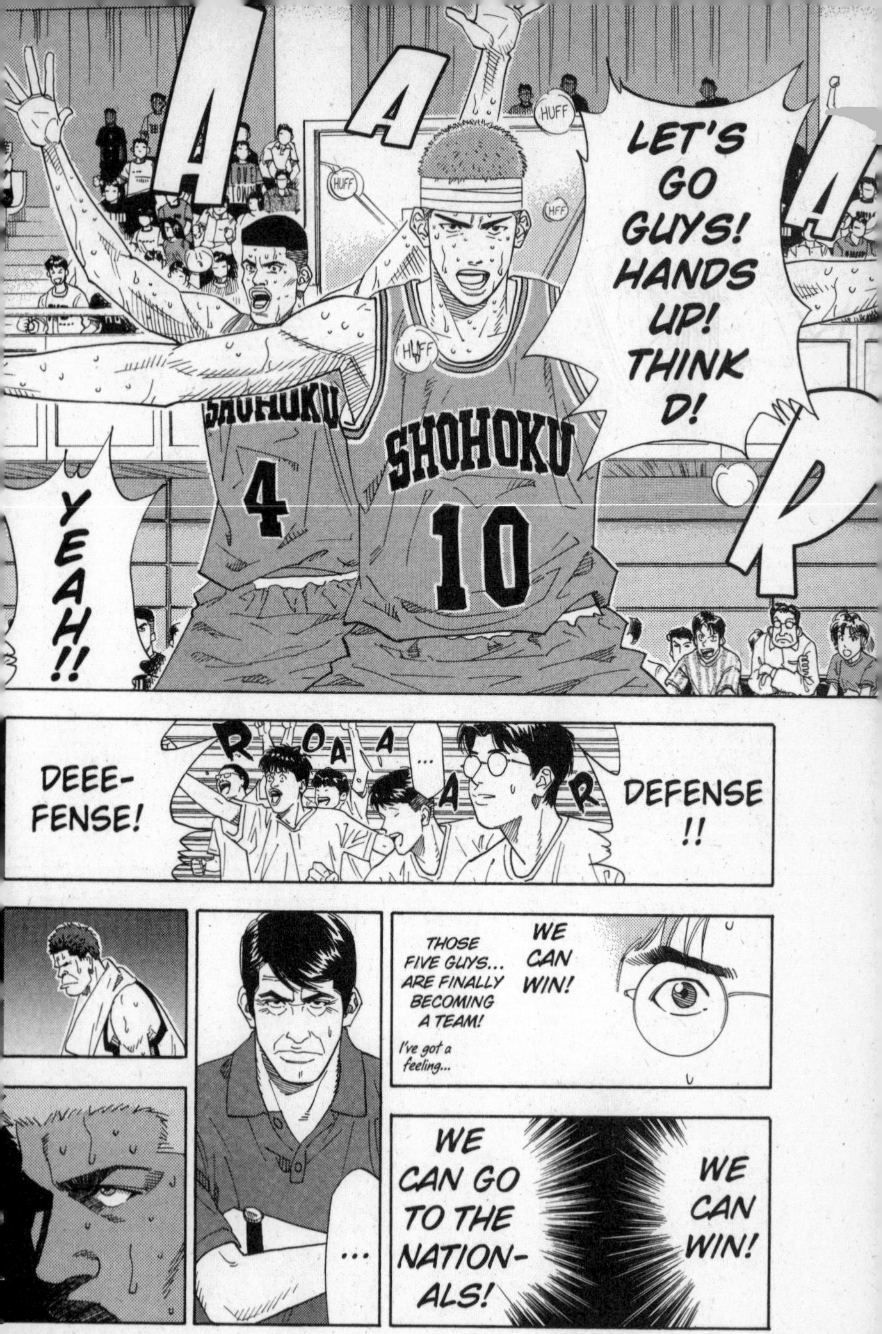
AAAR
HUFF
HUFF
HFF
HUFF
LET'S GO GUYS! HANDS UP! THINK D!
YEAH!!
DEFENSE !!
ROAAAR
...
DEEE-FENSE!
WE CAN WIN!
THOSE FIVE GUYS... ARE FINALLY BECOMING A TEAM!
I've got a feeling...
WE CAN WIN!
WE CAN GO TO THE NATION-ALS!
...

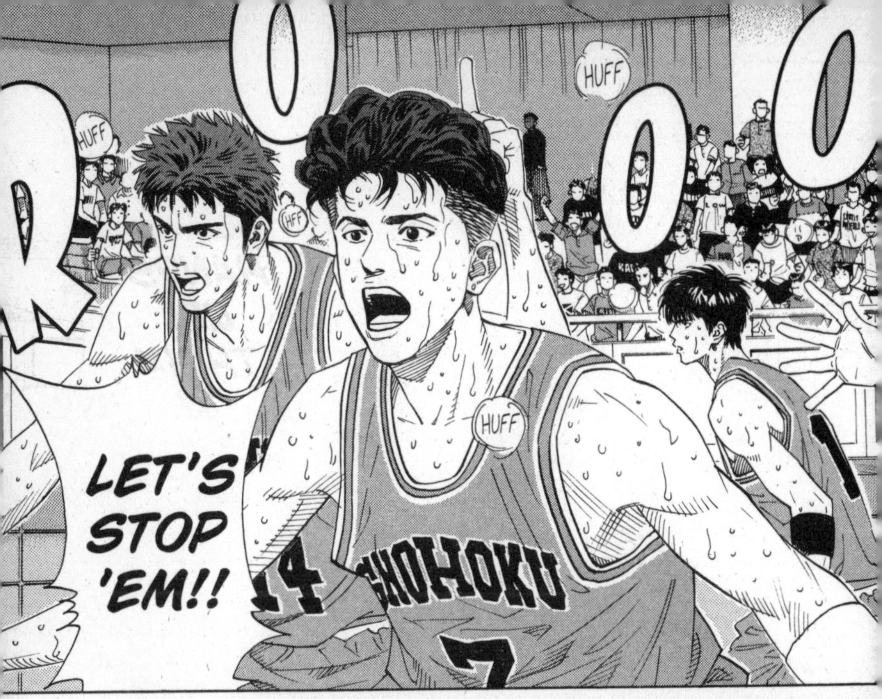
HUFF
HUFF
HFF
HUFF
LET'S STOP 'EM!!

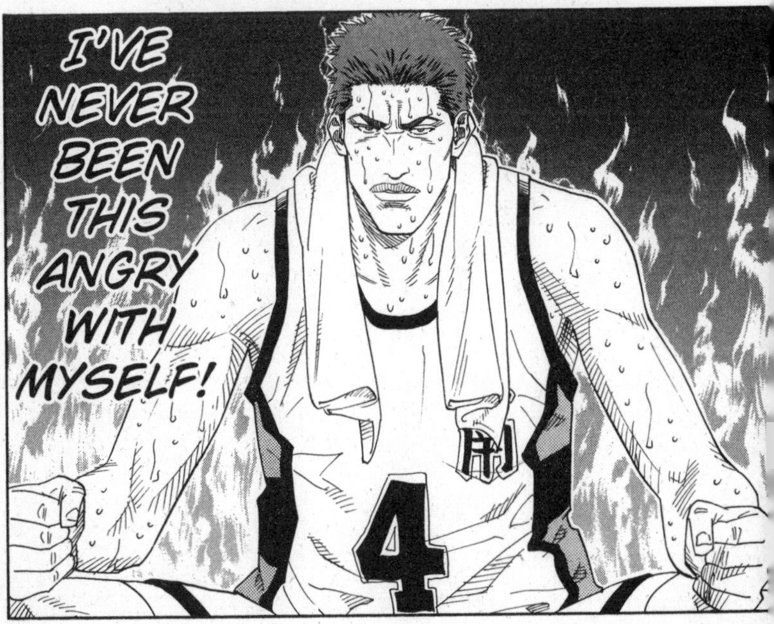
I'VE NEVER BEEN THIS ANGRY WITH MYSELF!

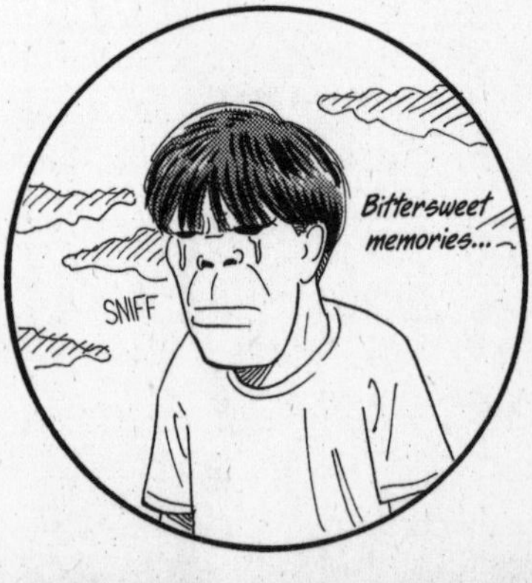
SNIFF
Bittersweet memories...

SLAM DUNK

#169 REBOUND KING – SAKURAGI'S STRUGGLES

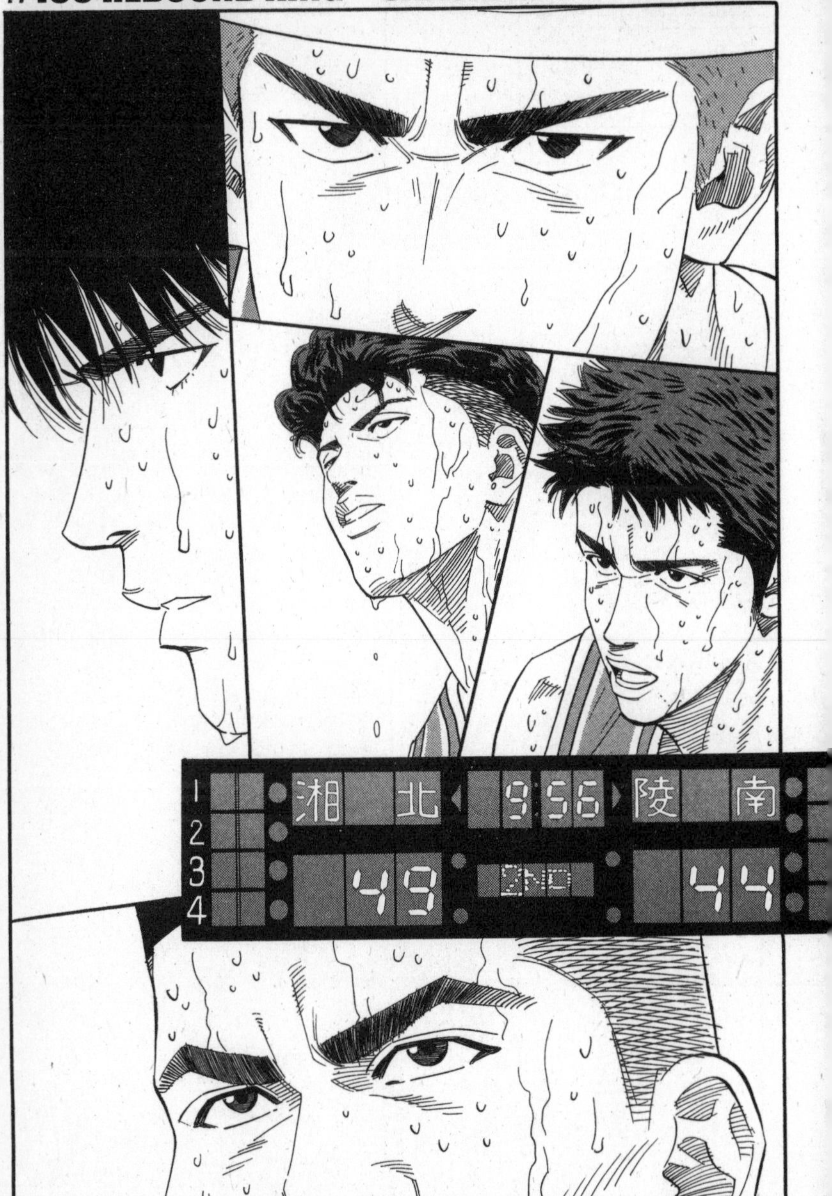
湘北
9:56
陵南
1
2
3
4
49
2ND
44

Scoreboard: Shohoku Ryonan

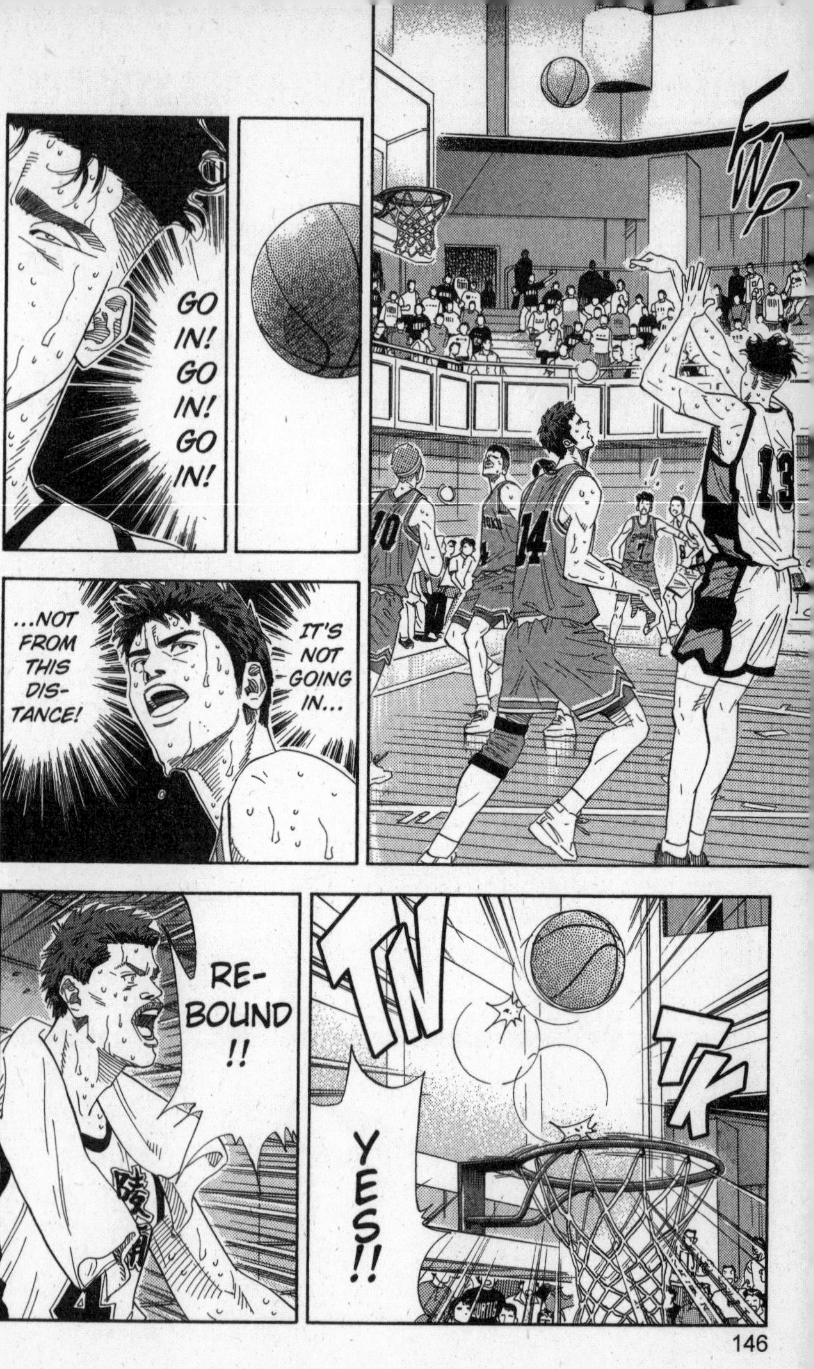
FWP
GO IN! GO IN! GO IN!
IT'S NOT GOING IN...
...NOT FROM THIS DIS-TANCE!
TN
TK
YES!!
RE-BOUND!!

READ THIS WAY

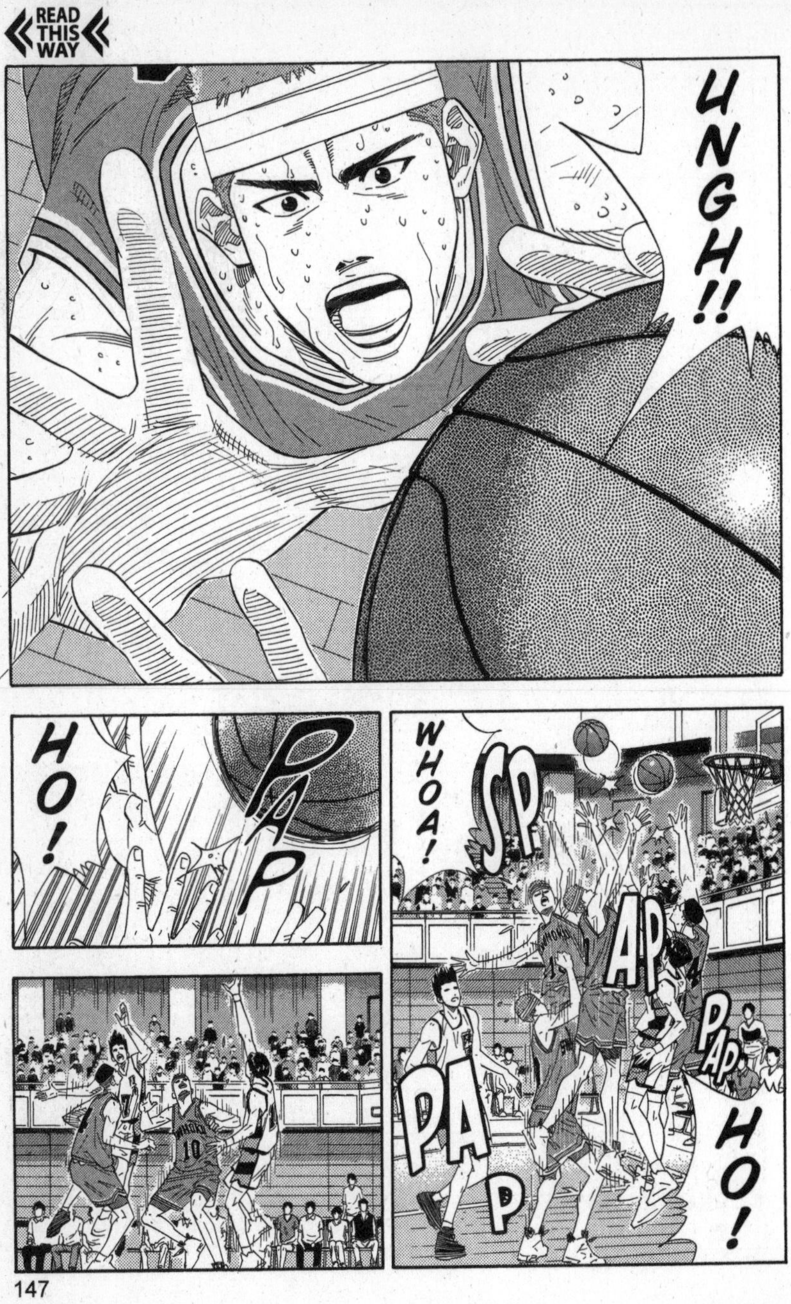
UNGH!!
SP
WHOA!
AP
PAP
HO HO!
PA
P
PAP
HO!

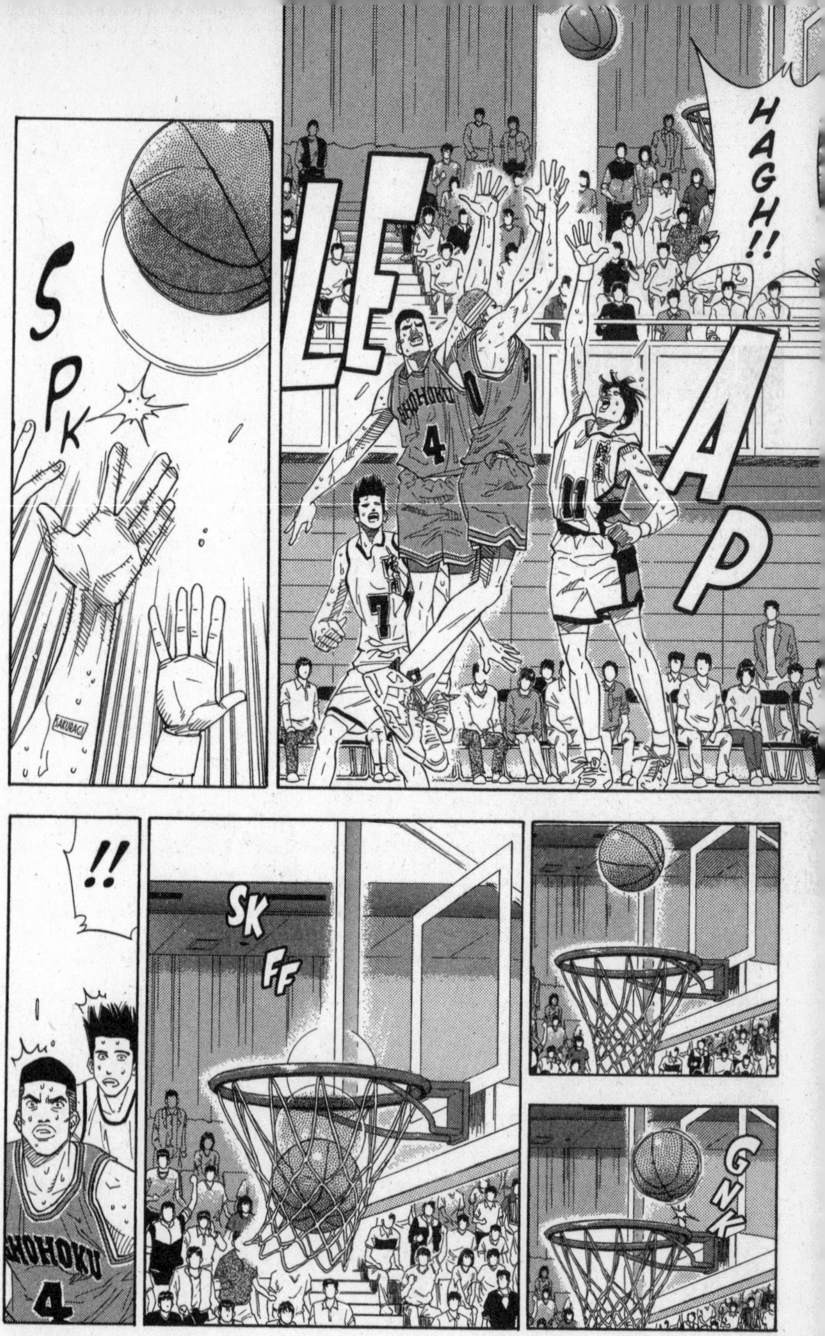
HAGH!!
LEAP
SPK
SAKURAGI
GNK
SKFF
!!

READ THIS WAY

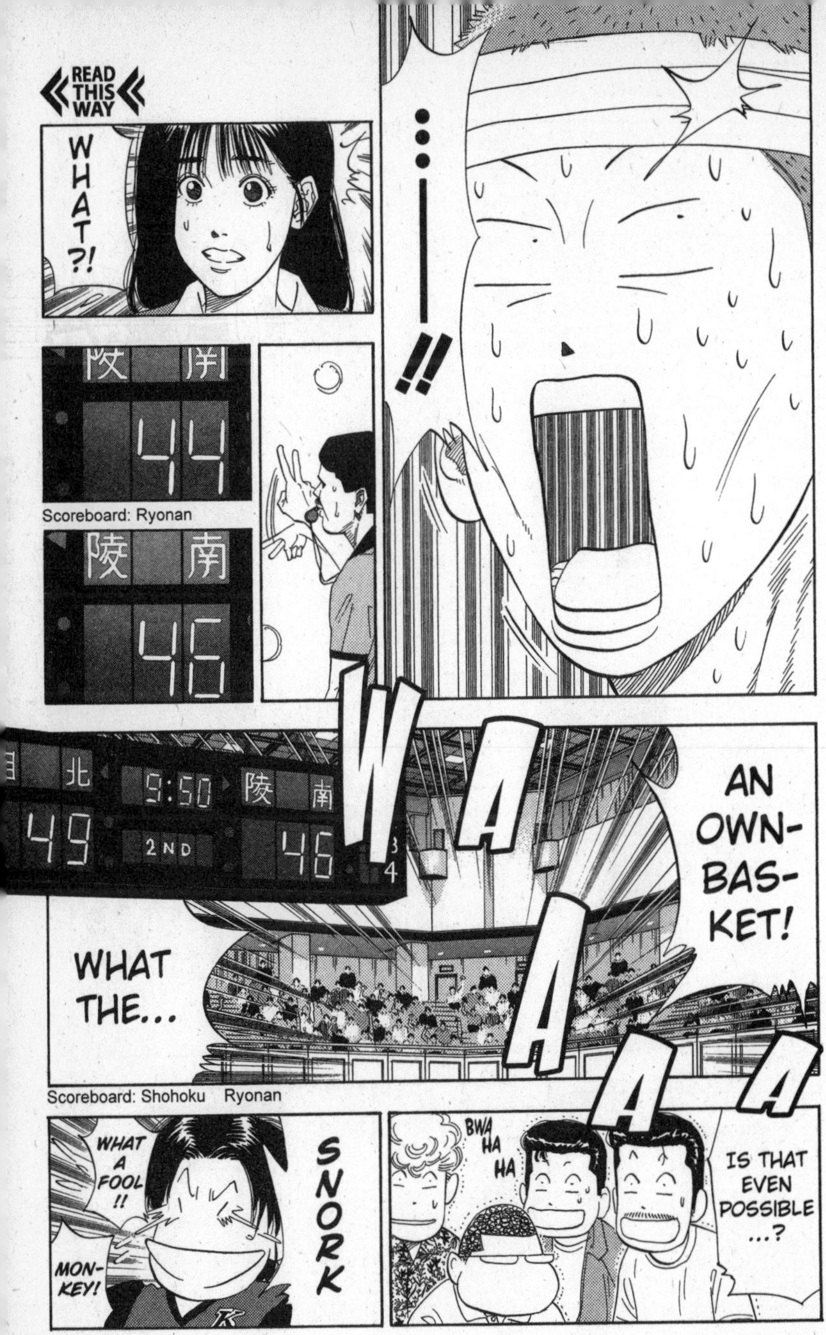
...!!
WHAT?!
Scoreboard: Ryonan
WAAAAAA
AN OWN-BASKET!
WHAT THE...
Scoreboard: Shohoku Ryonan
IS THAT EVEN POSSIBLE ...?
BWA HA HA
SNORK
WHAT A FOOL!!
MONKEY!

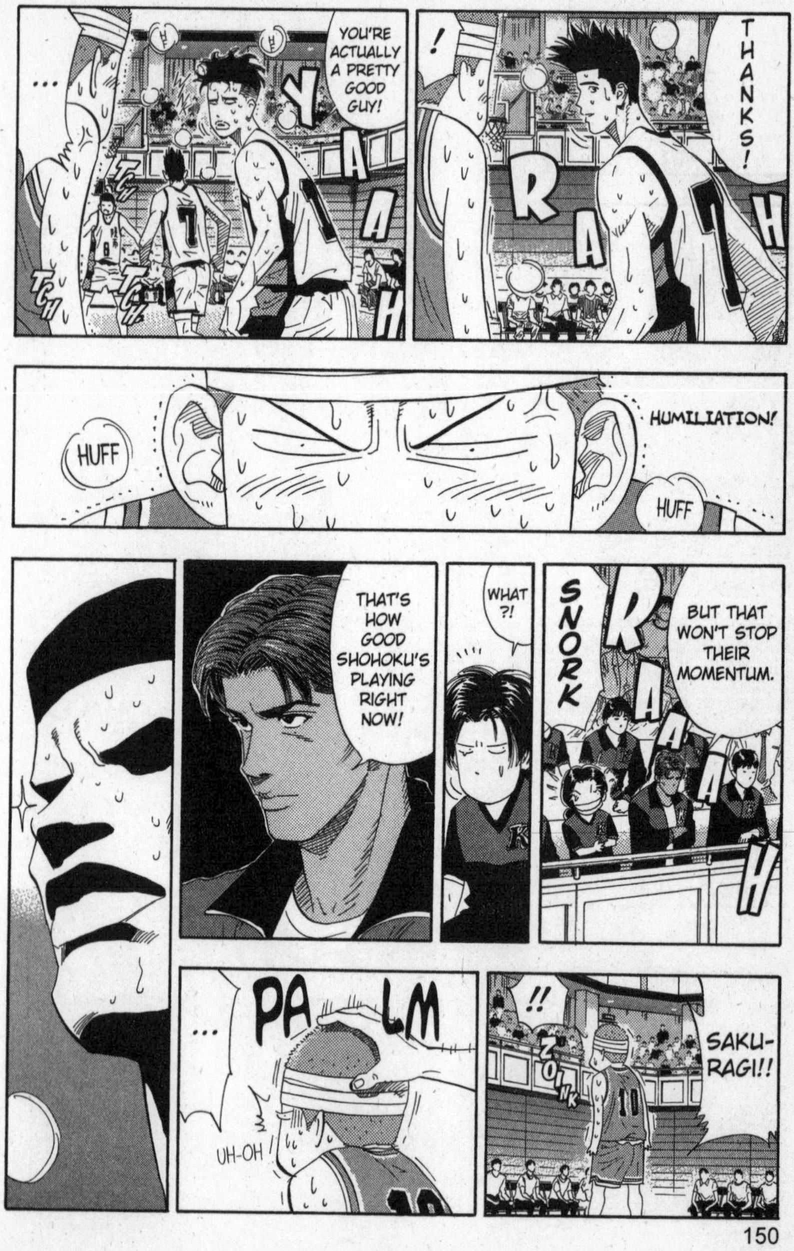
THANKS!
!
RAH
YOU'RE ACTUALLY A PRETTY GOOD GUY!
YAAH
HF
HF
...
TCH
TCH
TCH
HUMILIATION!
HUFF
HUFF
BUT THAT WON'T STOP THEIR MOMENTUM.
RAAAAH
SNORK
WHAT?!
THAT'S HOW GOOD SHOHOKU'S PLAYING RIGHT NOW!
SAKU-RAGI!!
!!
ZOINK
PALM
...
UH-OH

READ THIS WAY

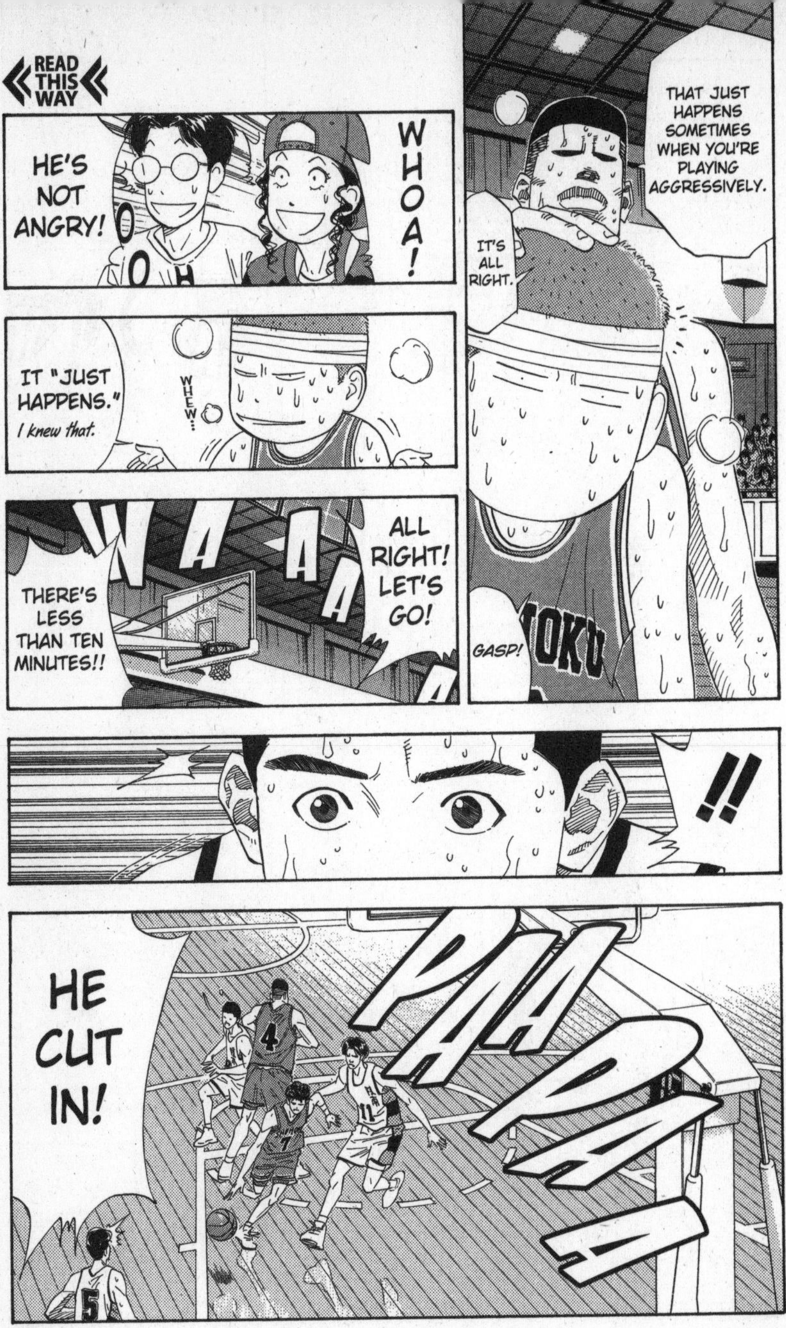
THAT JUST HAPPENS SOMETIMES WHEN YOU'RE PLAYING AGGRESSIVELY.
IT'S ALL RIGHT.
GASP!
WHOA!
HE'S NOT ANGRY!
WHEW...
IT "JUST HAPPENS."
I knew that.
ALL RIGHT! LET'S GO!
WAAAA
THERE'S LESS THAN TEN MINUTES!!
!!
PAPAPA
HE CUT IN!

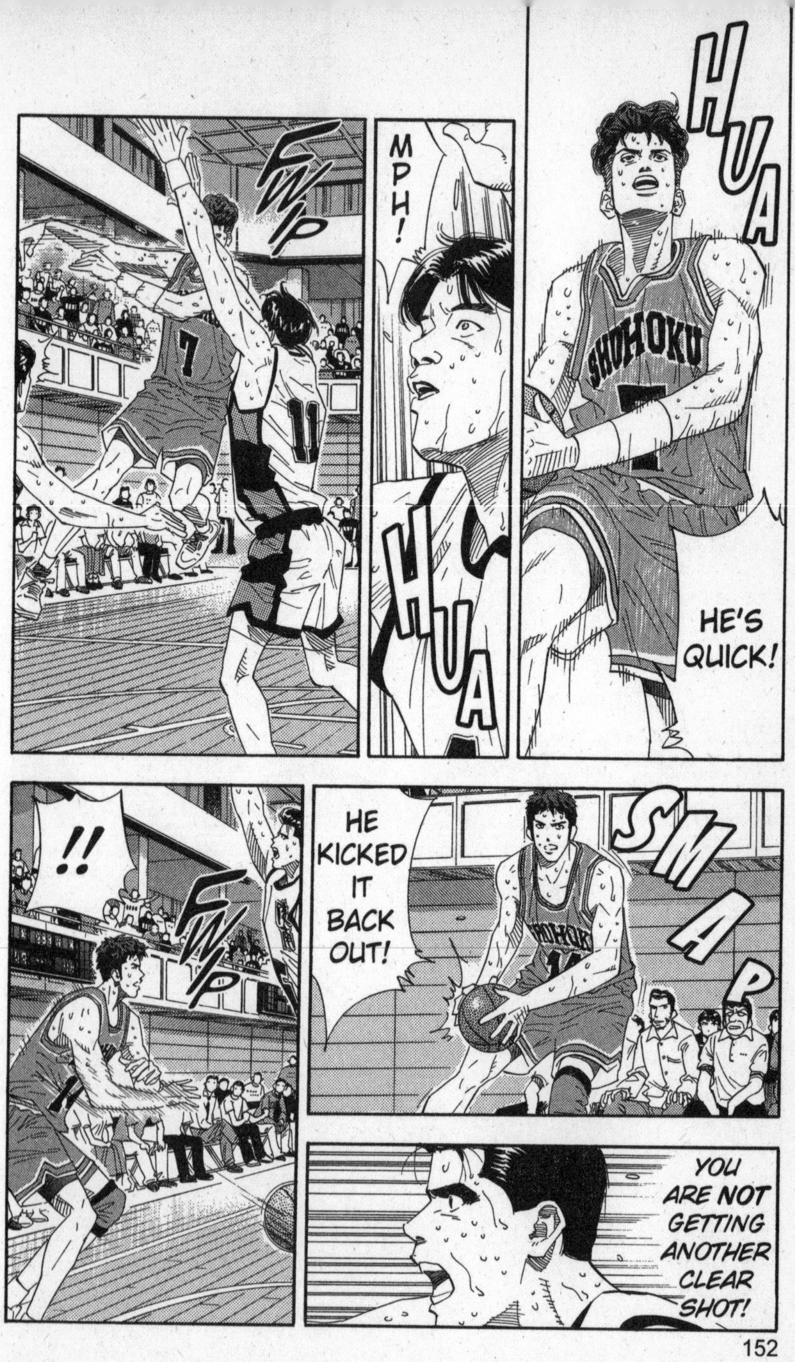
HUA
HE'S QUICK!
MPH!
HUA
FWIP
SMAP
HE KICKED IT BACK OUT!
YOU ARE NOT GETTING ANOTHER CLEAR SHOT!
!!
FWIP

READ THIS WAY

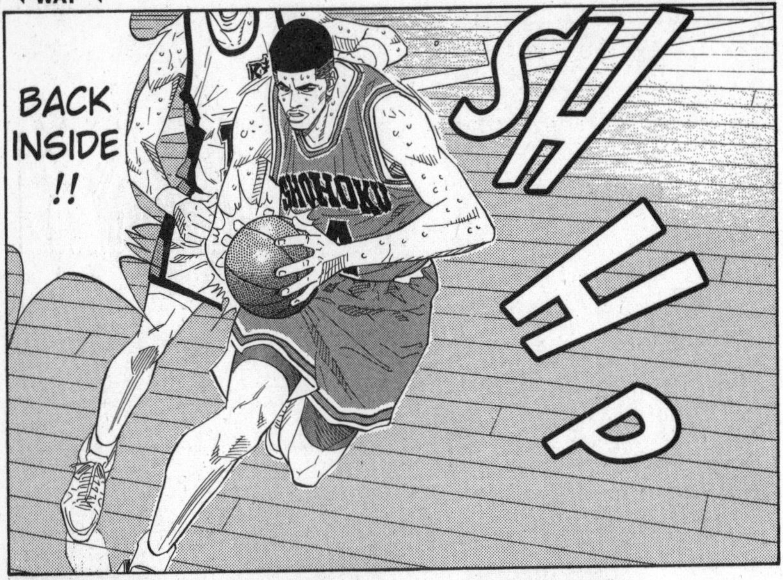
SHHP
BACK INSIDE !!

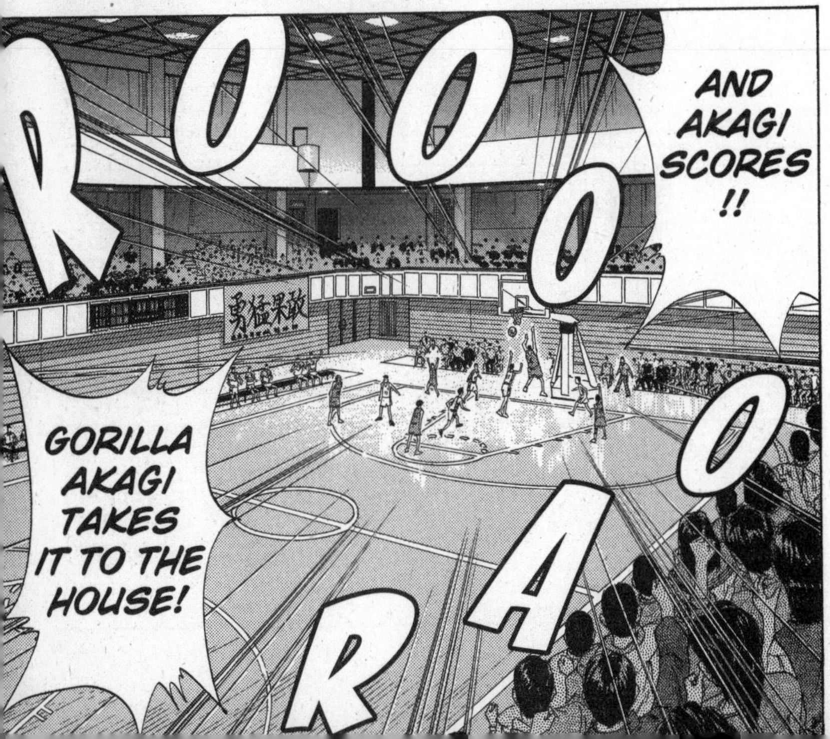
AND AKAGI SCORES !!
ROOOOOAR
GORILLA AKAGI TAKES IT TO THE HOUSE!

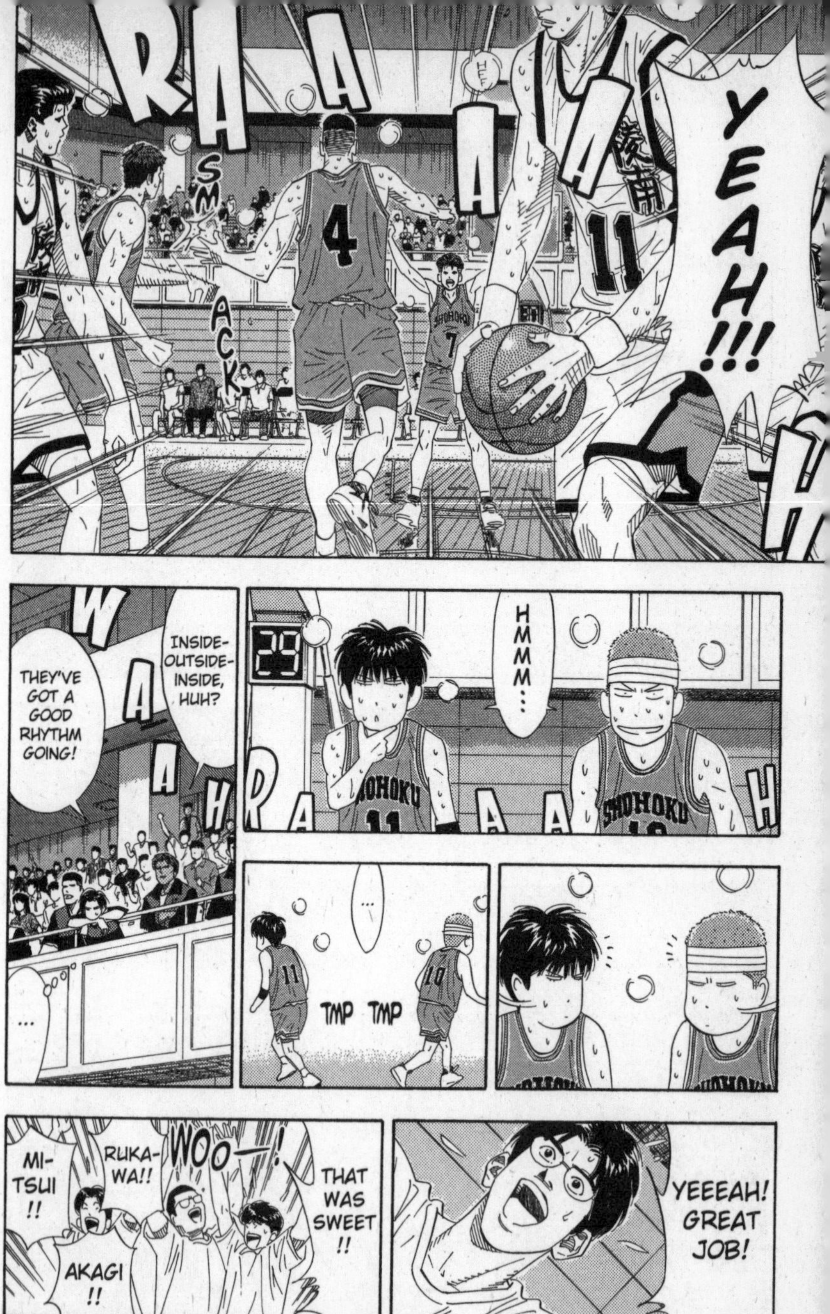
YEAH!!!
SMACK
RAAAAH
HMMM...
RAAAAH
INSIDE-OUTSIDE-INSIDE, HUH?
THEY'VE GOT A GOOD RHYTHM GOING!
WAAH
...
TMP TMP
...
YEEEAH! GREAT JOB!
THAT WAS SWEET!!
WOO—!
RUKAWA!!
MITSUI!!
AKAGI!!

READ THIS WAY

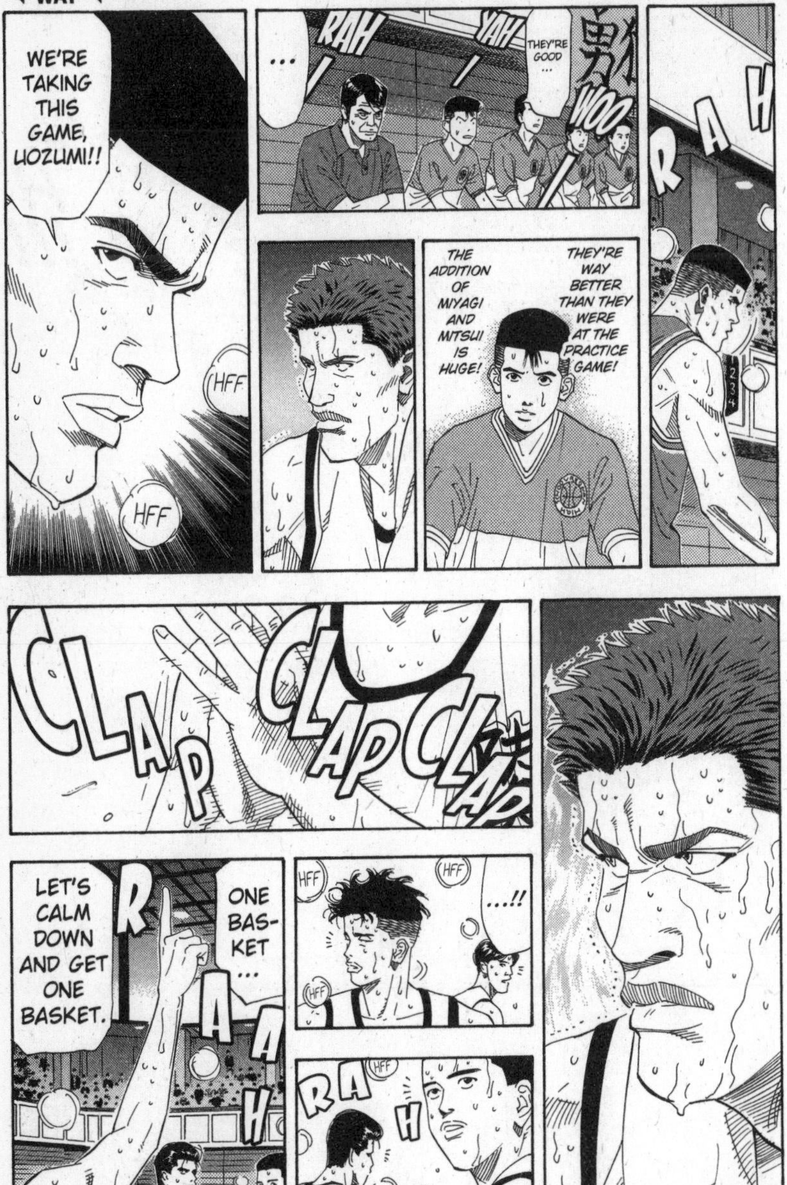
RAH
THEY'RE GOOD ...
WOO
YAH
RAH
...
THEY'RE WAY BETTER THAN THEY WERE AT THE PRACTICE GAME!
THE ADDITION OF MIYAGI AND MITSUI IS HUGE!
WE'RE TAKING THIS GAME, UOZUMI!!
HFF
HFF
CLAP CLAP CLAP CLAP
HFF
HFF
...!!
HFF
HFF
RAH
HFF
ONE BAS-KET ...
LET'S CALM DOWN AND GET ONE BASKET.
RAAH

THERE'S NO NEED TO PANIC YET.

YEAH !!

HF

HFF

SEN-DOH.

...!!

HFF

...

WELL SAID, SENDOH.

GOOD!

156

READ THIS WAY

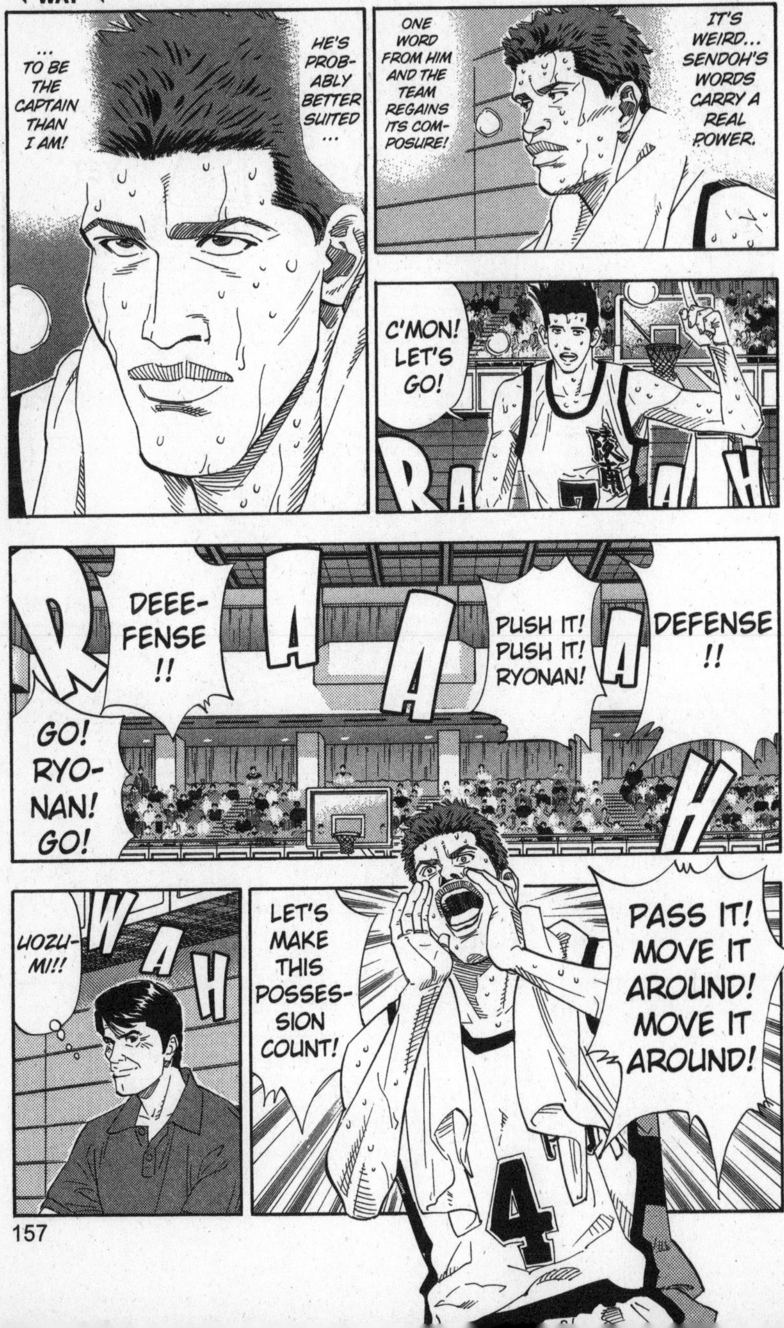
IT'S WEIRD... SENDOH'S WORDS CARRY A REAL POWER.
ONE WORD FROM HIM AND THE TEAM REGAINS ITS COMPOSURE!
C'MON! LET'S GO!
RAAH
HE'S PROBABLY BETTER SUITED ...
... TO BE THE CAPTAIN THAN I AM!
RAAAAH
DEFENSE!!
PUSH IT! PUSH IT! RYONAN!
DEEE-FENSE!!
GO! RYONAN! GO!
PASS IT! MOVE IT AROUND! MOVE IT AROUND!
LET'S MAKE THIS POSSESSION COUNT!
WAH
UOZUMI!!

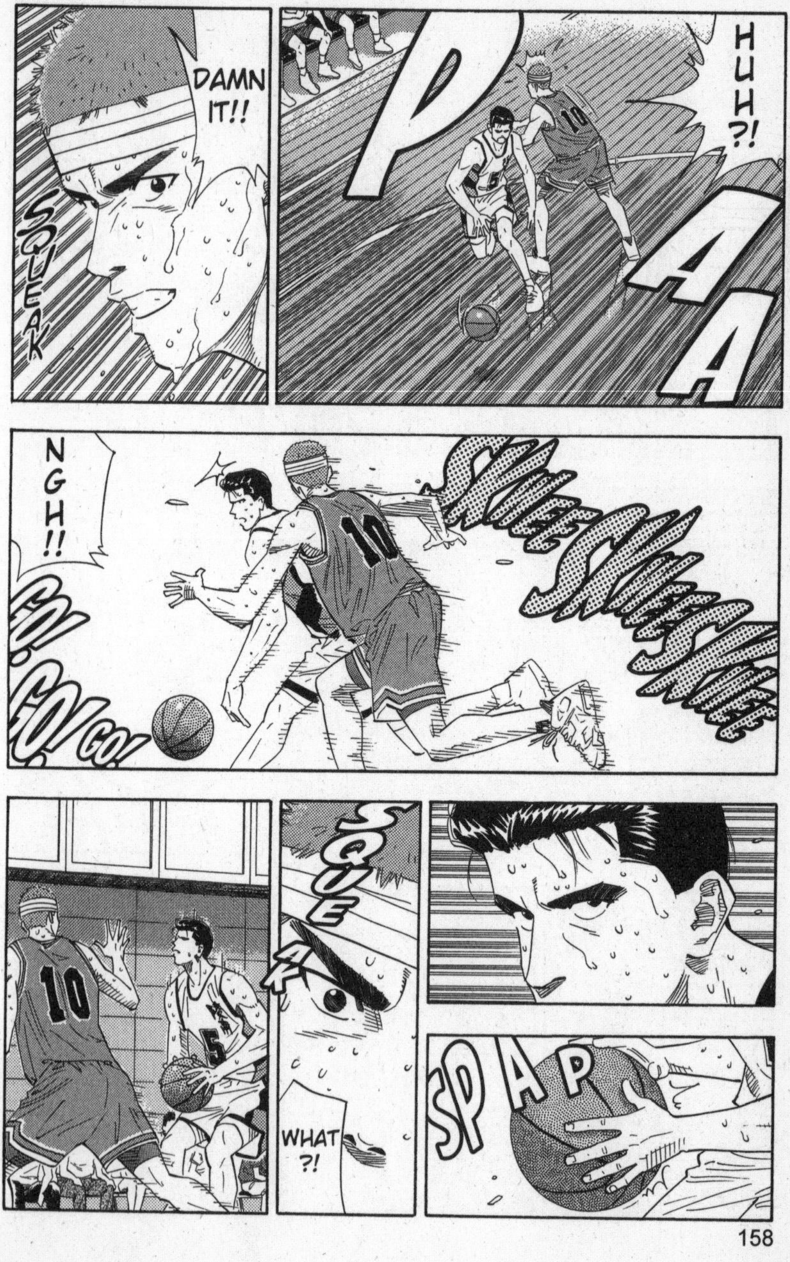
HUH?!
PAAA
DAMN IT!!
SQUEAK
NGH!!
GO! GO! GO! GO!
SPAP
SQUEAK
WHAT?!

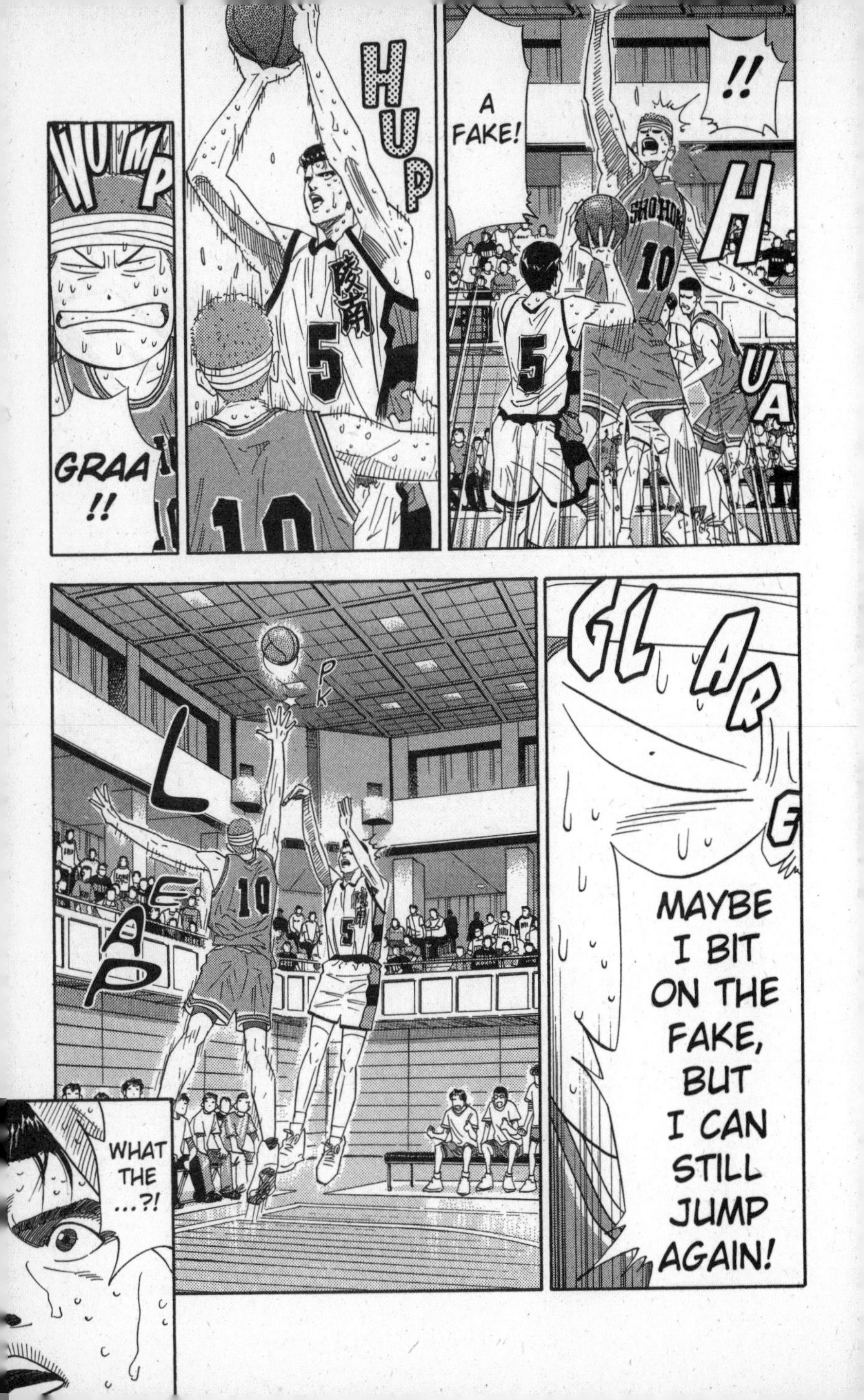
!!
A FAKE!
HUA
HUP
WUMP
GRAA !!
GLARE
MAYBE I BIT ON THE FAKE, BUT I CAN STILL JUMP AGAIN!
LEAP
PK
WHAT THE ...?!

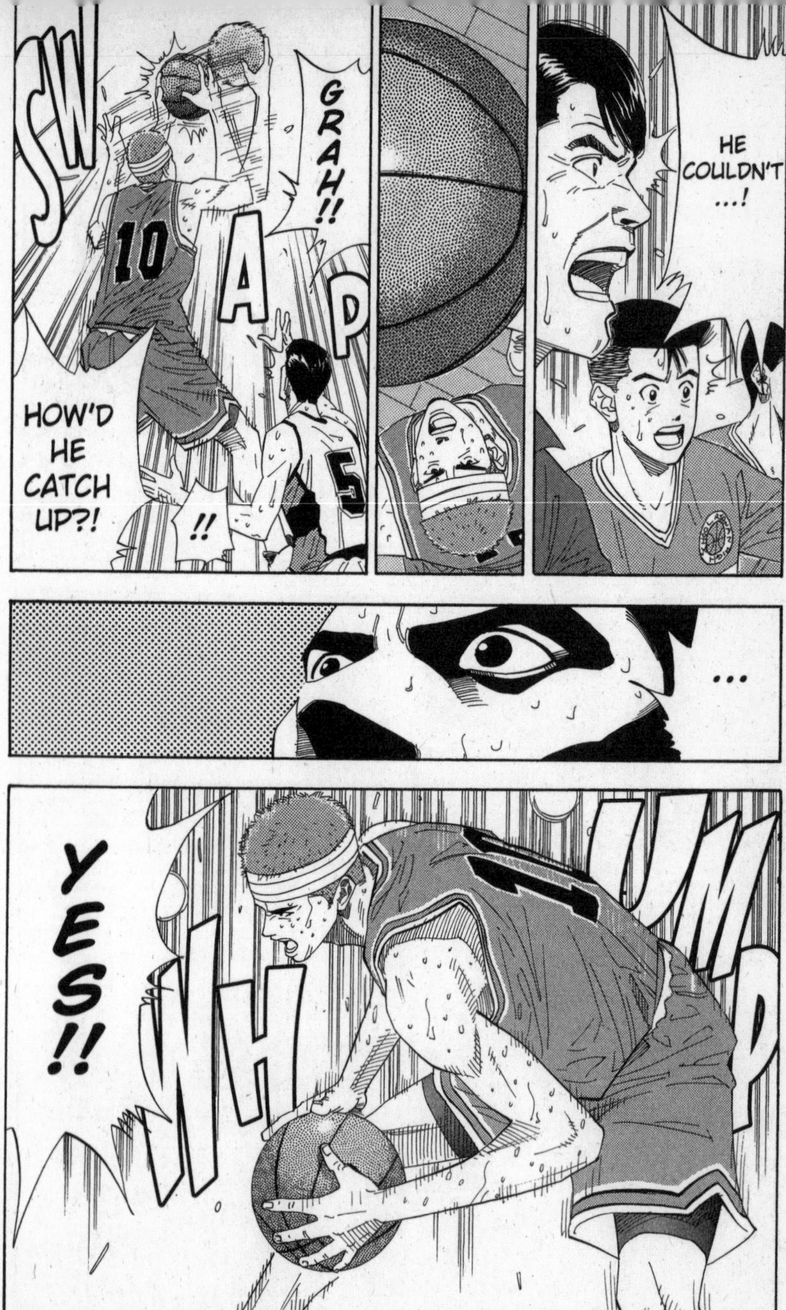
HE COULDN'T ...!
GRAH!!
SWAP
HOW'D HE CATCH UP?!
!!
...
WHUMP
YES!!

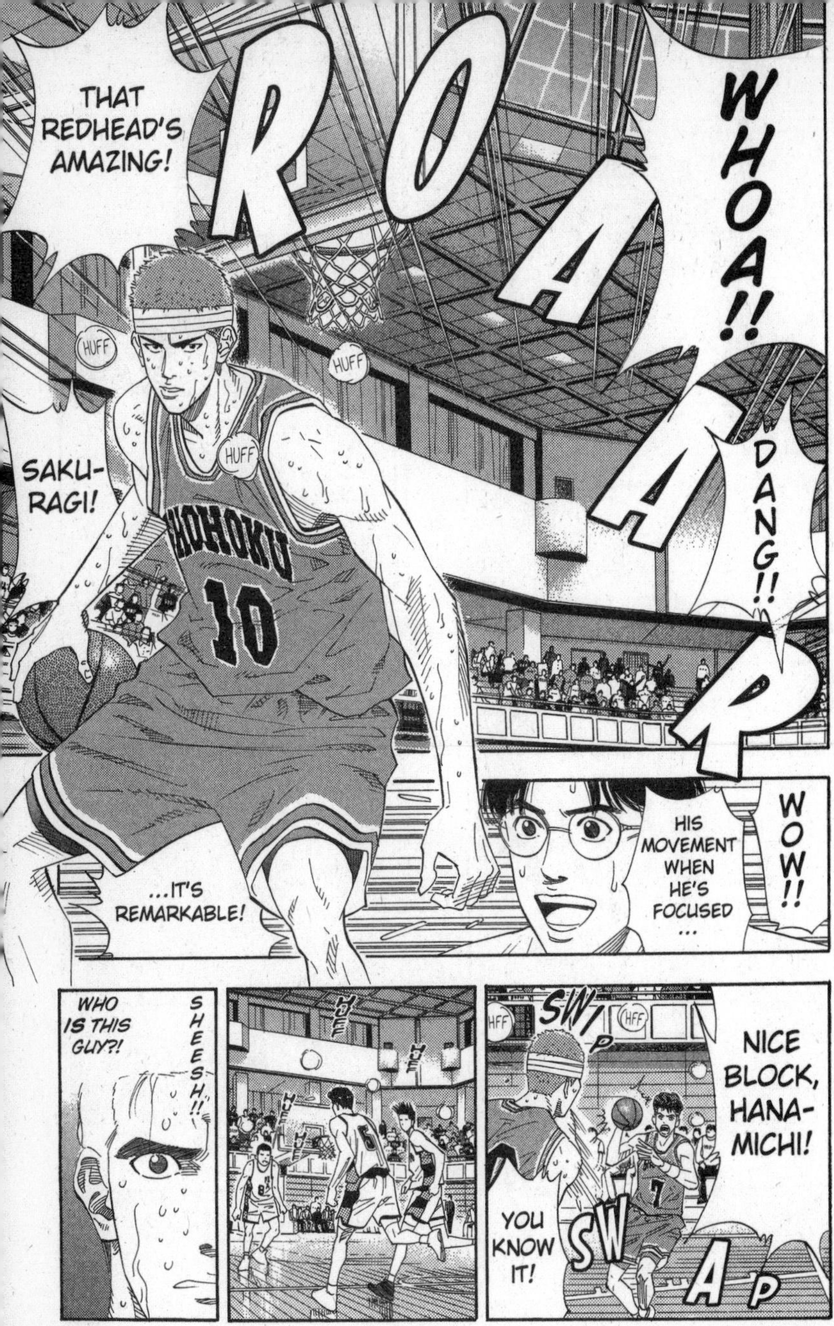
WHOA!!
ROAAAR
THAT REDHEAD'S AMAZING!
DANG!!
HUFF
HUFF
HUFF
SAKU-RAGI!
SHOHOKU
10
WOW!!
HIS MOVEMENT WHEN HE'S FOCUSED ...
...IT'S REMARKABLE!
NICE BLOCK, HANA-MICHI!
HFF
SWIP
HFF
YOU KNOW IT!
SWAP
HUFF
HUFF
HUFF
SHEESH!!
WHO IS THIS GUY?!

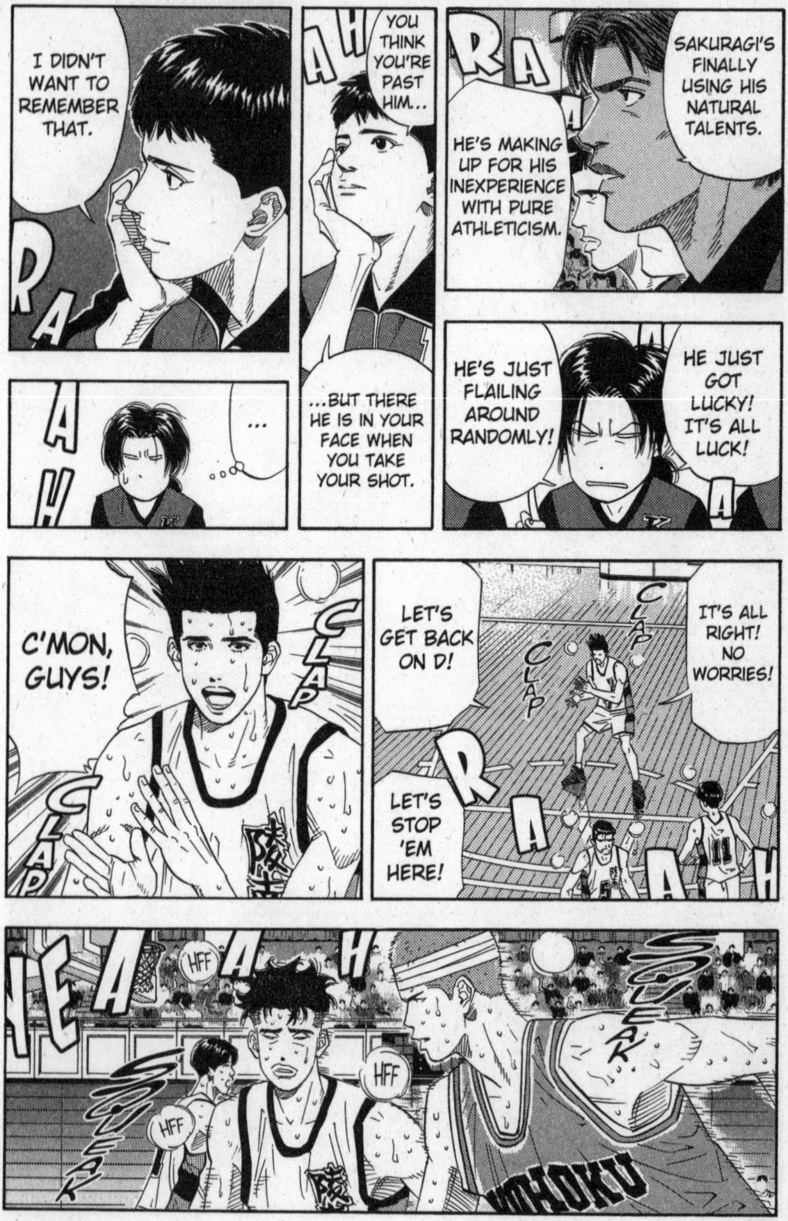

SAKURAGI'S FINALLY USING HIS NATURAL TALENTS.
HE'S MAKING UP FOR HIS INEXPERIENCE WITH PURE ATHLETICISM.
HE JUST GOT LUCKY! IT'S ALL LUCK!
HE'S JUST FLAILING AROUND RANDOMLY!
YOU THINK YOU'RE PAST HIM...
...BUT THERE HE IS IN YOUR FACE WHEN YOU TAKE YOUR SHOT.
I DIDN'T WANT TO REMEMBER THAT.
...
IT'S ALL RIGHT! NO WORRIES!
CLAP
LET'S GET BACK ON D!
CLAP
LET'S STOP 'EM HERE!
CLAP
C'MON, GUYS!
CLAP
SQUEAK
HFF
HFF
HFF
SQUEAK

READ THIS WAY

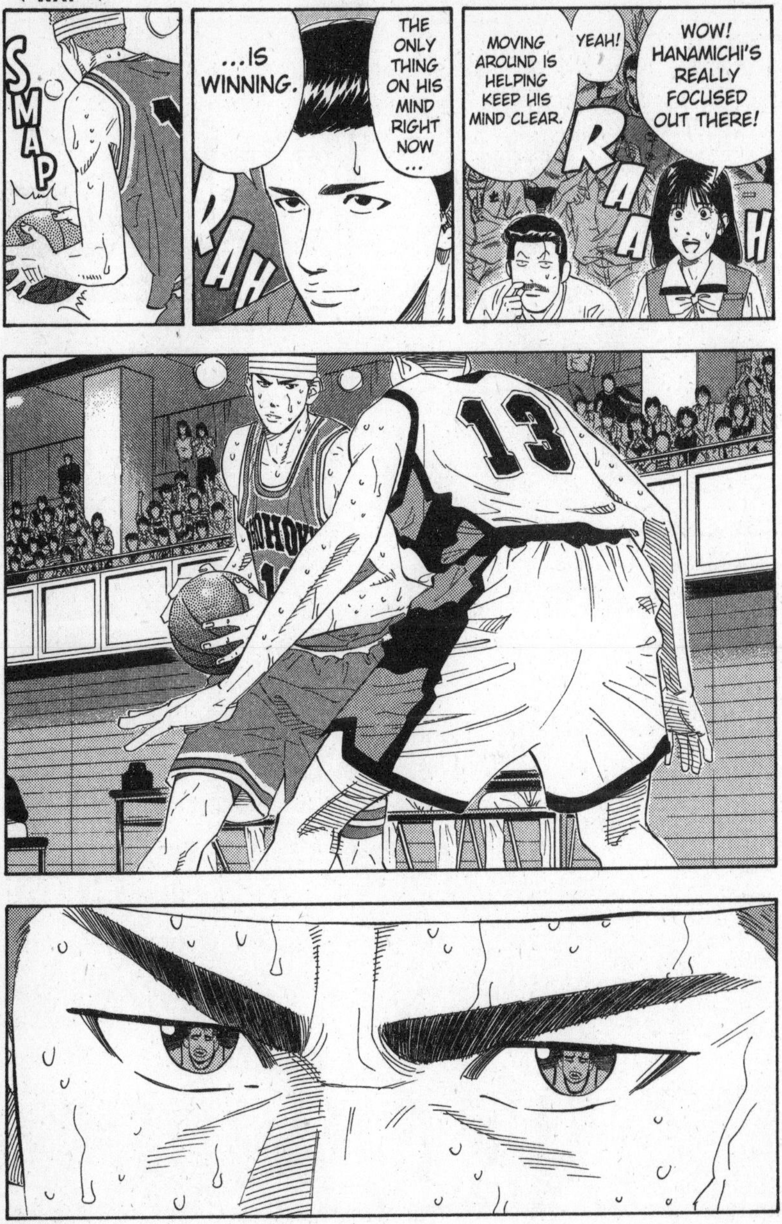

WOW! HANAMICHI'S REALLY FOCUSED OUT THERE!
YEAH!
MOVING AROUND IS HELPING KEEP HIS MIND CLEAR.
RAAH
THE ONLY THING ON HIS MIND RIGHT NOW ...
...IS WINNING.
RAH
SMAP

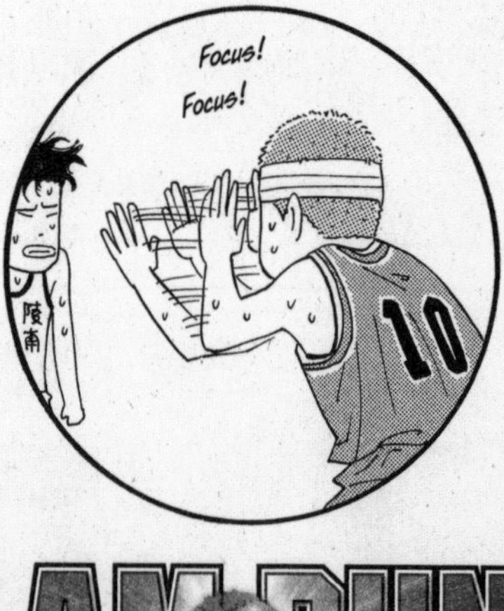
Focus!
Focus!

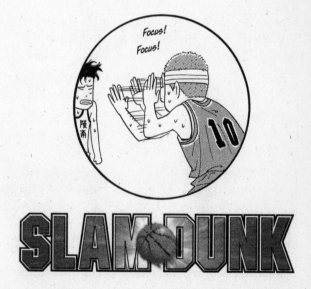

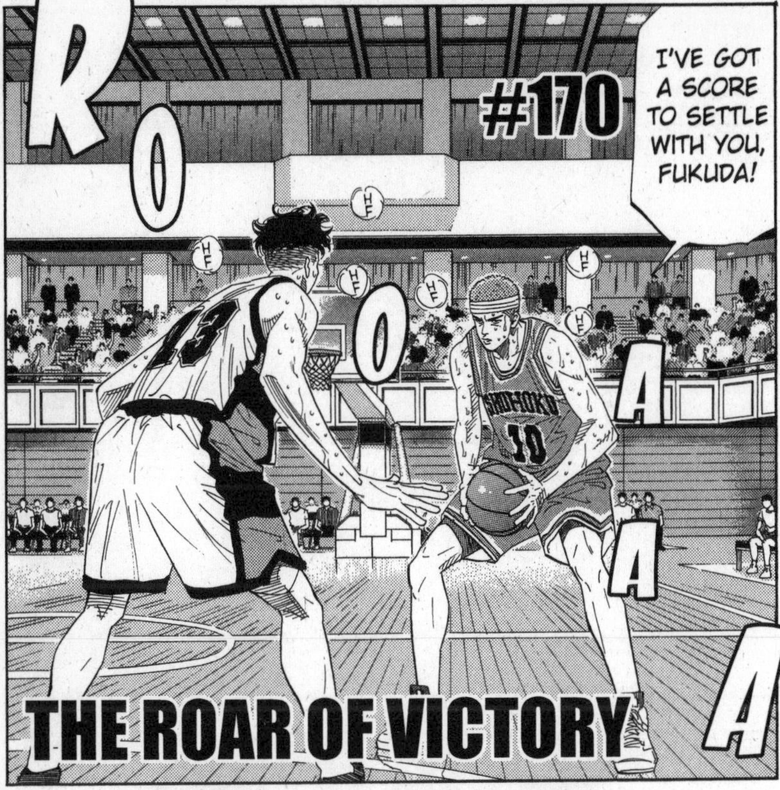
I'VE GOT A SCORE TO SETTLE WITH YOU, FUKUDA!
#170
R O O A A A
HF HF HF HF HF HF
THE ROAR OF VICTORY

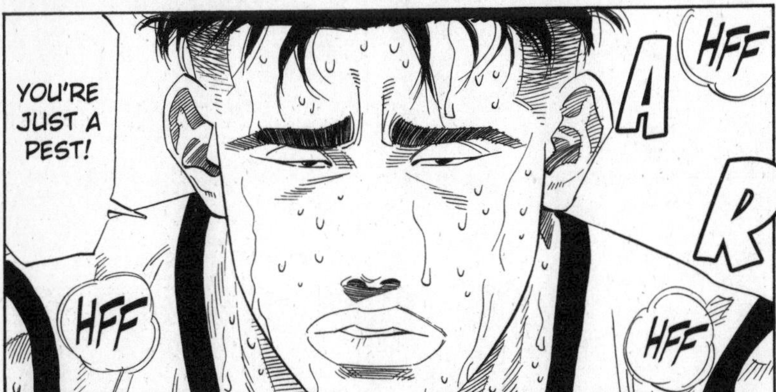
HFF
A A R
YOU'RE JUST A PEST!
HFF
HFF

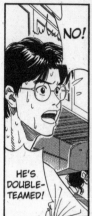

HFF
...
HFF
HFF
HUH?!
SQUEAK
NO!
HE'S DOUBLE-TEAMED!
HANAMICHI! DON'T HOLD ON TO IT TOO LONG! MOVE IT AROUND!
RIGHT HERE!
YES!!
CON-TAIN HIM!
I CAN'T SHOOT! NOT FROM HERE!
I GOTTA BE CLOSER TO THE BASKET!
HNNGH!!
SHWP

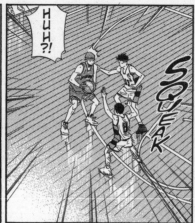

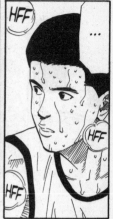

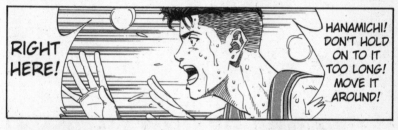

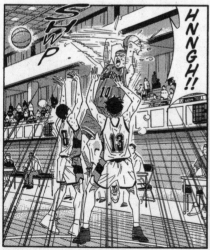

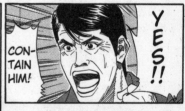

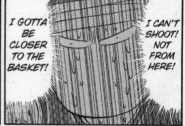

READ THIS WAY

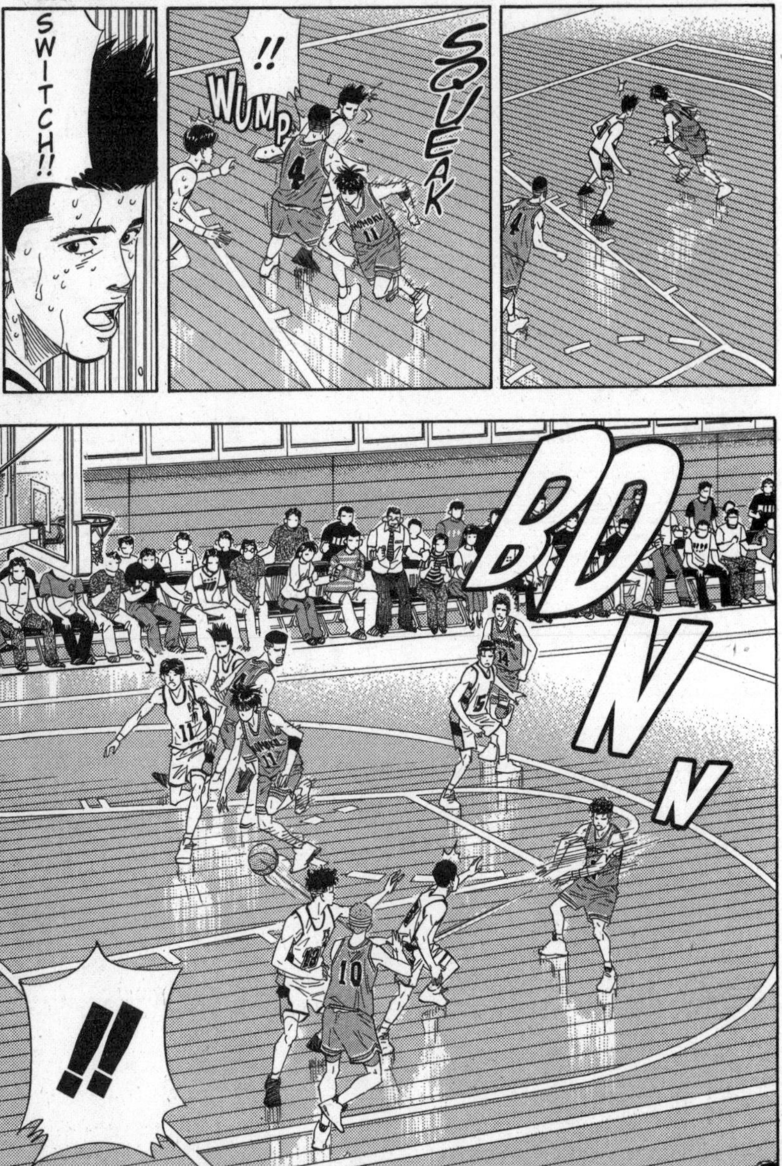

SQUEAK
!!
WUMP
SWITCH!!
BDNN
!!

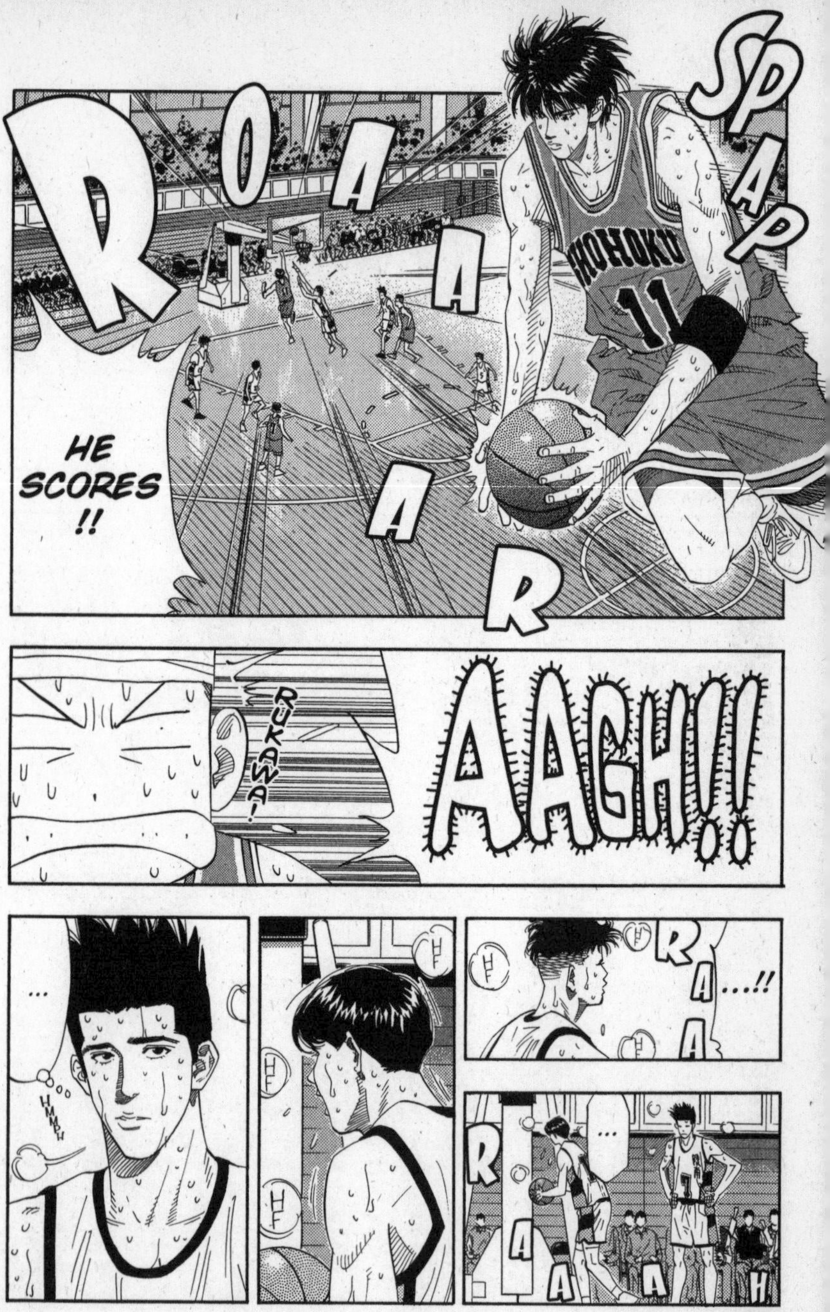
SPAP
ROOAAAR
HE SCORES !!
AAGH!!
RUKAWA!
RAA
...!!
...
RAAAAH
HF
HF
HF
HF
...
HMMPH

READ THIS WAY

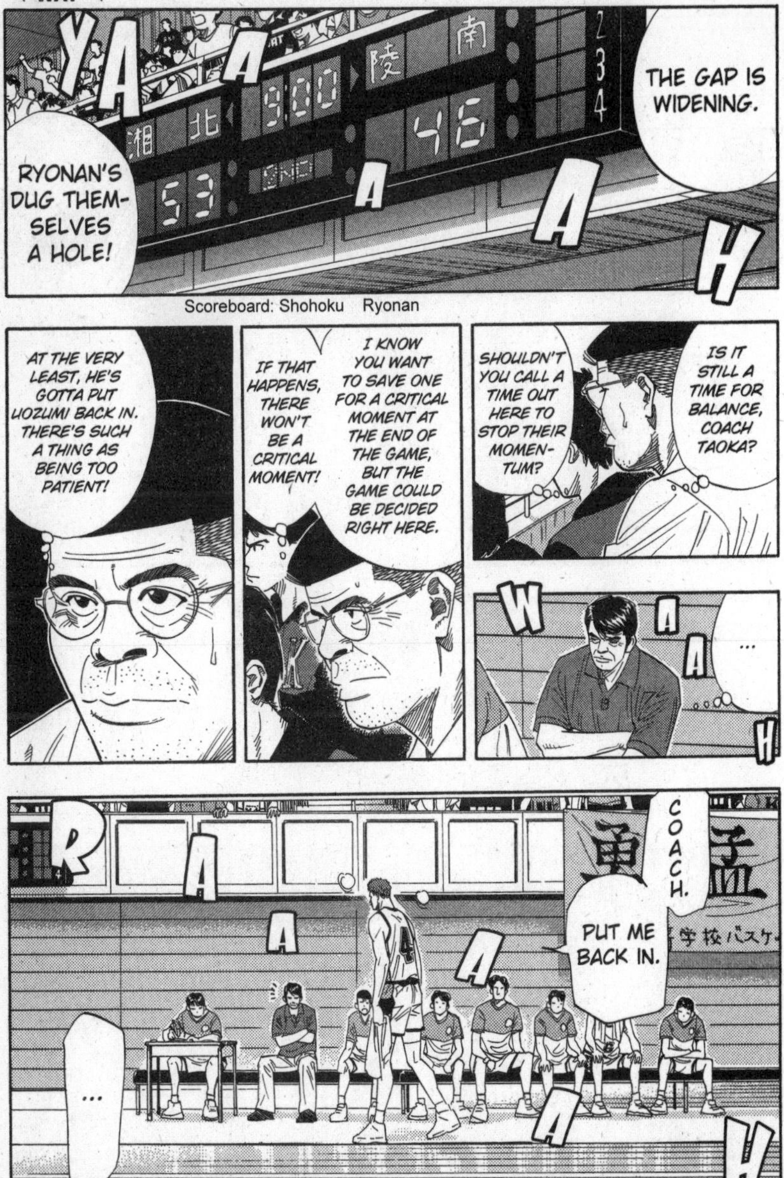
YAAAAAH
湘北 53
陵南 46
9:00
2ND
THE GAP IS WIDENING.
RYONAN'S DUG THEMSELVES A HOLE!
IS IT STILL A TIME FOR BALANCE, COACH TAOKA?
SHOULDN'T YOU CALL A TIME OUT HERE TO STOP THEIR MOMENTUM?
...
WAAAH
I KNOW YOU WANT TO SAVE ONE FOR A CRITICAL MOMENT AT THE END OF THE GAME, BUT THE GAME COULD BE DECIDED RIGHT HERE.
IF THAT HAPPENS, THERE WON'T BE A CRITICAL MOMENT!
AT THE VERY LEAST, HE'S GOTTA PUT UOZUMI BACK IN. THERE'S SUCH A THING AS BEING TOO PATIENT!
COACH.
PUT ME BACK IN.
...
RAAAAH
Scoreboard: Shohoku Ryonan

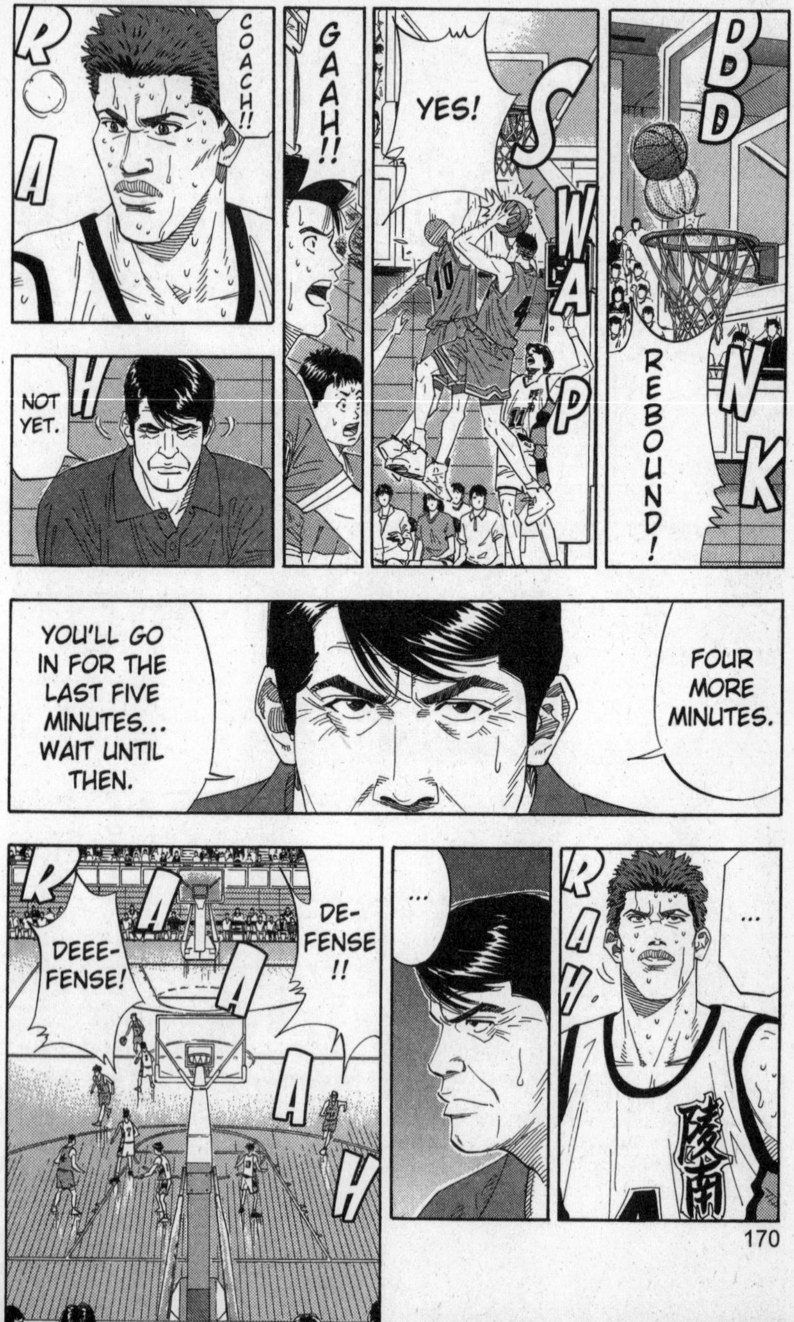
BDNK
REBOUND!
YES!
SWAP
GAAH!!
COACH!!
RA
NOT YET.
H
FOUR MORE MINUTES.
YOU'LL GO IN FOR THE LAST FIVE MINUTES... WAIT UNTIL THEN.
RAH
...
...
DE-FENSE!!
DEEE-FENSE!
RAAAAH

READ THIS WAY

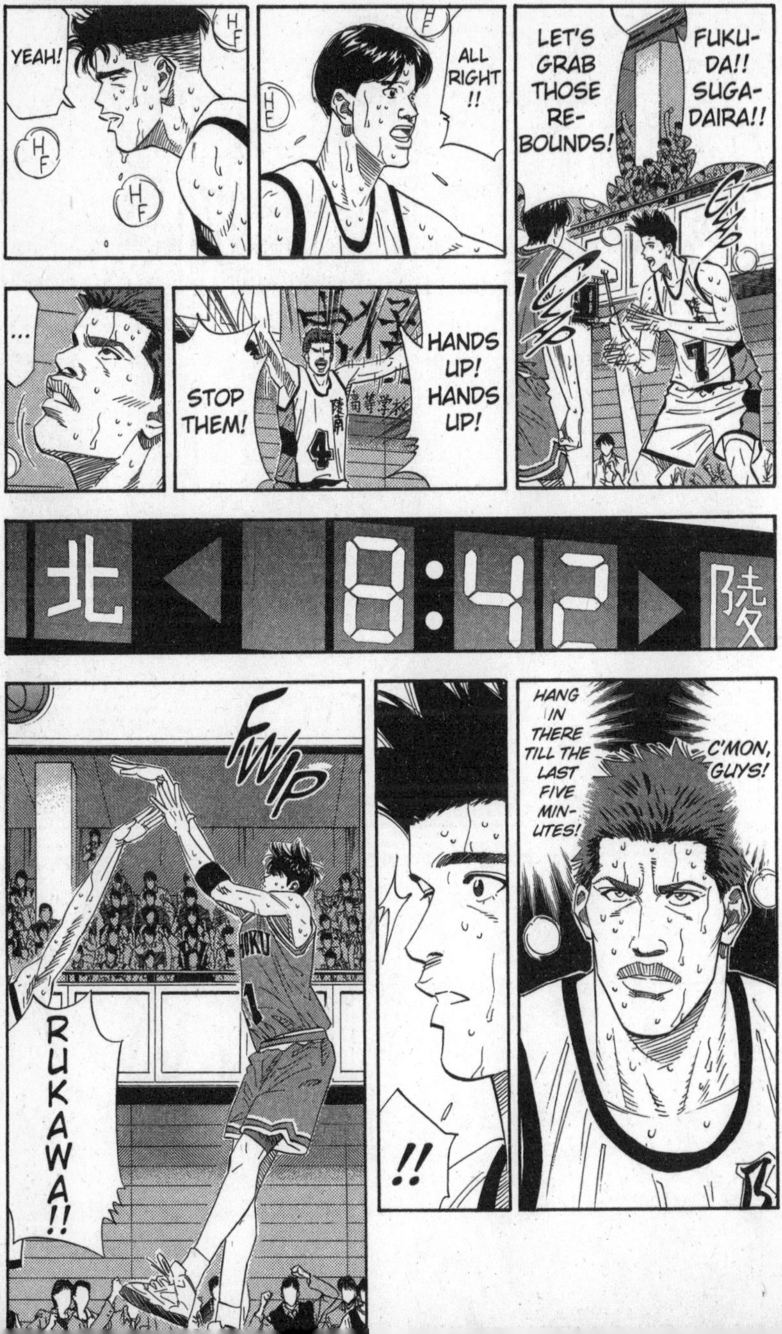
FUKU-DA!! SUGA-DAIRA!!
LET'S GRAB THOSE RE-BOUNDS!
GLOMP
GLOMP
ALL RIGHT!!
HF
HF
HF
YEAH!
HF
HF
HANDS UP! HANDS UP!
STOP THEM!
...
北
8:42
陵
C'MON, GUYS!
HANG IN THERE TILL THE LAST FIVE MIN-UTES!
!!
FWIP
RUKAWA!!

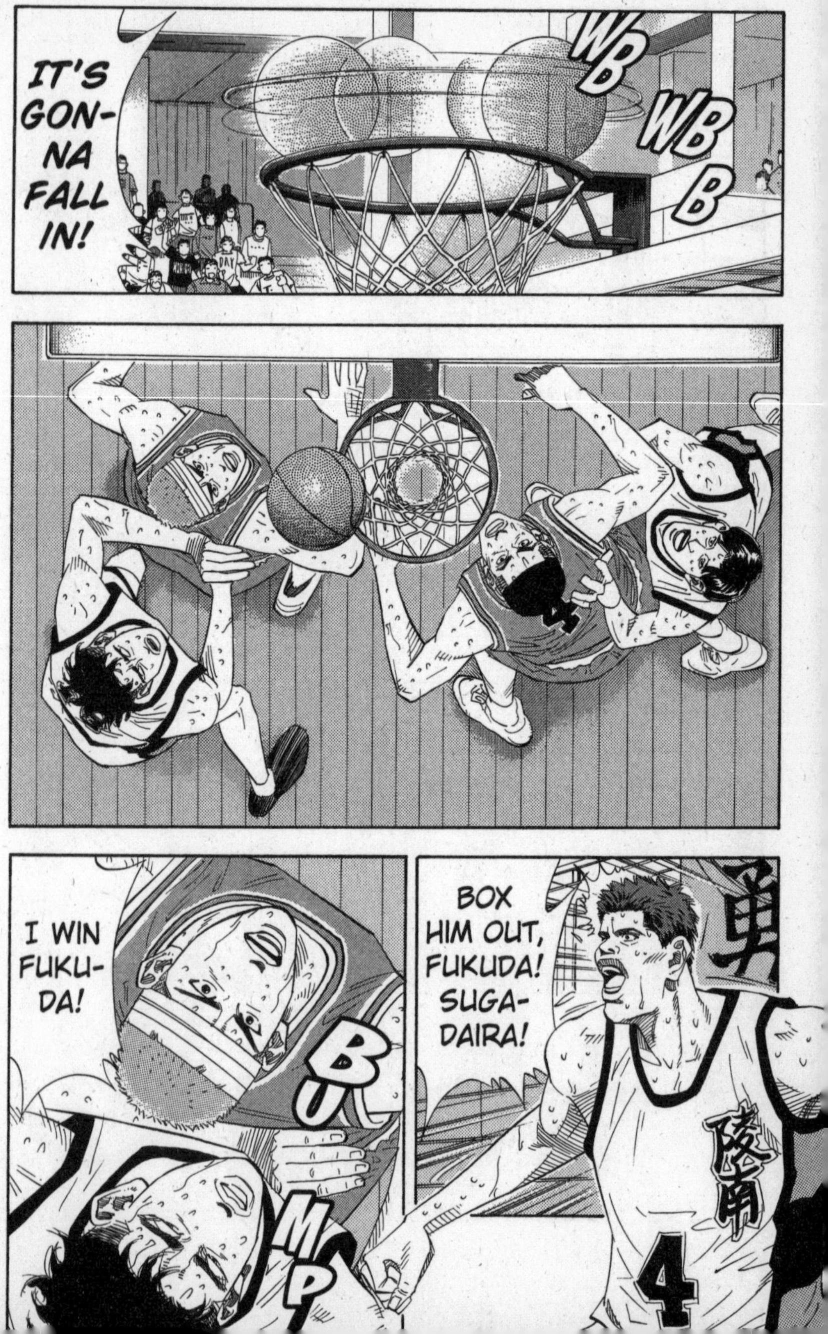
WB WB B
IT'S GONNA FALL IN!
BOX HIM OUT, FUKUDA! SUGADAIRA!
I WIN FUKUDA!
BUMP

READ THIS WAY

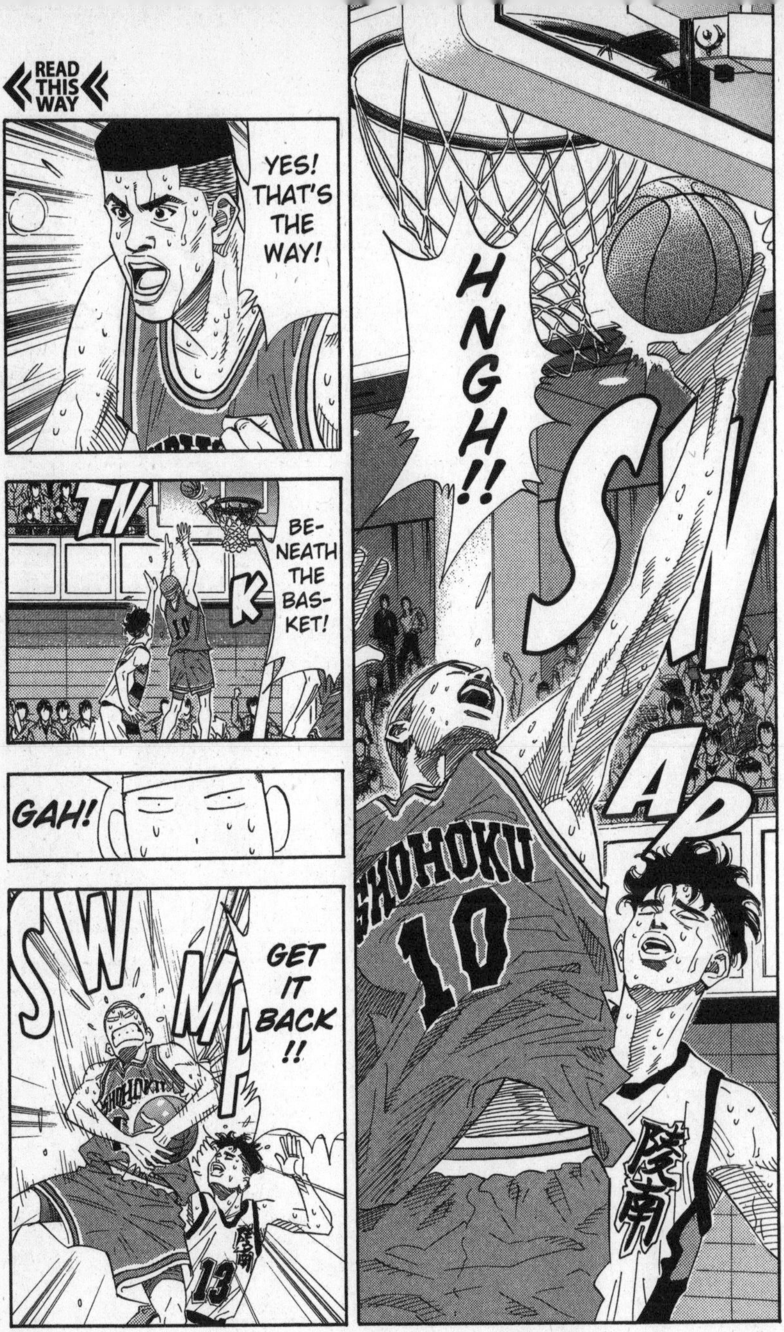
HNGH!!
SW
AP
YES! THAT'S THE WAY!
TN
K
BE-NEATH THE BAS-KET!
GAH!
SW
MP
GET IT BACK!!

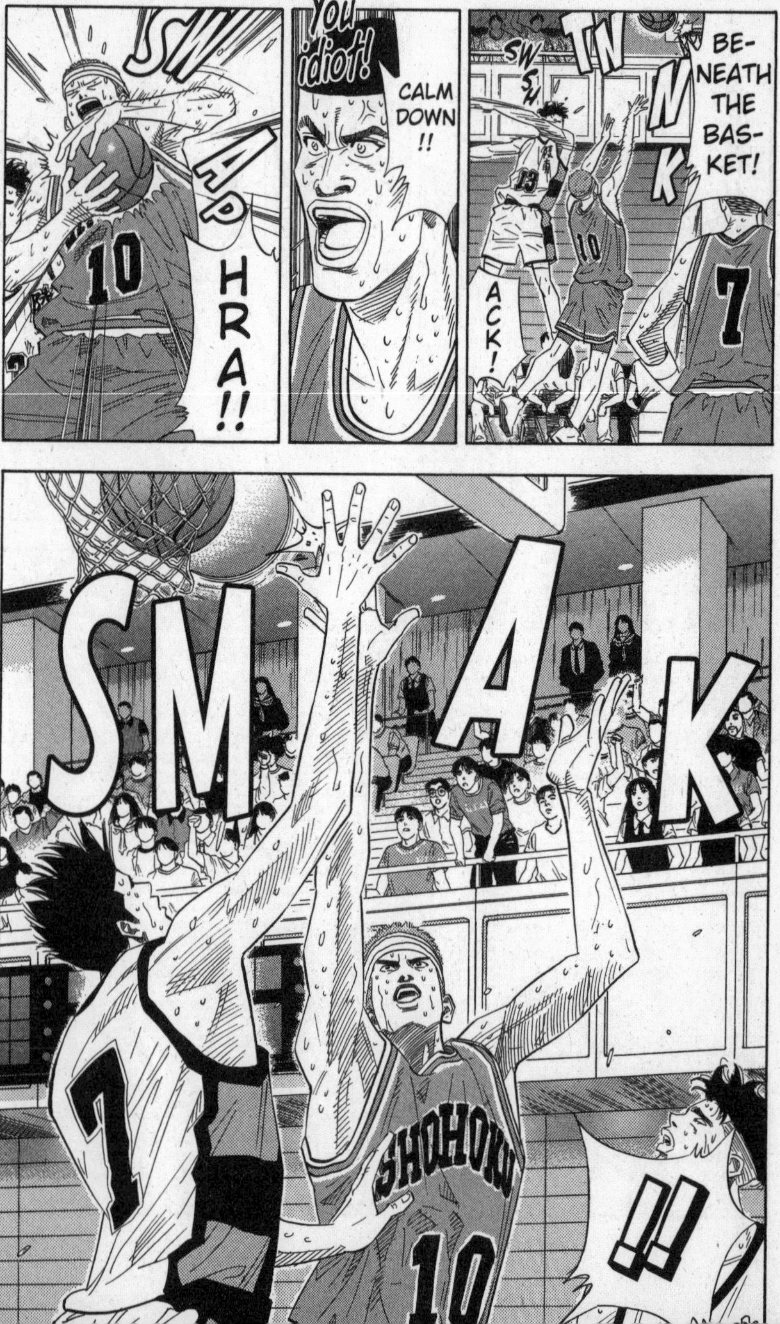
BE-NEATH THE BAS-KET!
TN NK
SWSH
ACK!
You idiot!
CALM DOWN !!
SWAP
HRA!!
SMAK
!!

READ THIS WAY

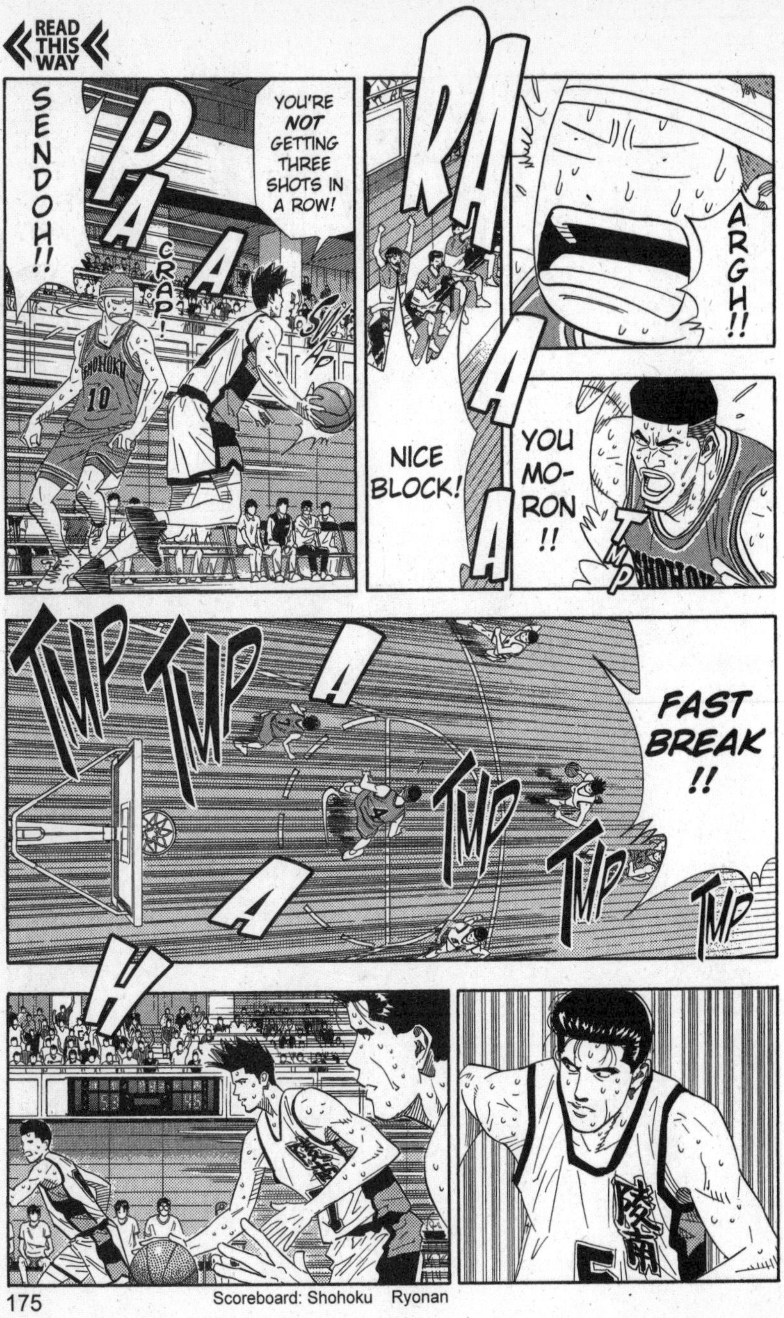
RAAAA
ARGH!!
YOU MO-RON!!
TMP
NICE BLOCK!
PAAA
YOU'RE NOT GETTING THREE SHOTS IN A ROW!
SENDOH!!
CRAP!
FAST BREAK!!
TMP
TMP
TMP
TMP
TMP
AA

Scoreboard: Shohoku Ryonan

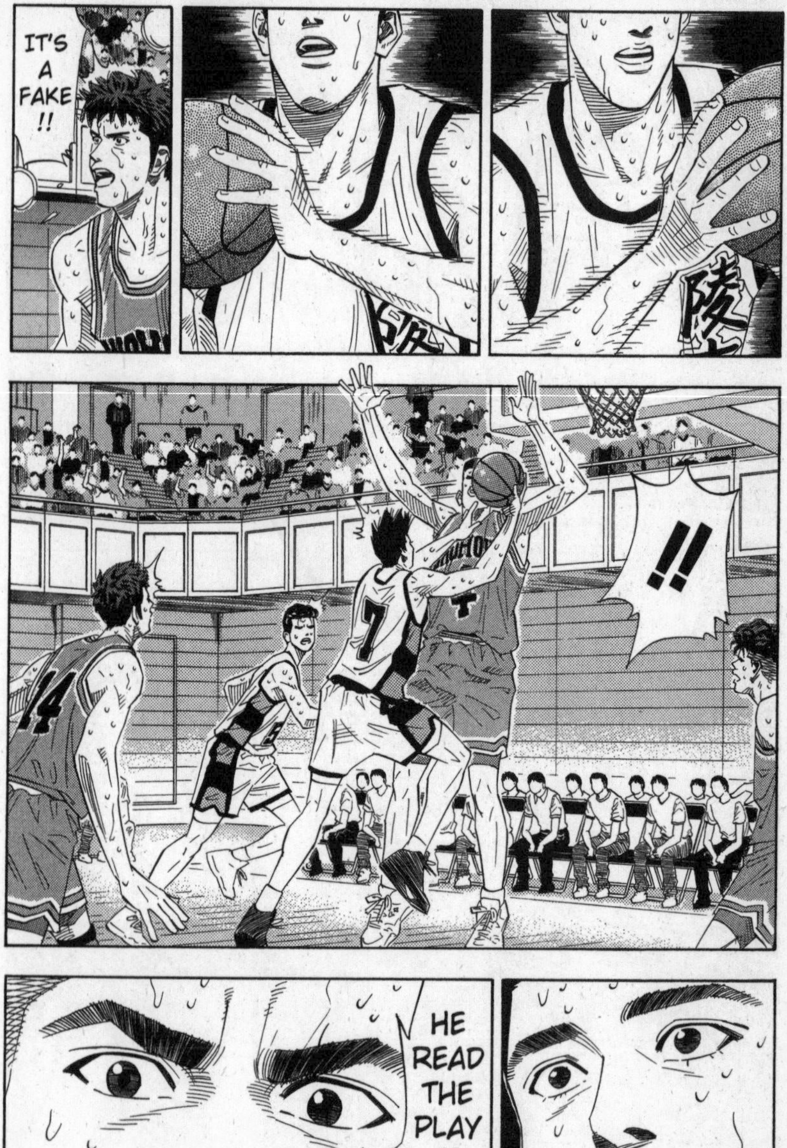
IT'S A FAKE !!
!!
HE READ THE PLAY !!

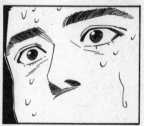

READ THIS WAY

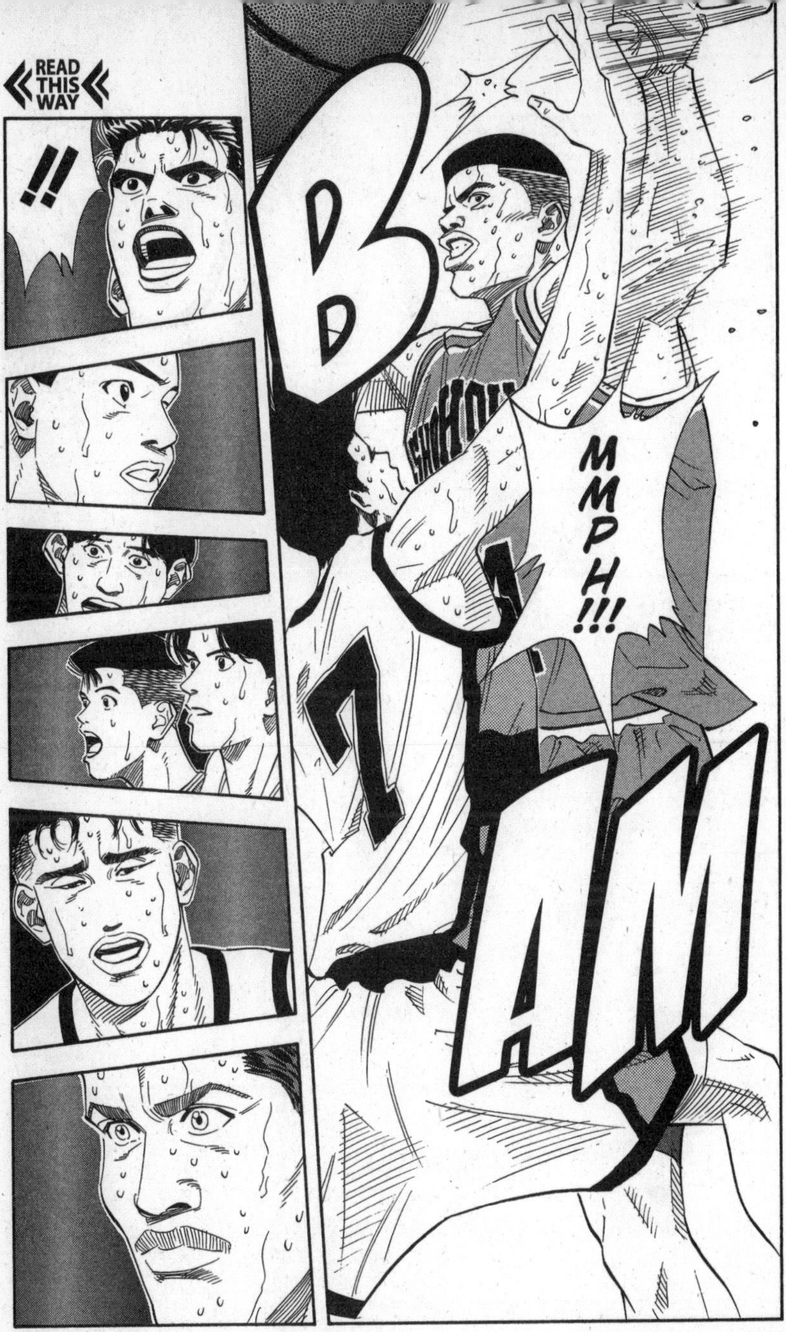

BAM
MMPH!!!
!!

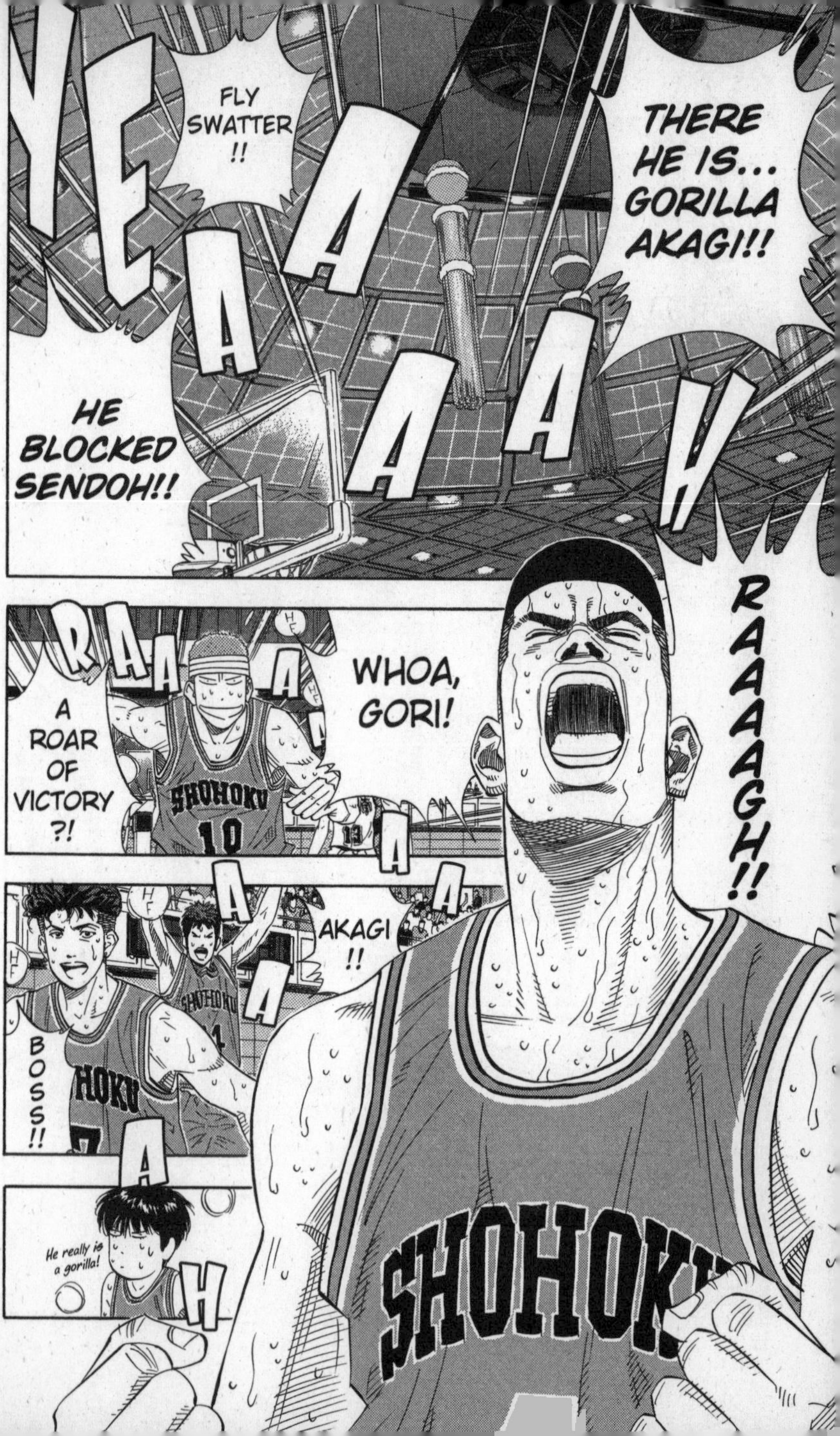
YEAAAAAH
THERE HE IS... GORILLA AKAGI!!
FLY SWATTER !!
HE BLOCKED SENDOH!!
RAAAAAGH!!
WHOA, GORI!
A ROAR OF VICTORY ?!
AKAGI !!
BOSS!!
He really is a gorilla!

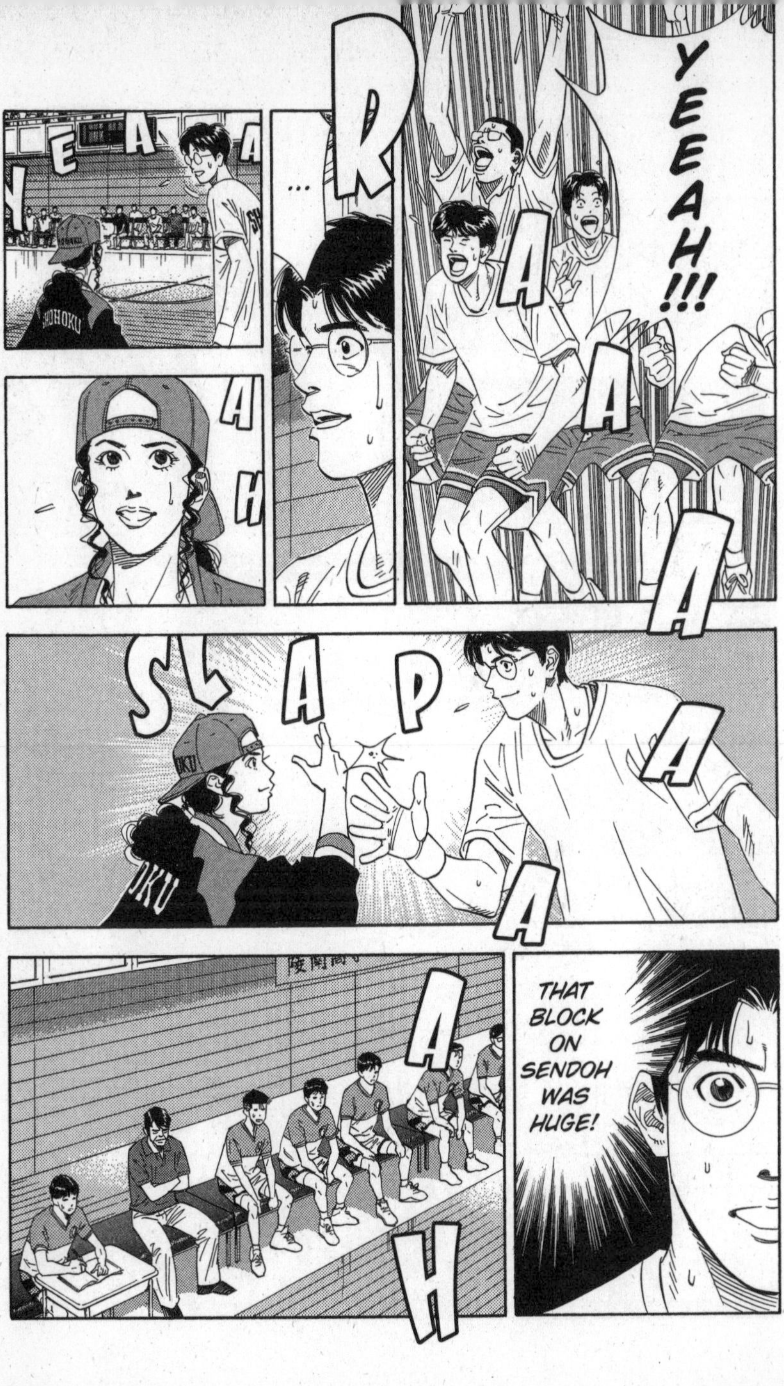
YEEEAH!!!
RAAAAAAH
...
YEAA
AH
SLAP
THAT BLOCK ON SENDOH WAS HUGE!

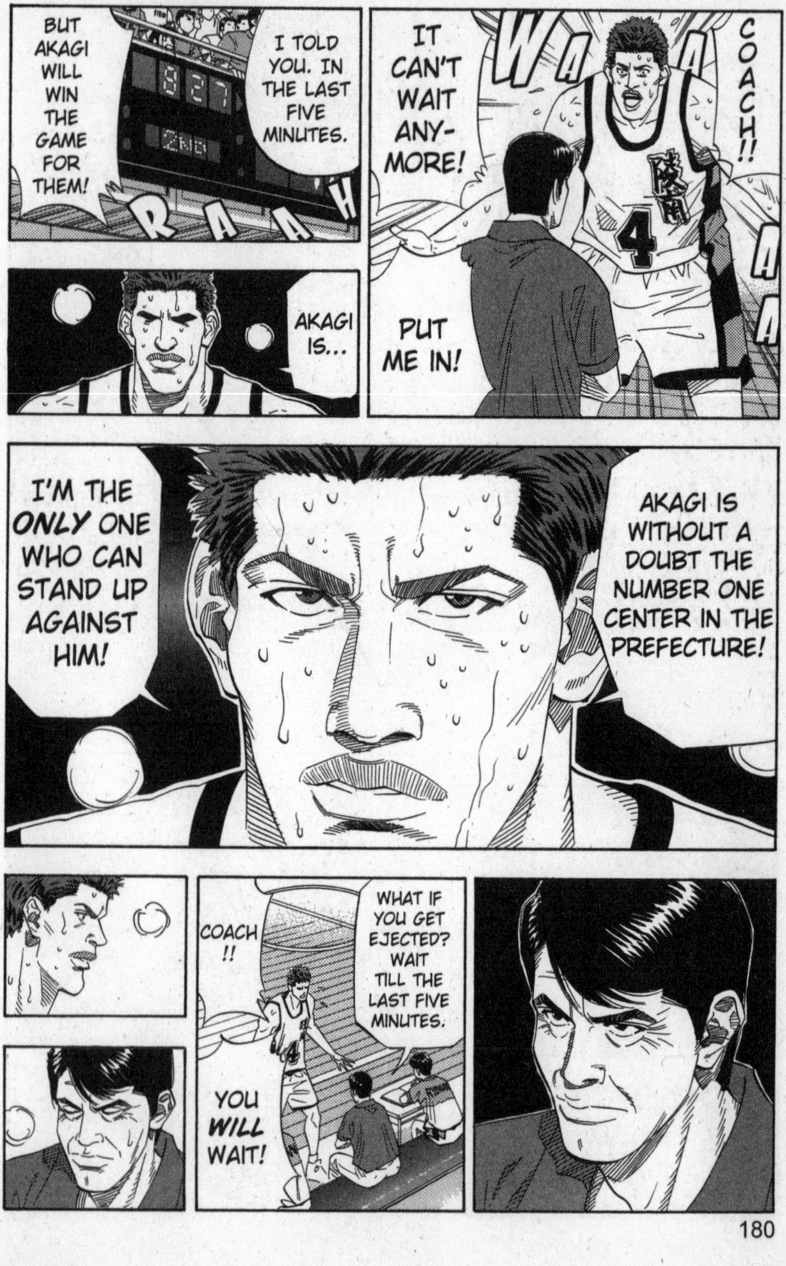
COACH!!
IT CAN'T WAIT ANY-MORE!
WAAAA
PUT ME IN!
I TOLD YOU. IN THE LAST FIVE MINUTES.
BUT AKAGI WILL WIN THE GAME FOR THEM!
RAAH
AKAGI IS...
AKAGI IS WITHOUT A DOUBT THE NUMBER ONE CENTER IN THE PREFECTURE!
I'M THE ONLY ONE WHO CAN STAND UP AGAINST HIM!
WHAT IF YOU GET EJECTED? WAIT TILL THE LAST FIVE MINUTES.
COACH !!
YOU WILL WAIT!

READ THIS WAY

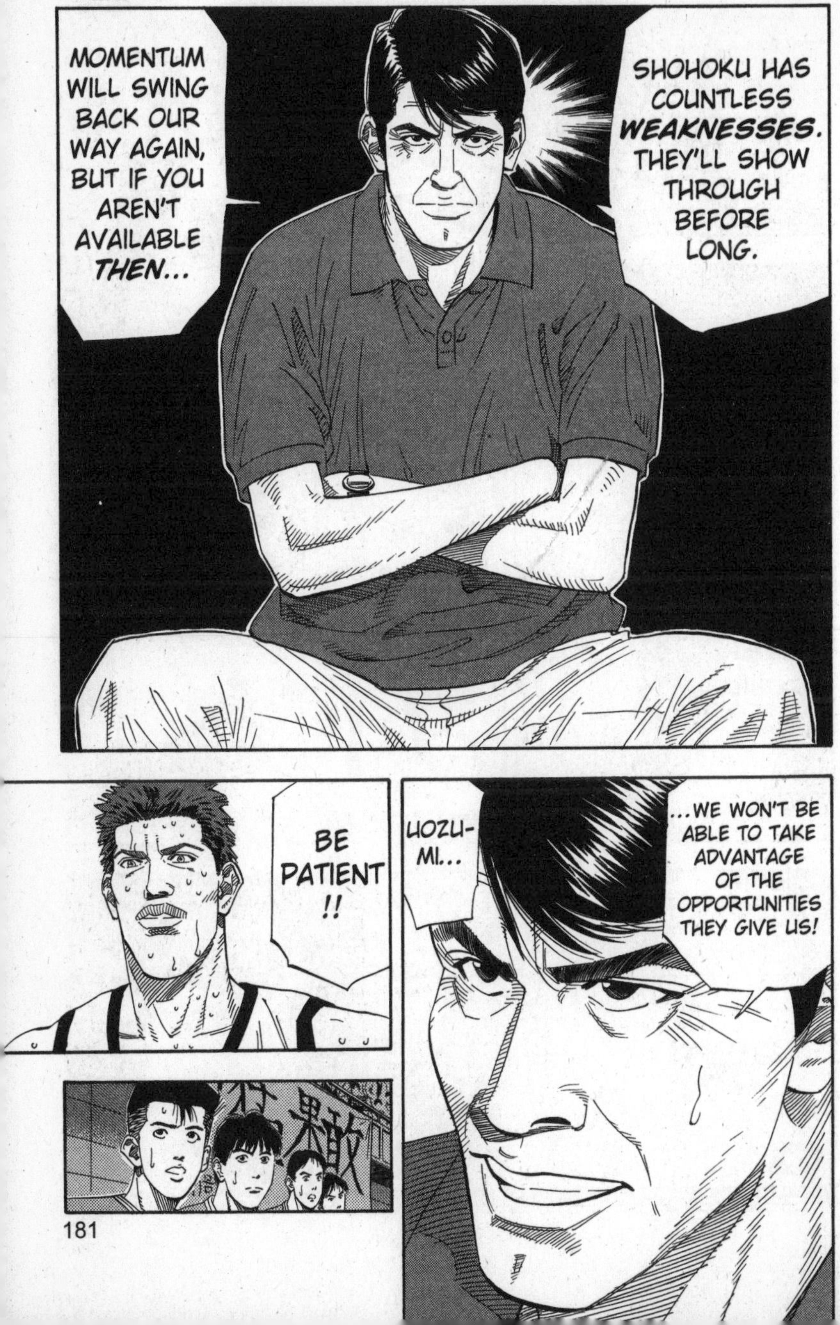

SHOHOKU HAS COUNTLESS *WEAKNESSES*. THEY'LL SHOW THROUGH BEFORE LONG.
MOMENTUM WILL SWING BACK OUR WAY AGAIN, BUT IF YOU AREN'T AVAILABLE *THEN*...
...WE WON'T BE ABLE TO TAKE ADVANTAGE OF THE OPPORTUNITIES THEY GIVE US!
UOZU-MI...
BE PATIENT!!

DE-FENSE!!
RAAAAAAH
...
DE-FENSE!!
RYONAN
RYONAN
DE-FENSE!!
DE-FENSE!!
DE-FENSE!!
RAAAAH
DEEE-FENSE!!
SQUEAK
HF
HF HF
EIGHT MORE MINUTES...
SQUEAK
SQUEAK

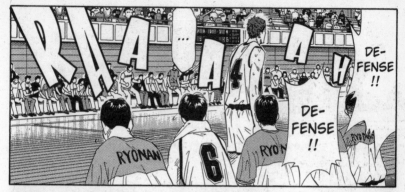

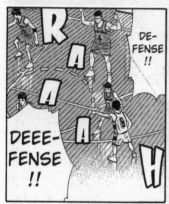

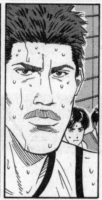

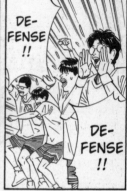

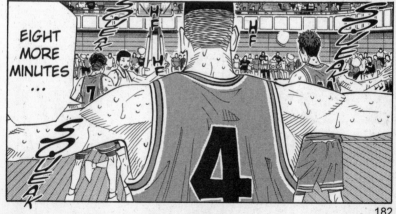

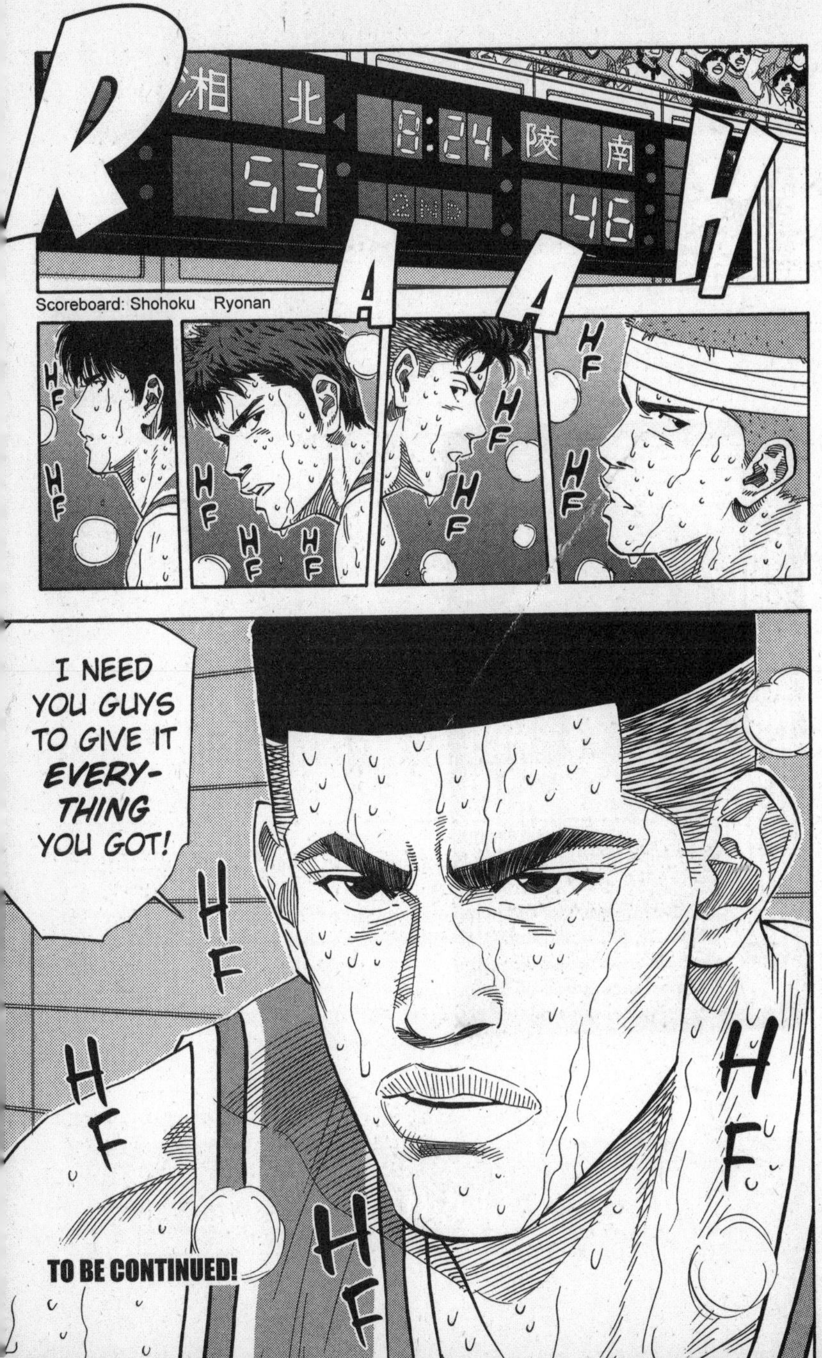
RAAH
湘北
8:24
陵南
53
2ND
46
Scoreboard: Shohoku Ryonan
HF HF
HF HF
HF HF HF HF
HF HF
I NEED YOU GUYS TO GIVE IT *EVERY-THING* YOU GOT!
HF
HF
HF
HF
TO BE CONTINUED!

Coming Next Volume

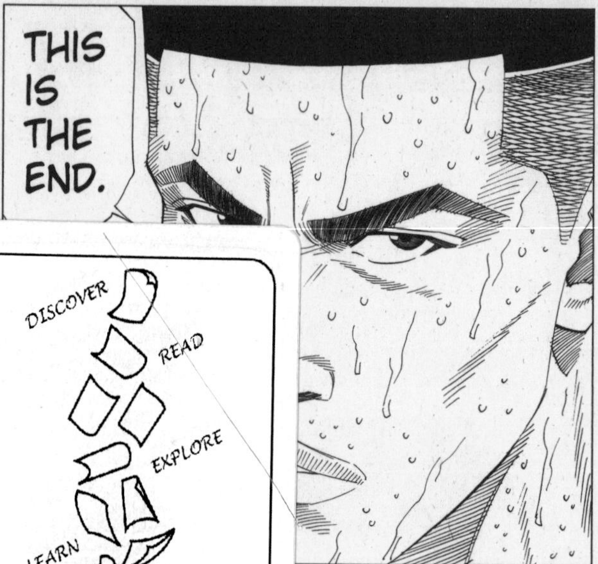

THIS
IS
THE
END.

...heir lead against Ryonan ...emaining in the game. But ...noku down and fatigue ...Without Coach Anzai's ...to hold on against Ryonan ...sed one by one. Sakuragi's ...biggest and the margin for ...n the court. Is this game going to push Shonoku to the edge of total collapse?

ON SALE F...RY 2012